MECHANICS-
MERCANTILE
LIBRARY.

Arthur F. Mathews '06

THE LOTTERY WARS

THE LOTTERY WARS

LONG ODDS, FAST MONEY, AND THE BATTLE OVER AN AMERICAN INSTITUTION

MATTHEW SWEENEY

B L O O M S B U R Y

New York   Berlin   London

Published by Bloomsbury USA, New York

All papers used by Bloomsbury USA are natural, recyclable products made
from wood grown in well-managed forests. The manufacturing processes
conform to the environmental regulations of the country of origin.

LIBRARY OF CONGRESS CATALOGING-IN-PUBLICATION DATA

Sweeney, Matthew.
The lottery wars : long odds, fast money, and the battle over an American institution/
Matthew Sweeney.—1st U.S. ed.
p.   cm.
Includes bibliographical references and index.
ISBN-13: 978-1-59691-304-2 (alk. paper)
ISBN-10: 1-59691-304-5 (alk. paper)
1. Lotteries—United States—History.   I. Title.

HG6126.S94 2008
795.3'8097—dc22
2008030835

First U.S. Edition 2009

1 3 5 7 9 10 8 6 4 2

Typeset by Westchester Book Group
Printed in the United States of America by Quebecor World Fairfield

For my parents

CONTENTS

GARBAGE STORIES

FOR FOUR DAYS in February 1983, Don Temple searched for his ticket. Family helped out and neighbors watched. Television cameras filmed and newspaper reporters took notes. He took a break from sifting through the three-ton pile of garbage to talk to ABC News. Over those days he repeated his story over and over: He was in a store near his home, playing a $1 scratch ticket. He saw two matching $5,000 amounts and a shamrock on the card. Thinking he'd lost—you need three matching numbers to win—he threw the ticket into an ashtray inside the store. But the Washington State Lottery had changed the rules of the game: The shamrock was like a wild card—it counted as a third matching number and doubled the prize. The new twist had been added to make the game more exciting. It also helped brand the game, since the lottery's logo was a four-leaf clover. Temple, an unemployed carpenter, didn't know about the new rule. Days later he learned about the shamrock rule on a television commercial. He realized he had been holding $10,000 and thrown it in the trash. When he went back to the store, the trash was gone.

What he did next was not so unreasonable, given the circumstances: He tracked the contents of the garbage can to the dump and had several tons of trash dumped in his father-in-law's driveway. They sifted through damp store receipts, old cigarette butts, and half-eaten food around the clock. There were plenty of used lottery tickets to check, but some were too filthy to read.

Temple's story is not unique by any means. Media coverage has even given it a kind of genre—the lost winner. Another such story happened in the late 1970s, when a mother of four wrote to the director of the Michigan lottery begging for help. She had bought a $5,000 winning ticket. She celebrated with her husband and hid the ticket before bed. The next morning she had a hangover and no memory of her hiding place. She was near a nervous breakdown, she wrote, after literally tearing her house apart in search of it. Amused by the story, the lottery director awarded her the money.

There are many stories like these, and we love to tell them. They fall under the general umbrella of the lengths to which we'll go for wealth. We have the pleasure of rooting for someone but also the freedom to laugh at their slapstick predicament. Each situation, each plight, lets us make a reflexive value judgment about how far we would go for wealth. And what is it worth? Lotteries can answer that. It costs a dollar or two—and a momentary suspension of disbelief. When we're presented with lottery tickets as a repository of hidden riches, the question becomes: How long and how hard are you willing to dig among the tickets for a winner?

Technically, Don Temple's story also fits into another subgenre of lottery stories that appear in papers and on television—the ticket lost in the garbage. You'd be surprised how often it happens.

In 1995, Beatrice Esquivel, a Californian, plucked from the trash a three-week-old lottery ticket. She had remembered, suddenly, that she had never checked the numbers. She and her husband won an $8 million jackpot. It came out to $288,000 after taxes, delivered every year for the next twenty years.

In Chicago, in 2003, Zeek Garnett lost his lottery ticket when his mother threw it out with the garbage. "I bought it, went home, and put it on the TV," he told ABC News. "That's where we put tickets." His mother, a daily player herself, thought the numbers had already been checked against the drawing. Because the Teamsters were on strike, no garbage was collected and the ticket was still there the next morning. Garnett, and his sister Karen, won $10.5 million. Karen, an airport baggage checker, dreamed of using the lump-sum payout to pay for a trip to Hawaii. Zeek, a UPS worker, thought of looking after his mother.

The Teamsters said they were happy to be of help.

Not all the stories end so sweetly. In October 2005, Edward St. John pawed through the garbage at a Massachusetts convenience store and pulled out a $1 million Hold 'em Poker scratch ticket. St. John, eighty-three, was well known in the small town of Blackstone, where he ambled around with the help of a cane, sifting through garbage. People rushed to the store after St. John's good fortune was announced. Sales there jumped 25 percent, and the store's owner got a $10,000 commission for its winner. Soon after St. John's lucky find was publicized, a local man, Kevin Donovan, laid claim to the ticket, saying he had mistakenly thrown it away. Before he got far, he died of a heart attack. The state lottery rejected his claim, but his family hired a lawyer and pursued St. John's new wealth in the courts. St. John, who wanted to enjoy the money before he died, settled for $140,000.

One could archive lottery stories into a handful of categories. There's the basic heartwarming story of a person with little money who wins a fortune. There's the winner who falls from grace and loses it all. There are popular narratives built around the group of co-workers who all chip in for tickets and share a jackpot. There is the guy who faithfully plays his lucky numbers day after day and one day hits; or the flipside of the story, where he skips a day and his lucky numbers come up. It's not just the media that broadcasts these stories. The lotteries themselves use them in advertising, by reminding their customers not to forget to play their numbers, portraying happy winners, and encouraging the idea that, whether by luck or fate, good fortune in the form of lottery dollars may arrive at any moment.

All this is another way of saying that the experience of winning, losing, and coming close in the lottery has become a commonplace— no more exotic than a brightly painted park bench. The lottery can catch your eye, hold your attention for a moment, but you're already familiar with the shape of the thing. It is all around us, yet we are usually hardly aware of it. Winning numbers, drawn twice per day, are broadcast every night on the local news channels, printed in nearly every newspaper. The games are advertised on television, radio, and billboards. The tickets are sold in gas stations, liquor stores, convenience stores, and newsstands, and now, in a long-sought breakthrough for the industry, are starting to show up in major retail chains, such as CVS, Costco, and Sears.

But as accustomed as we are to lotteries, the stories about them rarely go beyond the experience of winning or losing. It is seldom asked how the ticket got into the players' hands. Were they regular players or was it the first time? What compelled them to buy it? If they won, how did their lives change? Were they stingy or generous? Did the money affect their relationships ? Did it lead them to ruin or to God or to both? Did the money buy freedom?

Then, embedded in the ticket itself, is a whole other set of questions that never seem to get asked: Who decided its price, color, name, the amount of its prizes, and place on the shelf? Because someone was involved in all of these decisions. And what did the state do with the dollars the players just spent? Did it build a school? Did it seed a children's baseball field? Did it go to a private corporation? Or did it pay for a lobbyist? Did someone pocket it?

Lotteries have funded the United States for centuries. Newspaper accounts of happy lottery winners, reckless lottery winners, lost tickets, and lottery addicts go back to the early 1800s. But fewer accounts exist of the companies, such as Yates & McIntyre, that administered lotteries privately, or how Harvard, Princeton, Yale, Columbia, and other universities relied on lotteries to build their campuses.

And not all lottery stories are what they seem. Ed Rader found a big winner in a garbage can too—someone else's. Like Edward St. John, he was looking through trash cans for winning scratch tickets that, like Don Temple's, had been misread and thrown away. A surprising number of "scroungers" do this habitually.

"I was trying to pride myself on the fact that it wasn't coffee grounds," Rader told me. "It was 'clean' garbage." He paid off some debts and spent some on more tickets, upping his ante from the $1 and $2 scratch tickets to $5 scratch tickets with his newfound wealth. Soon most of the money was gone. "This is one hell of an addiction," he said.

Rader's story fits several categories—the lucky ticket in the garbage and the winner who lost it all. It also fits one less common to newspapers or television—the addicted gambler. It's not a particularly happy story, but not all lottery stories are. Officially, the lottery is a form of entertainment, not gambling. But not all of its players are after entertainment.

Just after New Year's Eve 2004, an Ohio woman named Elecia Battle called police and reported that she had lost a winning ticket in the $162 million Mega Millions drawing that had just been held in eleven states. She filed suit against the state lottery to stop payment of the prize to another woman who was holding the winning ticket, claiming that the money belonged to her. Battle, who said that she had dropped her purse after buying the ticket in a convenience store, was not helped in her argument by her rap sheet for credit-card fraud and assault. She had also once tried to sue McDonald's, alleging that her daughter drank a bad milk shake. ("My wife can stretch things out of proportion," her ex-husband said.) Battle eventually dropped her lawsuit and cried when she apologized to the real winner. "I wanted it so bad. I wanted it to change my life," she told the Associated Press. "The numbers were so overwhelming. I did buy a ticket and I lost it. I wanted to win so bad for my kids and my family. I apologize." She received nationwide coverage. Less than a year later, she was back in the news again. This time she was pursuing a boxing career under the ring name Mega Battle.

Desire, as crazily as it is sometimes expressed, is what ties all lottery stories together, the good and the bad, and what is behind all lottery marketing. When we buy a lottery ticket, we engage in reckless hope. Knowing full well that the odds of winning are infinitesimal, we spend money on the chance of a life-changing fortune (or at least some free pocket money).

Whether the ticket is casually or compulsorily purchased, the lure of the lottery is that all the player has to do is give in to his or her own wishful thinking. For most of us, that hardly needs encouragement.

"It pays to dream," New Jersey has told its customers.

The New York Lottery generally gets credit for having the best slogans: "All you need is a dollar and a dream." "You've got to be in it to win it." "Hey, you never know."

Connecticut admonished its citizens, "You can't win, if you don't play."

To counter the skeptics of the lottery's long odds, Michigan paid for a television ad that shows a man condemning the lottery by saying (accurately) that he is more likely to be struck by lightning than to win. Then a lightning bolt comes down and hits him.

Across the Atlantic, the British National Lottery offered the tantalizing "It could be you."

Maryland encouraged people to "Let yourself play."

A Washington State Lottery marketing campaign simply stated, "They're recyclable." That campaign didn't go far.

The ultimate point of all this effort is the bureaucratic task of raising money for the government. Unlike tax collectors, lottery officials are in retail sales. There is little "government" in their government jobs. If Americans treated the lottery like any other government agency, it would flop. Who wants to gamble to help the state pay for services? Would anyone enter a state-sponsored raffle? "Investing in New Mexico's Education" is about as sexy a slogan as Vietnam's "The lottery is useful for both the country and the individual family."

Some states have tried trickier ways to suggest the public benefit of lotteries and still market to the players' desire to beat the odds. In Oregon they came up with "There's no such thing as a losing ticket." Massachusetts, which has a wildly profitable lottery, came up with a similar concept. Not surprisingly, marketing campaigns like that usually run into complaints that they are misleading. But lotteries exist to raise as much money for the public good as they can. It is a strange position to be in, trying to convince the public to gamble in furtherance of their own good.

Lotteries are the most accessible form of gambling because the state has a monopoly on them; tickets can be sold in almost any store that's willing to stock them. Yet lotteries have terrible odds. Perhaps the worst are in the multistate jackpot lottery: 1 in 150 million. A mathematician at Stanford University, Keith Devlin, described the odds of winning a Powerball drawing this way: "Imagine a standard NFL football field. Somewhere in the field, a student has placed a single, small, common variety of ant that she has marked with a spot of yellow paint. You walk onto the field, blindfolded, and push a pin into the ground. If your pin pierces the marked ant, you win. Otherwise you lose. Want to give it a go?"

Put a dollar down. Guess right and you're a multimillionaire. The odds are somewhere between getting hit by space debris—1:5 billion—and the 1:6,500 chance of being injured by a toilet seat. And yet, why not risk a buck on a goof? Who can argue with spending $1 for the chance of making $200 million? We gamble for the thrill of it. We gamble to entertain ourselves. The expectation and the hope of winning money is a part of that thrill, and so is the fear of losing our money.

It's all momentary, especially in lottery games that depend on a few different gambling impulses. The first is the jackpot draw: the allure of life-changing money won by sheer luck. The second is compulsion: a $2 or $10 scratch ticket offers money, whether it's $100 or $10,000, in the blink of an eye or the scratch of a ticket. You know it's there. Some of the cards behind the counter hold money, maybe a lot. If one card is a loser, maybe the next one is a winner. Or in a keno game, the ball on the screen may not have bounced to all of your picks this game, but a new one is starting in five minutes and you are due for a winner.

Lottery games have a no-frills quality. They are the closest we can come to wagering on pure chance. The daily numbers offer no cards to hold, no real competitors, and nobody cheering us on. They're not social. Without the trappings of a casino to showcase the games and the fun, or dice or cards to give the added allure of interaction and the seduction of skill, lotteries have to rely on emotion and anticipation. Is it this one? Maybe the next one? This thin veil of mystery is enough to sell tickets at 150 million to 1. The average blackjack hand, meanwhile, has slightly less than a 50 percent chance of winning.

Some buy into their state lottery with good humor, some with mechanical regularity, some with passionate certainty. There are different kinds of players, but in the end more than half of the country buys a lottery ticket or scratch card at one time or another.

The state lotteries wouldn't spend money on slogans and ad campaigns if they didn't work. Lotteries are the most popular form of gambling in the nation.

We spent $57 billion on lottery tickets in the United States in 2006. Even including the eight states that don't have lotteries, the average American household spends about $500 on lottery tickets every year. Americans spend more money on gambling than they do on movie tickets, videos, DVDs, CDs, and books combined.

Lotteries have swung through our history and culture like a pendulum: first in our good graces, then out, only to return as a financial "necessity" to raise government revenue. In each era, the same positions for and against them have been staked out over and over. Lotteries are a voluntary means to raise funds for public works; lotteries are a vice; lotteries are ruinous to personal industry, particularly among the poor; lotteries are a popularly approved alternative to increasing taxes.

In one form or another, we've always had the lottery. And for as long as we've had it, we've had a troubled relationship with it. We've depended on it to build vital infrastructures and universities. We've called it sinful, and a sucker's bet that takes advantage of the poor. We've subtly, semiconsciously, allowed it to shape our dreams of wealth and how it's attained.

Over the centuries of lottery play we've celebrated lottery winners who were stable hands and parking-garage attendants. We celebrate sudden wealth, particularly when it comes to someone who never had it. But outside of the storybook, when someone wins the lottery, a part of us has always worried that such sudden riches are destructive to the value of hard work. Politicians may still talk in the language of Horatio Alger's tales, but a survey by the Consumer Federation of America found that 21 percent of Americans believed that winning the lottery was the most likely way they would ever see several hundred thousand dollars in their lives. About one third of people with low incomes and senior citizens believed this. Thirty percent of people without a high school degree say winning the lottery is an important strategy for building wealth. We may be less judgmental, less elitist, about the lottery, but we continue to be morally ambivalent about it. This is particularly true when we consider that the government's role in controlling, encouraging, and profiting from lotteries has been a source of controversy from the beginning. At different periods, depending on the prosperity of the country, the lottery has been popular or maligned.

The pattern that has repeated over the centuries starts with broad encouragement to play and a munificent goal for the proceeds. As public eagerness for the game increases, public and political dismay grows over how much money people throw at the slim hope of winning more. The games are then reined in through legislative measures, and continue on until their popularity increases enough to bring notice again. At the end of the nineteenth century, the game grew so wildly out of control and so corrupted public officials that the president stepped in and banished it from the United States. But even then it didn't disappear. Americans didn't want it to disappear. A large

American appetite existed for a cheap game that gave chances at large amounts of sudden money. Games of blind chance, in which everyone faces the same odds, had a strong appeal among all groups, particularly the lower-income and working classes, who had a chance at upward mobility that they would otherwise have little expectation of ever seeing. Lotteries were absorbed into the American dream. There was no reason you couldn't work hard and hedge against uncertainty with long-shot lottery tickets. The less you had, well, the less you had to lose.

When the government outlawed it, the lottery simply went underground and flourished as the illegal numbers racket, until the government decided that the only way to control it was to legalize it again. The modern lottery was directly modeled on the illegal games. Today, some lottery opponents cite the same moral and ethical arguments that their predecessors did two hundred years ago. Lotteries, they argue, undermine personal initiative, unduly tax the poor, who play more than others, and are an improper business for government to be in. The response is much the same as it was two hundred years ago as well: Government needs funding and taxes are unpopular.

New Hampshire sold its first lottery ticket in 1964, and less than fifty years later the profitability of a state lottery is one of the surest bets in the country. More than half of Americans say they "strongly disapprove of gambling." Yet today lotteries are in forty-two states and the District of Columbia.

The desire, the aspiration that good fortune will strike despite expectations, is a common, if not universal, trait of humanity. We all want good things to happen to us, and the lottery industry counts on our belief that they will.

"I firmly believe that what's really indigenously different about the lottery industry is that people who play the lottery are optimistic people," said Constance Laverty O'Connor, chief marketing officer for GTECH Holdings, the lottery-industry giant.

After more than twenty-five years in the industry, working for two of the biggest state lotteries, in New York and Georgia, and now on the corporate side of the industry, she may know more about lottery players than anyone.

"They believe that maybe it could be them," she said. "Even though in their intellect they know it won't be. But in their sort of imagination, their heart, there's this wonderful, wonderful sense of anticipation. So to me the articulation of that from a marketing perspective can be as simple as people with warm eyes looking at the camera, saying, 'What if?' Or, 'It could be me.' Or, 'Hey, you never know.'"

Boiled down to a basic desire, or hope, the lottery has a marketing appeal similar to that of other products. A makeup ad may suggest that we can all be beautiful; a tropical-vacation ad may promise to rekindle romance; a car can promise entrée into a world of class and luxury. These work because they encourage an optimistic belief in our ability to change our lives—with a little help. The product is simply the catalyst for the change we already believe is possible. But the lottery offers something even bigger: life-changing wealth.

It could change your life. Lottery-industry marketing people talk about that draw all the time—the selling point of "life-changing" money. Who doesn't want to change his or her life in some way? Everyone dreams of *something*. By opening the possibility of life-changing wealth, the lottery is able to sell us on our own dreams. How did such a universal aspiration come to reside in a $5 scratch ticket at the corner grocery or highway gas station?

The winners from the early centuries of the lotteries and people such as Ed Rader, Elecia Battle, Don Temple, and all the others who play the lottery share something: the sliver of belief that they will win against stupendous odds. It's a belief that is at once basic to human character, but, at the same time, so defiant of reality that it almost takes an act of faith—or compulsion—to buy into it.

In September 2005, NBC premiered *My Name Is Earl*, a sitcom about a small-town ne'er-do-well and small-time crook who wins $100,000 in the lottery only to get run down by a car and lose the ticket. With help from a celebrity, he realizes that karma is to blame. He spends the show's episodes comically trying to make amends for all 258 bad deeds he has committed. The ticket finds its way back to him when he starts doing good.

Two months after the show first aired, life imitated television in the person of Mike Sargent of Alvarado, Texas. A former drug addict and alcoholic, Sargent had long since found sobriety through religion when he won $25,000 on a scratch ticket. He did the smart thing and made his ownership official by filling in the back of the ticket with his address and signature. He called home to his wife to say that Christmas had arrived early. But on the way home the ticket disappeared. It was nowhere in his car nor in his pockets. Sargent could only guess that God had snatched away the ticket for reasons known only to Him. He searched along the highway and in the store Dumpster. Nothing. Five days later, Gerardo Ruiz, a water-meter reader, called Sargent to say he'd found the ticket a short distance from the convenience store alongside the highway. Ruiz admitted he had thought about keeping the ticket, but his wife had warned that divine punishment would follow if he did. Instead of karma, Sargent thought his good fortune was from Jesus. He gave Ruiz $2,500 and vowed never to play the lottery again. "I think God was telling me . . . that I need to be dependent on Him and not on lotteries and jobs and anything else."

As for Don Temple, his search for his lost ticket came to an end after four days. He looked under the last scrap of trash and found nothing. The next day the *New York Times* ran a piece saying the search had ended. ABC followed up with its own report. Both moved on to other stories.

"I still believe it's in there," Temple told reporters. After four days of digging through garbage, he was still dreaming about how to spend the money.

CHAPTER 1

THE FIRST LOTTERY

AMERICA'S FIRST LOTTERY winner was a London tailor. Little else is known about Thomas Sharplisse. His name has survived history because of one lucky day in June 1612 when a two-shillings-and-sixpence ticket was pulled in the First Great Standing Lottery held by the Virginia Company of London. As recorded in *Stow's Chronicles*, Sharplisse's ticket was called out as the grand-prize winner—four thousand crowns in "fayre plate, which was sent to his house in a vary stately manner." It was a fortune at the time. Two Anglican churches took home smaller winnings. After the Virginia Company paid for the prizes, salesmen, managers, and other expenses, the remaining revenue covered the cost of shipping people and supplies to the struggling colony at Jamestown.

In America, we've had lotteries since the beginning and leaned on them for some of our most important achievements; the Continental Congress even enacted a lottery to fund Washington's bedraggled army. But lotteries were a medieval European invention used to elect leaders in Venice or sell off estates in other nations. When John Smith landed at Jamestown, the lottery was already the domain of ambivalent customers and seductive advertising tricks. Sharplisse may have been inspired to buy his winning ticket after hearing "London's Lotterie," the sales jingle sung to the tune of "The Lusty Gallant." It may not have the staying power of, say, "A Dollar and a Dream," but in its day it was a catchy piece of marketing doggerel:

> *The Merchants of Virginia now,*
> *hath nobly tooke in hand,*
> *The bravest golden Lottery,*
> *that ere was in this Land.*

> *A gallant House well furnisht foorth*
> *with Gold and Silver Plate,*
> *There standes perpard with Prizes now,*
> *set foorth in greatest state.*

> *To London, worthy Gentlemen,*
> *goe venture there your chaunce:*
> *Good lucke standes now in readinesse,*
> *your fortunes to advance.*

> *Full many a man that lives full bare,*
> *And knows no joyes of Gold,*
> *For one small Crowne may get a share,*
> *Of twice two Thousand fold:*

If he didn't hear the song, Sharplisse may have read about the lottery in one of the broadsides the Virginia Company distributed in London and surrounding towns "to inable us to make good supplies to the colonie in Virginia." He may have been moved to help the settlers, seeing purchasing a ticket as an act of patriotism for the furtherance of England's glory. Or maybe he dreamed of getting rich.

Sharplisse would have been among the jostling crowds that gathered from June 25 to July 20 in the specially constructed Lottery House near St. Paul's Church to watch the tickets drawn. The person who pulled the tickets—in some cases a child, whose innocence was visible proof of the fairness of the game—dipped his arm into the first drum. The number was pulled out and called. Then the second drum was opened and a corresponding slip, either a "blank" or a prize, was pulled out. In the words of one contemporary account, the scene was viewed by a gathering of "Knights and esquires, accompanied with sundry grave discreet citizens."

Unlike Sharplisse, most Londoners did not want to buy tickets; sixty thousand went unsold. Lotteries were not uncommon in England and were usually mandated by royal order, to meet some need for harbor repairs or military defense. Even if their fund-raising goal was worthy, lotteries were commonly shadowed by accusations of deception and fraud. The expensive tickets may also have discouraged sales. In general, lotteries were primarily a tool for generating public revenue, and only secondarily a form of gambling. Someone who purchased an expensive ticket—it was hoped—was someone who could afford a voluntary act of charity to the country.

The miserable Jamestown colony was not exactly a magnet for charity. It was a private venture of the Virginia Company, not an organization that inspired munificence.

By resorting to a lottery, the company was admitting it was in desperate financial straits. A Spanish ambassador reported back to King Philip III that the British had fallen upon "a generall kynde of begging" to prop up the Jamestown colony. In 1612, the Virginia Company's five-year-old toehold in the New World looked like a failed investment. Instead of profits, the colony had returned stories of death, disease, and starvation. Stockholders, unwilling to throw good money after bad, reneged on their promises to finance the venture, leaving it saddled with debt. Talk of the colony's failure so threatened Virgina Company investors that one wrote a passionate defense of it "to free the name it selfe from the injurious scoffer, and this commendable enterprise from the scorne and derision of any such, as by ignorance and malice have sought the way to wrong it."

King James I extended the struggling Virginia Company's charter and granted its request for permission to hold lotteries—at his pleasure—on March 12, 1612. Three months later the first drawing was held.

But the merchants and others who were repeatedly badgered by the Virginia Company to buy tickets agreed with the Spanish ambassador. Before long many in London, especially business owners, were fed up with the salesmen and circulars promoting the lottery, which was a drain on their profits.

In 1615, the Virginia Company arranged a second Great Standing Lottery, at five shillings per ticket. But sales dropped off when the drawing was held. To win over the public and inspire settlers and reluctant lottery-ticket buyers, the company changed tack with some creative advertising. Instead of promoting the lottery, they promoted the colony. In handbills and flyers the company put out word that the colony was now a thriving community of brave and skilled laborers, whose adventure was certain to show profits soon. No longer on the brink of oblivion, the Virginia colony was on the edge of establishing a new and soon-to-be prosperous world. And if one had some moral opposition to lotteries or mistrusted them, one could still buy a ticket, knowing, the advertisements stated, that "though all his lots come blanke; yet if his minde be upright, he rests content in this, that his money goeth to a publike worke, wherein he hath his part of benefit, though he, never so meane and remote in his dwelling."

In the broadsides posted in taverns and markets the company

admitted that, yes, it could no longer finance the colony on its own. But the advertisements also reminded readers of the colony's patriotic purpose: to further the glory of the kingdom and establish the gospel among the "savage and barbarous people" in the New World. Gambling in the name of spreading the gospel was allowed. In later years, religious leaders would have a mixed response to lotteries, sometimes accepting them in the name of public good and at other times lashing out at the games as destructive of good morals. As pitched by the Virginia Company, buying a lottery ticket was an act of charity that could save a savage's soul. And selling the public on buying tickets for the good of the colony was not entirely cynical salesmanship. There was a genuine feeling for the colonists. Several winners returned their prizes to the company.

If God, king, and country didn't sway seventeenth-century Britons, there were illustrations of the prizes—silver cups and plates—awaiting ticket buyers, who, in the language of the day, were called adventurers. The company tried to sweeten the lottery with rewards such as stock membership for anyone who spent more than twelve pounds, ten shillings.

Still, ticket sales remained low. Accusations of misappropriated lottery funds dogged the company. At least one manager was caught with his hand in the prizes. Poor sales delayed drawings, which further reduced public confidence. The money that did come in helped keep the company afloat for a time. Fortunately, the king did more than just give permission to hold lotteries. James I had also ordered that public officials such as mayors, sheriffs, and justices of the peace help the company sell tickets. The success of the lottery, and the Virginia Company, was a government concern.

In 1616, armed with the king's order to public officials to cooperate, the managers sent the lottery on the road to the larger towns and cities across England. They soon hit upon a successful formula. "Running lotteries" were held in smaller locales than London, towns that were not yet jaded by the Virginia Company's begging. Ticket prices were just twelve pence, and, just as important, the company amplified the public's excitement by holding "instant" lotteries. Instead of buying numbered tickets and waiting weeks or months for the drawing, bettors were given rolled-up slips of paper from a drum. They could unroll them on the spot to discover whether they held a prize or an empty blank. To overcome mistrust, the company handed local officials much of the work of securing and running the lottery. To put an incorruptible face on drawings, they made sure that a child drew the lots from the drums. The lotteries ran for weeks in each town. Business boomed, sales soared. Finally, the company had a successful lottery. With a growing, if unpredictable, source of income, the Virginia Company shipped hundreds of settlers and supplies across the Atlantic to Virginia. In 1620, the company estimated that the small-scale "instant" games had brought in a total of £29,000 over their first four years. For 1620, the company estimated that the lotteries had covered £7,000 of its nearly £10,000 costs. The company projected an increase in lottery revenue to £8,000 in 1621. It would be the last year of the lottery.

For all its rising sales among the far-flung towns and cities, the Virginia Company lotteries were still unpopular where it counted—the government. In 1621, the House of Commons asked the king to withdraw his permission to hold them. Some members argued that the drawings were distasteful; others that the king improperly stepped on Parliament's rights to make such grants by giving his personal approval to the Virginia Company; one member said that the lotteries traveling around the towns of England left the "Common sort greatly cozened"—"fooled," in modern language. It was a common criticism

against lotteries. At least one of the towns had instructed lottery operators not to sell any tickets to the poor. Desperate for a chance to
rise above their station, or just to put a better roof over their heads,
the poor were considered more easily duped into playing. Certainly,
in the seventeenth century, there was a perception that if ticket sellers
weren't restrained, it might leave some districts penniless. The complaint still registers today, particularly when ads seem misleading. A
Massachusetts advertisement said, "No matter what you do for a living,
there's an easier way to make money." One notorious Chicago bill-
board loomed over a poor neighborhood with the slogan "This could
be your ticket out."

Some things have not changed much since the reign of James I.

But concern for the poor was equally rooted in concerns over
maintaining social stability—a town of people who had spent all
their money on lottery tickets was not good for local merchants. Envy
was also behind the opposition. Why should the crown grant such a
profitable license to the Virginia Company and not to anyone else?
Again, the past repeats itself. Today, private lottery companies fight
bitterly over government contracts to operate the state lotteries.

The antilottery campaign was influential enough that a minister
was sent to King James I with a request to rescind the lotteries. The
king assented, telling the messenger that "he never liked the lotterie; he ever suspected it would prove hurtfull and distasteful." The
king added that he only gave his permission because the Virginia
Company had no other options. On March 8, 1621, the king issued a
proclamation: "Now forasmuch as We are given to understand, that
although We in granting the sayd License, had Our eye fixed upon a
religious and Princely end designe, yet the sayd Lotteries, having now
for a long time been put in use, doe dayly decline to more and more
inconvenience, to the hinderance of multitudes of Our Subjects." In

1621, twelve years after he left the colony, Captain John Smith pointed out, too late, that the lotteries had been "the reall and substantiall food" that kept Virginia alive.

AS THE AMERICAN colonies grew, they did so with help from lotteries. Even so, the problems that harassed the operations of the Virginia Company lottery continued. Throughout their roughly two-hundred-year life span in the United States, lotteries have always been accused of supporting immorality, corruption, mismanagement, and greed.

The first notable American lottery opponents were the Puritan father and son duo Increase and Cotton Mather. More famous for chasing New England witches, they also used the pulpit of Boston's North Church to warn against the evils of games of chance. Adventurers in these games were sinners because they put themselves in the hands of luck, not God. One has to wonder how Increase, the sixth president of Harvard College, would have reacted to the university's later heavy reliance on lotteries to build up the campus in the decades after his death. The Mathers fought a losing battle against necessity. Harvard and Yale defended the use of lotteries based on their benefitting a larger good.

As long as there was a public benefit, the games were permissable. This reliance on "public benefit" carried lotteries for some time. In *Fortune's Merry Wheel*, his definitive history of early American lotteries, John Samuel Ezell writes that the first known government lottery in the colonies was held in Massachusetts in 1744 to pay for military defenses against the French. The goal was to raise £7,500. Only whites were permitted to purchase tickets for fear that a ticket in the hands of an Indian or Negro could result in "mischievous consequence."

Only the Puritans and the Quakers were steadfast in their opposition to lotteries in these early years. The Quakers had settled in Pennsylvania and fought lotteries there by passing law upon law in the late seventeenth and early eighteenth centuries punishing participation in them with hard labor. The British crown struck each of the laws down. Government reserved for itself the right to hold lotteries. The colonial rulers, on the other hand, were driven to distraction by private lotteries.

Unsanctioned, privately managed lotteries were a commonplace method of auctioning off estates, settling a deceased person's debts, or getting a good price for rare possessions, such as a personal library or scientific equipment. They were structured like a raffle. Players bought prenumbered tickets that were later picked out of a drum. In the colonies, lotteries were used—as they were in Europe—to settle private debts or as public entertainment. Estate sales might take place as a lottery, with homes, cattle, and land going as prizes to ticket buyers. This raffle version of the early lottery had been in use for centuries. Lotteries were used on an ambitious scale by monarchs of Europe to raise money for their armies, harbors, churches, and bridges. The Flemish painter Jan van Eyck's wife sold off his paintings in a lottery in 1446. The small homemade lotteries in colonial America became popular.

In 1719, Samuel Sewall, a Puritan merchant and Harvard graduate, was troubled by the public appetite for the game. Sewall was a leading citizen of Massachusetts, a veteran (to his deep regret) of the Salem witch trials, member of the Governor's Council, and chief justice of the colony. After a talk over dinner with the colonial rulers one night, he wrote to his cousin William Dummer, "I dined with the court last Friday, where many expressed their dislike of the lotteries practised of late, as differing little from Gaming for Money; and as being really pernicious to Trade. Taking notice of no less than four lotteries in the enclosed News-Letter I would propound it to Consideration, whether it will not be expedient to put some stop to the progress of it?"

They did. That same year Massachusetts outlawed any lottery not authorized by the government. Many colonies feeling overrun by similar financial schemes followed suit. No doubt, Sewall objected to lotteries on moral grounds as "gaming," but he, and others, also saw that they disrupted business. Money that was spent on lotteries couldn't be spent on goods. Within a decade, New York, Connecticut, and Pennsylvania had banned private lotteries. Almost invariably, the colonial governments based their decision on the belief that the games were pernicious to the servants, children, and other "unwary" folk who lost their money chasing an easy fortune. When New Jersey banned its thriving trade of unsanctioned lotteries in 1748, gamers found a loophole, moving their business to the unclaimed islands in the Delaware River. Decades before painter Emanuel Leutze made Washington's crossing of the Delaware legendary, lottery operators made the crossing the Delaware notorious for covert drawings on Biles, Petty, and Fish islands, Ezell writes.

The colonies continued to approve lotteries with sanction of their royal governors. In the hands of the government, lotteries covered the costs of infrastructure and other immediate and serious needs. One of the game's great beneficiaries—alongside churches, colleges, streets, harbors, and bridges—was war. In October of 1754, the French and Indian War kicked off with Virginia's authorization of a lottery to raise a military force against the French after a skirmish over Ohio. The previous July, French forces had defeated a young colonel named George Washington.

The gentlemen farmers of Virginia, like Washington, were a far cry from the Quakers of Pennsylvania. In their eyes, a little gambling, especially in the furtherance of a social benefit, was no sin. Virginia did not ban private lotteries until 1769, which was fortunate for Washington, who was an inveterate player. From his fastidious records of his personal expenses we know that in 1768 he won land along the James River in a private lottery, having bought £50 in tickets. He bought tickets in other lotteries in 1760, 1763, and 1766. On occasion he even helped organize lotteries. Washington's ticket buying was, in no small part, done in public spirit. Lotteries were the province of social leaders. Tickets were usually expensive. Winning was not the be-all and end-all of the ventures. The money usually went to a "worthy" cause, though the chance of winning must have made it more fun. Well into retirement, Washington continued to spend money on the game.

In 1769, Washington helped manage a lottery in Williamsburg, historian Henry Wiencek recounts in *An Imperfect God*. The first five prizes were parcels of land ripe with orchards, woods with valuable lumber, and fertile fields. Near the top of the list of prizes to be won was "A Negro man named Billy, about 22 years old, an exceeding trusty good Forgeman, as well at the Finery as under the Hammer, and understands putting up his Fire; Also his wife named Lucy, a young Wench, who works exceeding well both in the House and Field." They were valued at £280. Joe, was next on the list, age twenty-seven, a "a very trusty good Forgeman," then Mingo, about twenty-four; Ralph, about twenty-two; Isaac, about thirty; and Sam and his wife, Daphne. It is disturbing to think of Washington involved in such an endeavor. Thirty years later there would be some measure of justice, perhaps, when a slave won a lottery and purchased his freedom with the winnings.

Prior to the Revolutionary War, these private lotteries, which more closely resembled raffles, were run by merchants and gentlemen such as Washington. They outnumbered the state-sponsored games despite the individual bans on them. They were so heavily used that they became a threat to colonial governance. In 1769, private lotteries were forbidden in nearly all of the colonies. The Lords of Trade, a committee of the king's Privy Council that oversaw the operations of the colonies, handed down the prohibition. They declared that all lotteries would now require approval from England because they "tend to disengage those who become adventurers therein from that spirit of industry and attention to their proper callings and occupations on which the public welfare so greatly depends" and that "great frauds and abuses have been committed." The Lords had no supervision over Connecticut, Maryland, or Rhode Island under their charters.

Under the 1769 law, the crown had a legal monopoly on lotteries in the colonies and did not sanction any over the next three years. This strangling of lotteries happened while many of the colonies were still soaked in debt from the French and Indian War. The colonies had come to depend on lotteries as a way of raising funds without resorting to unpopular taxes. But Britain was also in debt and had its own national tickets to sell in the colonies. The English State Lottery was always available in the colonies, but Parliament changed the rules of the game as it pushed aside colonial lotteries. Under the new guidelines, the English State Lottery would pay out less to players in the form of prizes and take a larger cut of sales for the government. Among the significant allocations from the lottery was £30,000 to go toward "defending, protecting, and securing the British colonies and plantations in America." It was essentially a forced tax, and like the Stamp Act, it was unpopular.

In 1776, Adam Smith described the revolutionaries in *An Inquiry into the Nature and Causes of the Wealth of Nations* as lottery players: "Instead of piddling for the little prizes which are to be found in what may be called the paltry raffle of colony faction; they might then hope, from the presumption which men naturally have in their own ability and good fortune, to draw some of the great prizes which sometimes come from the wheel of the great state lottery of British politics."

It was not necessarily a compliment. Smith marveled at the horrific odds of lotteries and how still "the soberest people scarce look upon it as a folly to pay a small sum for the chance of gaining ten or twenty thousand pounds." Given the odds against the revolutionaries, Smith's metaphor was apt. It was appropriate then that the Continental Congress authorized the first true "American" lottery. Two months after Washington was routed in the Battle of Long Island and retreated across the Hudson River to New Jersey, a lottery scheme was hatched to raise just over $1 million for the Continental Army. The flyers went out on January 11, 1777:

"This lottery is set on foot by a Resolution of Congress passed at Philadelphia, the 18th day of November 1776, for the purpose of raising a sum of money on a loan, bearing an annual interest rate of 4 per cent, which, the sum arising from the deduction, is to be applied for carrying on the present most just and necessary war, in defense of the lives, liberty and property of the inhabitants of these United States . . . As this lottery is established for the sole purpose of raising a sum of money for carrying on the present just war, undertaken in defense of the rights and liberties of America, in which every individual and posterity will be so deeply interested, it is not doubted but every real friend to his country will most cheerfully become an adventurer, and that the sale of tickets will be very rapid, especially as even the unsuccessful adventurer will have the pleasing reflection of having contributed, in a degree, to the great and glorious American Cause."

It's hard to imagine a more compelling advertisement. It was a deadly earnest business. The Continental Congress was so terrified that fraud and counterfeit tickets would undermine the lottery that Rhode Island made these offenses an act of treason, punishable by execution and confiscation of property. Several states enacted their own lotteries to help the war effort. But in the final tally, lotteries did not provide significant aid to independence. Despite the rousing advertisement, tickets were slow to sell, money was slow to collect, and drawings were delayed. The Continental Congress also had to compete with some state lotteries that continued to raise money for schools, streets, and churches during the war years.

Lotteries blossomed after the war. How else could the newly independent state and municipal governments pay for their most expensive needs? They governed a population that had just won a violent war over taxation; laying a tax on them seemed unwise. Little currency was around, so the banknotes that could be gathered for expensive projects were gathered by lotteries. The games flourished throughout the decades after the Revolutionary War.

A typical lottery was created on October 15, 1798, when Charleston passed an ordinance authorizing the East Bay Street Lottery. As the cosmopolitan cultural and commercial capital of the South, Charleston had approval from the South Carolina legislature to hold lotteries for improvements as it saw fit. The lottery hoped to raise $6,000 for paving East Bay Street on the bustling waterfront, where Denmark Vesey, a slave, worked in his master's store. He must have seen the handbill the city put out on September 30, 1799, advertising the drawings to begin in one week. Vesey bought ticket No. 1884. On November 9 the *Charleston City Gazette* announced ticket number 1884 was a winner, with a prize of $1,500. It was a fortune. A laborer made roughly $8 a month at the time. No one knows how Denmark Vesey reacted to the news. The *City Gazette* did not run a human-interest piece about this lucky winner. Vesey bought his freedom from Captain John Vesey, a retired slave trader turned ship supplier, for $600.

Vesey's remaining money dwindled over the next twenty years. He hired himself out as a carpenter and, at one point, went back to work for Captain Vesey. A free black man in Charleston had to compete for work with slaves for hire. Vesey was said to be quick to anger and resented the bowing and scraping of the slaves around him. Decades after buying his freedom, Vesey began to plot a citywide slave uprising. Inspired by the slave revolt in Haiti, Vesey and his cohorts wrote letters to that country seeking asylum and assistance. They planned to strike in July 1822, but Vesey was arrested on June 22. On July 2 he was hanged.

George Evans, a slave who knew him, told those investigating the plot that even as he planned the rebellion, Vesey bought several tickets in the "Grand Lottery for the Benefit of the South Carolina Academy of Arts" in hopes that lightning would strike again. With little left from his first win, he hoped to fund the revolt with a second jackpot.

The response to Vesey's plan was violent. The prospect of a slave revolt confirmed the worst nightmares of South Carolina's ruling slaveholders. Charleston, once relatively liberal, cracked down. New state laws required free blacks coming off ships in the port to be put under house arrest. Forced detention of free men violated federal law. It was the first of many conflicts with Washington, D.C., that led to talk of secession. South Carolina's white populace demanded the state create an arsenal to be at hand in the event of a future slave rebellion. The Military College of South Carolina, later known as the Citadel, was built in response. Citadel cadets fired the first volley of the Civil War.

When Vesey bought his lottery ticket, Charleston was a like a lot of other late-eighteenth-century cities: a mud-splattered assemblage of crooked wooden homes and fewer brick buildings. But the country and its cities were trying to lift themselves from the mud. After the Revolutionary War people flooded into cities. The urbanites of the 1790s crammed into a few short blocks of one another. And just as Charleston needed to pave East Bay Street along the waterfront in the interest of commerce, the towns and cities also desperately needed clean water, sewers, and streets. Municipal buildings were needed to house and give respectability to democracy. Other edifices would be needed to take care of the new local governments' responsibilities: courthouses and jails, hospitals and poorhouses, marketplaces and libraries. As America tried to enter the modern world, the morals of the Puritan forefathers were put on hold. Bills had to be paid. Lotteries were the obvious and, for a time, the only solution.

CHAPTER 2

THE PROFESSIONALS

MOST OF THE Founding Fathers supported lotteries before and after the war as a convenient way to fund government. Benjamin Franklin, George Washington, Alexander Hamilton, and Thomas Jefferson were all, at one time or another, involved with lotteries. In 1793, Hamilton laid out his "Ideas Concerning a Lottery" for a New Jersey scheme. Hamilton's rules for success included cheap tickets, a no-frills, easily comprehended game, and ticket offices near the borders to reach buyers in neighboring states. He also understood that the actual odds of winning were less important than igniting the mind of the player with the hope of a grand prize. "Everybody, almost, can and will be willing to hazard a trifling sum for the chance of considerable gain." The big jackpot, not an offering of numerous small prizes, was the avenue to a well-run lottery: "Hope is apt to supply the place of probability—and the Imagination to be struck with glittering though precarious prospects."

It was a bankable formula. The new nation—poor and striving to create a representative government with an independent economy—relied on lotteries to finance its growth. States used lottery money to build water supplies and city halls, streets, bridges, and canals, churches, prisons, and universities. Sometimes lotteries directly funded states' general budgets. As the states' ambitions increased, so did their budgets. The lotteries grew accordingly and became, over time, national businesses run by specialists.

At the heart of the games was either a wheel, a drum, or whatever container that could hold tickets and be shaken. Contemporary accounts usually describe two wheels, sometimes with glass sides. In one wheel are slips of paper with the prizes written on them. In the other are the rolled-up, numbered tickets purchased by players. Amid great ceremony, a child or a prominent public official or a blind person would draw a ticket. The ticket number would be called out, then a slip would be pulled from the second wheel and the prize—usually a blank, but sometimes a prize—would be awarded.

The lotteries' overwhelming success and popularity with the public would, as in the colonial years, send a wave of concern through government and some citizens and ultimately bring their demise.

But first the lotteries had to grow. Historian John MacMaster described the lotteries' spread after the Revolution as a result of a flood of municipal need: "In a short time there was a wheel in every town large enough to boast of a court house or a jail. Wherever a clumsy bridge was to be thrown across a stream, a public building enlarged, a schoolhouse built, a street paved, a road repaired, a manufacturing company to be aided, a church assisted, or a college treasury replenished, a lottery bill was passed by the legislature, a wheel procured, a notice put in the papers, and often in a few weeks the money was raised."

Running these early American games were men like P. T. Barnum, the great showman, impresario, and bellwether of the public's appetites. Barnum, born in 1810, came of age in the tail end of America's lottery golden age. He learned the lottery business from his grandfather, for whom he was named. Barnum recounts in his autobiography that in 1819, his grandfather Phineas Taylor was appointed manager of a lottery to benefit the Fairfield Episcopal Society in Connecticut. The tickets cost $5 each—half the price of the usual lottery at the time. Besides touting the relatively cheap price, Barnum's grandfather also advertised that the Episcopal Society lottery contained no "blanks." Every single ticket would produce a prize, the elder Barnum proclaimed. It was a seductive marketing pitch. Nearly every lottery placed unsold tickets into the lottery wheel with the purchased tickets. If a lot of tickets went unsold, the odds of winning were greatly reduced. The practice protected the people running the lottery.

Grandfather Barnum also insisted that nearly everyone who played would get half of their money back. Of the 12,000 prizes to be won, 11,400 were worth $2.50. No one seemed to notice that the odds of making a profit were horrendous—95 percent of the players would lose half their money. In recounting his grandfather's lottery scheme Barnum was astounded: "One chance in thirteen hundred and thirty-three! But customers did not stop to think of that." Compared to today's lottery odds, Grandfather Barnum's game seems like a good bet.

The tickets sold out, but the drawings left many customers unhappy. They had ignored the fine print that "all prizes are subject to the usual deduction of 15 per cent." The 11,400 people who were certain they would at least get half of their money back instead received $2.12½, "payable in 60 days." Barnum tells the tale with evident pride—it presaged his own future as a master huckster. As Barnum recounts it, his grandfather became a subject of derision for a time, nicknamed "old two dollars and fifty cents." But the hard feelings did not last forever: "As time wore away, he was declared to be the cutest man in those parts, and the public generally became reconciled to consider his famous 'Scheme' as a capital practical joke."

Barnum, who made a fortune on the art of bamboozling the public, wrote that the lottery was his first lesson in humbug. He soon ginned up his own lottery out of the general store where he clerked. The store dealt mostly in barter, so the prizes were items from the store. The top prize was $25 worth of merchandise. The next fifty prizes consisted of $5 worth of items of Barnum's choosing, mostly surplus items the store couldn't sell—flyspecked tinware and glass bottles. The same went for the other prizes valued at $1, 50¢, and 25¢ each. Barnum, still a teenager, posted large signs: MAGNIFICENT LOTTERY!, $25 FOR ONLY 50 CTS.!!, OVER 550 PRIZES!!! This was the new shorthand of lottery advertising. The thousand tickets were sold out at 50¢ each in less than two weeks. "Customers did not stop to consider the nature of the prizes," he wrote. "A young lady who had drawn five dollars would find herself entitled to a piece of tape, a spool of cotton, a paper of pins, sixteen tin skimmers, cups, and nutmeg graters, and a few dozen glass bottles of various sizes!"

When it was all done, the villagers, who worked in nearby factories manufacturing hats and combs, trundled home their worthless prizes. According to Barnum, most laughed it off just as he did. "My grandfather enjoyed my lottery speculation very much, and seemed to agree with many others, who declared that I was indeed 'a chip off the old block.'"

The ambitious Barnum left behind these small, unsanctioned lotteries and starting selling government and other lottery tickets on commission. He entered the growing professional national market of lotteries. He had much to learn. He traveled to New York to meet with a director of Yates & McIntyre, the nation's largest lottery-management firm, about opening a lottery office in Pittsburgh. The director was not interested, but offered Barnum a position as the company's sales agent in Nashville, where he could handle the state of Tennessee. Barnum declined the offer, but picked up some tips as to how the lottery—on a professional level—could be made more profitable. He expanded his coverage by selling tickets through the mail. Soon he had agents in a thirty-mile radius around Bethel, Connecticut, working for him. He sold anywhere from $500 to $2,000 worth of tickets a day. He advertised in thousands of flyers that boasted of his winners, and invented a fictional lucky operator—Dr. Peter Strickland—portrayed in newspapers as a man of science who brought fortune to his customers. When the state of Connecticut—fed up with the glut of games— prohibited any new lotteries in May 1834, Barnum gave up. He moved to New York City, where he switched to the business of entertainment and spectacle.

In the lottery world, Barnum had been a bit player, running games in the circumscribed surroundings of his hometown. Meanwhile, the lottery had gone national and been taken over from the amateurs. Lotteries were no longer games for small-time profit; they were the precursor of modern finance: a tool for gathering investment capital.

Every middling town had a lottery broker like Barnum. A lot of them supplemented their ticket-sales business with currency exchange. They accepted whatever banknotes were offered and assessed their value. With no national currency, Americans carried banknotes of various and negotiable worth and validity. If Barnum had taken the job with Yates & McIntyre and joined the major leagues of the lottery business, who knows what might have happened to Tennessee, or to Barnum. He might have been a financier as other lottery managers became.

Along with Yates & McIntyre, S&M Allen was one of the specialized firms that did nothing but manage sanctioned lotteries through a network of branch offices that sold tickets around the country. In any given lottery only 15 percent or so went to the "cause," whether it be road, church, school, or library, so the managers made steep profits.

Lottery offices dominated the landscape in some cities where ads for tickets crammed newspapers. S&M Allen was the second-largest lottery-management company, after Yates & McIntyre, but it had greater foresight than its rival. S&M Allen saw visions of a future in pure finance through stock and bond issuances—all backed by lottery revenue. The men who worked for S&M Allen and other lottery managers took their training in the lottery to investment-banking firms such as Smith Barney. Over a generation or two they so modernized the means for raising capital that lotteries became unnecessary as a tool of public or private finance.

Solomon Allen started out running a printing business at 45 Court Street in Albany. In 1808, the state capital was a sleepy government town just beginning to wake up. Robert Fulton had opened his Hudson River steamboat line linking Albany with New York City. The Erie Canal to connect the city to the Great Lakes had recently been dismissed by President Jefferson as "little short of madness." Ground would not be broken for almost another decade. Allen was young—in his early twenties—and had a decent business printing the *Albany Register*. He was in a central location, a stone's throw from City Hall, and he used the newspaper to advertise his sidelines in lottery tickets and other wares such as patent medicines, sealing wax, pencils, legal blanks, and, on request, gunpowder by the keg.

He also ran a successful, though small, currency exchange for the many different state banknotes in circulation. Business was good enough that in April 1812 he announced in the *Register* that he was leaving the printing business and would "devote his whole time, to the service of his friends, and customers in the Lottery, Exchange & Broking Business." With his brother Moses, he formed S&M Allen.

Their timing was admirable. The years following the War of 1812 were a period of widespread speculation in America. More and more state-chartered banks were opening and issuing notes, many of them in support of business ventures. For someone holding the notes it was difficult to determine their value. Brokers such as the Allens took the reins of the new business. In their early years they traded bank notes, sold shares in privateers, and took a wide variety of payments for lottery tickets. They opened a New York City branch dubbed Allens' Lucky Office. They sold tickets in the Harvard and Union College lotteries managed by Yates & McIntyre. They sold tickets in Pennsylvania's massive Union Canal Lottery, a project to bring coal and lumber into Philadelphia from the state's interior. The Allens sold tickets in New York's Medical Science Library Lottery, which raised money to purchase a doctor's twenty-acre botanic garden near what is now Fifth Avenue and Forty-seventh Street for the use of Columbia College. The garden of herbs was a piece of valuable real estate that would become the financial backbone of Columbia University. All of these transactions were precursors to today's bond issuances.

The Allens bought tickets in bulk and, like other brokers, sold them at a price of their choosing based on demand. Some tickets were expensive and naturally bought by wealthy players; others were sold for a few cents. The Allens publicized winners they knew would appeal to the public—widows or wounded veterans. Business boomed. Over their first twenty-five years they opened offices in thirteen states from Massachusetts to Alabama.

As they entered the 1820s their interests moved deeper into the emerging world of dealing in banknotes, securities, and stocks. In 1817, the New York Stock and Exchange Board was founded, named for a room at a coffeehouse where people met to exchange offers and securities. The Allen brothers jumped in with both feet, moving more and more of their business from lotteries to stocks and bonds. But while the New York Exchange was largely limited to local security issuances in its early years, the Allens had national ambitions. With branches around the country, they were a precursor to diversified investment banking firms, exchanging paper as capital through a network of commissioned brokers.

The firm went belly up in 1836 after a series of bad investments, but not before Allens hired a cousin, Enoch Clark, and taught him the lottery and brokerage businesses. When the firm failed, Clark went on to form his own successful securities-exchange business, E. W. Clark and Company. Clark made a fortune selling Texas state bonds in the years leading up to the war with Mexico. The bonds were a bet that the United States would defeat its neighbor and annex the frontier territory. More significantly, Clark soon hired an eighteen-year-old clerk, Jay Cooke. In 1861, Cooke struck out on his own and made a fortune selling nearly $1 billion in federal treasury notes to fund the Civil War. But E. W. Clark and Co. went bankrupt after stretching itself beyond the breaking point in railroad speculation, which helped start the financial panic of 1873. Cooke's son-in-law, Charles Barney, started his own firm the year of the panic. When he was ninety-four his company, Chas. D. Barney & Co., merged with Edward B. Smith & Co. to create Smith Barney & Co. Barney lived to be 101 years old.

As a whole, lotteries provided a valuable service to municipalities and states in need of finance. They pooled and assigned value to the various confusing notes on the market. The business overlapped with securities brokerage, bond sales, and other forms of debt marketing, and led into more sophisticated investment banking. Another broker who moved from lotteries to finance was John Thompson, a former math teacher from Albany. He sold tickets for Yates & McIntyre until 1833, when he left the dying lottery business and opened a brokerage firm on Wall Street. In 1836, he launched *Thompson's Bank Note and Commercial Reporter*, a newsletter that listed rates on the myriad banknotes on the market. The newsletter became today's *American Banker*. In 1863, he formed the First National Bank of New York, the largest holder of government bonds during the Civil War. And in 1877, he opened Chase National Bank, later renamed Chase Manhattan, then J. P. Morgan Chase.

Under the guidance of such ambitious men—and with the loosening of restrictions on private business as government and industry were pressed to raise large amounts of capital—an era of speculation took hold in the first two decades of the nineteenth century. On the street, this fever translated into lottery schemes that blanketed cities around the country. In 1809, three storefronts sold lottery tickets in Philadelphia. By 1833, more than two hundred were catering to the city's eighty thousand residents, who spent $30,000 a week on tickets. In 1826, New York City had more lottery vendors than there are Starbucks outlets today. In 1833, the city's roughly 160 lottery shops collected about $1.5 million from a population of about two hundred thousand. Portland, Maine, had twenty-five lottery vendors and a population of just twelve thousand. There were a variety of games to play from states around the country. In Baltimore or any other city, one could purchase a ticket in the lottery to fund the rebuilding of Faneuil Hall in Boston. Indeed you could buy tickets for just about any state-sponsored lottery, anywhere you pleased. Most of these lotteries ran for years, sometimes decades.

As lotteries blossomed, states banned the sale of "foreign" or out-of-state lotteries to protect local lottery profits and curtail the omnipresent vendors. But the practice continued. Vendors sometimes had to pay fines, but penalties were easily worth the high risk. A multitude of games and their salesmen jostled for customers in storefronts, in taverns, and on street corners. They also shouted from the newspapers with ads like Barnum's that promised good fortune and easy riches. Lottery dealers bought more ad space in newspapers than anyone else except patent medicine salesmen. They used direct marketing by sending flyers around the country and selling tickets through the mail. They used psychology to entice new players.

An ad that ran in 1808 in *Relfs Philadelphia Gazette* encouraged women to buy tickets: Hope and Company had tickets available in the Universalist Church lottery and the Holy Trinity lotteries for strong-minded ladies who did not have to "consult their cautious plodding husbands." The "one or more of the many dazzling prizes" awaited "the claim of beauty," the ad promised.

Over the next decades the sophistication of lottery marketing—and the ambitions for its profits—grew alongside the country's financial needs.

ONCE SMALLISH CITIES such as New York, Philadelphia, and Boston were quickly growing into busy trading ports with large populations hungry for entertainment. Lotteries were a popular way to pass the time. Players could choose from several different drawings, some running in different styles. Lottery vendors and managers thought up new ways to increase sales. Some found tickets difficult to afford. Rhode Island's School Fund Lottery of the 1830s and 1840s, which was the primary source of revenue for public schools, might have cost more than others at $5, but poverty was no barrier to playing. Ingenious vendors regularly split tickets into "shares"—a practice from the eighteenth century that became a standard part of play. Tickets were commonly broken down as small as one-sixteenth shares when it benefited sales, which were unpredictable. Lotteries were not guaranteed of success. Competition in the crowded market was an obstacle to gaining public interest. New games were developed and another old practice was quickly expanded—insurance or, as it became known, policy.

To opponents, the growth of policy was one of the most disheartening aspects of the nineteenth-century lotteries. Rather than buy a ticket, policy players bet a few pennies on what ticket numbers would be pulled on a given day in the lottery drawing. Or they could bet against certain ticket numbers. Insurance was invented by lottery retailers as a cheap side bet. One could buy a lottery ticket, or a share in a ticket, and as an afterthought place an insurance bet on the side. It was a cheap hedge, just a few cents, against losing, so they called it insurance. But many played insurance precisely because it was cheap. It quickly became the game of choice among the poorer classes. It was looked down on by some players. And from government's perspective, it was a nuisance. Bets on policy were not ticket sales, so the pennies didn't go to the official beneficiary of the lottery. Policy was a private side enterprise run by ticket brokers. States hated the policy game. The players and the ticket vendors loved it.

One of policy's great attractions was that players chose their own numbers. Picking numbers through the policy game eventually became the most widespread form of illegal gambling in the twentieth century. It still survives today as the numbers racket. In the nineteenth century the game had varying odds, determined by how many tickets were left in the lottery wheel. Because policy players picked their own numbers, it was an excellent outlet for superstition. Lottery vendors sold "dream books" that assigned certain numbers to various images that might occur in one's dreams or waking life. A rabbit might be 3-6-9, for example. The books grew in popularity in the late nineteenth and early twentieth century.

Insurance games grew rapidly in the nineteenth century, mostly because they were cheap and because they allowed the player the added excitement and "control" of choosing his own numbers. A century later it would become the cornerstone of the modern lottery.

Since only ticket sales were shared with the government, states, not surprisingly, began to ban policy because it undermined their lottery profits. They handed down fines to any vendors involved. But when a single lottery office could take in $30,000 in a day on policy bets, it was worth the risk. It was pure profit. Policy shops went underground.

Seeing the popularity of policy, lottery-management companies, hired by the states to raise money for various infrastructure projects, adopted their own legitimate number-picking system. In one popular variation, three numbers were picked from a large field—1 to 78 or 1 to 66. The first three-number combination to come out of the wheel won the grand prize. The next three-number combination took the second-place prize, the one after that took third place, and so on. In a game with tickets numbered 1 through 78, there were 76,076 possible combinations, so that many tickets could be sold. The drawings could be held in as little as fifteen minutes, allowing multiple drawings per day. With so much excitement and small, familiar numbers, sales of the number-picking game—a version of the old Renaissance Italian *lotto* game—skyrocketed.

In addition to banning "foreign" tickets and policy, states also began to rein in lotteries by requiring vendors to purchase licenses.

Ostensibly, the goal of licensing was to weed out fraudulent lotteries, but the licenses also allowed the state to take an extra piece of the pie. Since the states were only getting about 15 percent of sales, the extra licensing fees were welcome. The licenses might cost a few hundred dollars, or they could be even more expensive. In Louisiana in 1822, out-of-state lotteries paid $50,000 for a license to do business. Some legislatures enacted another regulatory measure by demanding that lottery managers post bonds to back up their drawings.

When these restrictions failed to curtail the availability of lottery games, a movement grew to ban them outright. Starting in the 1830s, states began prohibiting lotteries, repeating the same arguments used against the Virginia Company—they were immoral and destructive to business and public welfare. Two groups of citizens lined up in opposition to lotteries. First came the moralists. The puritanical and religious had always disliked lotteries, but in the nineteenth century, the Second Great Awakening focused on them as a clear target. A second, overlapping attack on lotteries came from the birth of the urban reform movement, whose members hated and feared the lottery offices that sprouted up like mushrooms in the less genteel corners of cities.

The civic reformers concentrated on Philadelphia, New York, and Boston. By the 1830s, the urban antilottery movement gained enough momentum to bring the entire lottery system into question. It took different avenues of attack. In some states the moral argument was predominant. In others, the discovery of local corruption or the erosion of public welfare motivated opponents and legislatures to reject new lottery applications, abolish existing lotteries, and in many cases write a lottery prohibition into their state's constitution.

Since day one, the Quakers had opposed the lottery on moral

grounds. In 1746, when Benjamin Franklin organized a lottery to fund the military defense of Philadelphia against a feared French invasion, he worried about the reaction of his Quaker peers. A Quaker friend did buy tickets but insisted he would not accept any prize he might win.

One of the leading tracts of the 1830s antilottery movement came from Philadelphia. Job Tyson had previously written for small audiences against the lotteries, but *The Lottery System in the United States*, financed by the Pennsylvania Society for the Suppression of Lotteries, was addressed to the whole country. Tyson, an erudite lawyer, employed the moral argument that lotteries were destructive to human behavior and particularly subversive to American society. The poor succumbed to idleness when they played, or even won, lotteries. He made examples of lottery winners, relating a piece of foreign news about a coachman in Brussels who had "drawn a prize of 5 million florins"—about $2 million—from a German lottery.

"The publication of such intelligence cannot but be injurious to the whole tribe of coachmen and servants in this country, whose ambition, it is well known, is already sufficiently magnificent," Tyson wrote. To Tyson, and fellow moralizers, every lottery player was a potential Icarus, who would doubtless crash and burn should he ever win. The "sudden elevation of a person beyond his natural condition, usually causes his ruin," Tyson wrote.

Unearned wealth destroys character because "it raises him to a sudden pinnacle which renders him dizzy; he looks with contempt upon the humbleness of useful labors below. His brief career, marked by wasteful extravagance and licentious folly, ends in bankruptcy."

Lottery winners, opponents feared, inspired the lower strata of Philadelphia to chase their own fantasy of wealth, causing them to become distracted from honest work and further eroding the burgeoning American urban society. Newspaper articles and antilottery tracts of the time traced a pattern of fallen character through lotteries. All around, Tyson saw otherwise respectable chimney sweeps, clerks, and the "man of slender means" overtaken with dreams of "sudden wealth" and in danger of turning into "degraded paupers." He retold newspaper stories from around the country, such as those of the bank teller who embezzled funds to cover the $10,000 he had lost to the lotteries and of a woman who stole from her husband to play and eventually ended up a prostitute. Suicide, which was treated not as a sign of psychological depression but as the result of moral depravity, was another popular end for lottery players in stories recounted by lottery opponents and in the press.

The year before Tyson's tract came out, Massachusetts had been abuzz over reports of the suicide of a young clerk, David Ackers. Although known among his colleagues at an importing house for "integrity and purity," Ackers was secretly hooked on the lottery. He stole $18,000 from his employers. When he was found dead, it was first thought that he had been robbed and murdered. Then his note was found: "The time I note my downfall, or deviated from the path of rectitude, was about the middle of June last when I took a share in a company of lottery tickets, whereby I was successful in obtaining a share of one half the capital prize since which I have gone for myself, and that too, not on a very small scale, as you can judge from the amount now due J.R. & Co., every dollar of which has been spent in that way." If Massachusetts lottery opponents needed any more evidence to make their case, Ackers's final sentence sealed the deal: "Oh wretch! Lotteries have been thy ruin. I cannot add more." The story was an effective weapon for opponents to use against the lottery. Within months of Ackers's death the legislature made participation in lotteries punishable by imprisonment.

Gradually, Presbyterian, Baptist, and Lutheran councils—churches that had all reaped windfalls from lotteries—joined the Quakers in opposition to them.

Tyson and others did not limit themselves to the moral arguments of the eighteenth century. They added fiscal criticism. "Can it, upon any just view of the subject, be regarded in the light of a tax?" Tyson wrote. "Does the ostensible sum to be levied constitute the whole of the assessment? And is it equal in its effects, in the imposition of a burden which is proportional to the ability of the citizen?"

The answer was no, and it was easily found by looking at a few of the largest and longest-running lotteries in the country. Lotteries created to benefit the public were often rife with financial waste. An 1812 scheme to restore Plymouth Beach in Massachusetts had legislative approval to sell tickets until the managers had raised $16,000. Over the next nine years the lotteries raked in $886,439.75, of which they returned a whopping $9,876.17—or 1 percent of sales—to the project. On Tyson's home front, Pennsylvania had authorized one of the largest lotteries to date to finance the Union Canal Company. The twenty-year grant started in 1812. It was a profitable twenty-year run but not for the canal. The lottery took in $21,248,891 and returned less than its goal of $340,000 to the canal project. Rather than cancel the lottery, the legislature renewed and enlarged its charter.

In New York, in 1818, Charles Baldwin, the editor of the *Republican Chronicle* in New York City, published accusations that the local Medical Science Lottery to benefit Columbia College was crooked. The managers of the lottery had hired children to draw the tickets as visible proof of an honest game, but children were in on the scam. Tickets were being palmed and then "drawn" from the wheel after heavy policy bets were placed on them.

On the fifth day of drawing, a little boy pulled out ticket number 3865. The ticket had been insured at several lottery offices for a large amount of money. Later in the day ticket number 30 was pulled. It had also been heavily insured. Whispers grew that the game was fixed. On the ninth day of drawings, ticket number 15,468 was pulled, and, surprise, it had a lot of insurance money riding on it. One of the winners said the number came to him in a dream. The winning-number slips were all worn and soiled, as if they'd been handled far more than the others. When Baldwin published his account of the dirty lottery, the managers sued him for libel. The mayor held hearings on the case, followed closely by the press and the public, which acquitted Baldwin and proved his accusations of fraud.

New York banned lotteries in 1833. The Pennsylvania legislature soon followed, prohibiting lotteries after December 31, 1834. Tyson was prescient in noting that the abolition of lotteries was not much more than the "vogue" of the hour, though he praised New York for taking the added step of carving the ban into its constitution. Nine states had stopped holding lotteries by 1835. The rest would follow suit over the next several decades. As new states entered the union at a fast clip in the 1840s and 1850s, most ratified constitutions that specifically banned lotteries. By the start of the Civil War nearly every state in the country had repudiated the lottery. There were sporadic lotteries, however, particularly in the South during the second half of the nineteenth century. Some lotteries financed Confederate troops and others took advantage of the confusion during Reconstruction to sell tickets. But they were scattered. Only the Louisiana Lottery, approved in 1868, would thrive. S&M Allen went out of business. So did fellow lottery manager Yates & McIntyre, which was the giant of the business. Tickets could still be purchased, but the business was a shadow of its former self. Lotteries operated illegally or were bought through the mail from Mexico, Havana, Spain, and elsewhere.

The lotteries were the victim of their own success, not to mention their susceptibility to corruption. Renewed moral and civic opposition drove them out. Another factor in their demise was the
increased sophistication of American finance. The country was ma-
turing. The first decades of the nineteenth century saw an increase in
foreign trade and a decrease in the number of obstacles to the creation
of corporations. As a result, a number of alternatives competed with
the lotteries for the raising of capital. Many of the new lottery men
were diversified and engaged in financial transactions either as a side-
line or as the main thrust of their business. They offered small loans
to governments or local municipal projects and held securities or
stocks in the project, which they might resell.

At first, most of the money for large-scale projects came from
private domestic sources. For some years foreign investors considered
America, with little credit history and an uncertain future, an unstable investment. Financial historian Fritz Redlich identified four other
sources of finance in this era that competed with lotteries. First were
the emerging princes of trade such as John Jacob Astor, who invested
his own and his friends' money in canals. Private commercial banks
were a second source of capital that provided long-term loans, particularly to railroads. A third were banks created to issue notes on specific commercial ventures, such as Chemical Bank, which began as a
division of the New York Chemical Manufacturing Company. From
the end of the Revolution through the 1820s banks had a difficult time.
Legislatures mistrusted them. By the 1830s the legal barriers that restricted their transactions were loosened. Men such as the Allen
brothers joined the new world of finance. New banks sprang up, taking more business away from lotteries.

The fourth financial force that hurt lotteries was, in fact, founded
with the express interest of putting the games out of business. The

first savings banks opened in America with the mission to get working people to save their hard-earned pennies and dollars. There was little upward mobility in the late eighteenth and early nineteenth centuries. Those with wealth could buy government bonds or private investments. For those with little or moderate income the lottery offered one of the few opportunities to increase wealth. Merchant bankers held the capital and created banks to hold their wealth and fund industry, public projects, and in times of need, such as the War of 1812, the government itself. They did not take small accounts. Those with a little bit of money stuffed it in their mattresses or played the lottery.

The New York Bank for Savings was the product of a group of civic reformers, men such as John Pintard, who were concerned about the rising tide of poor and immigrants. As they saw it, the lottery was a symptom of poverty. It was a problem of public welfare. Pintard was an importer and securities broker turned social reformer. He was one of the first Wall Street traders in the 1790s, when securities were sold on commission while brokers stood on Wall Street or in bad weather in a private room at the nearby Tontine Coffee House. Bad investments led him to bankruptcy and some time in debtors' prison. From then on he became a public servant in local offices and a busy man in the new era of civic reform. He and other urban reformers were informed by the growing Christian zeal to banish immoral habits—Pintard was active in the American Bible Society along with many civic improvement societies—but they also had a utilitarian agenda. On December 4, 1816, he wrote a letter to his daughter Eliza, in New Orleans, describing their savings bank plan: "It will remove one of the causes of mendacity & thereby lessen the burthens on the more favoured class of citizens in supporting paupers, by exciting thrift, frugality, a pride of character & independence which will be productive of moral & religious habits."

In other words, immoral behavior was common among the poorer classes, so Pintard sought to eliminate poverty. The full-service, central headquarters of this movement was the Society for the Prevention of Pauperism. Its purpose, he wrote Eliza in October 1818, was "not to afford alms but labour, so that there shall be no pretext for idleness, to give the means of occupation to the industrious, to educate their children & to expel the drones from Society."

Pintard chaired the society's Committee on Lotteries. He quickly learned that getting ahold of the lottery problem required a "more intricate" solution than creating a savings bank. "The evils and abuses are apparent but the remedies not so, for there is no possibility of laying the ax to the root & abolishing them," he wrote Eliza on November 16, 1816.

When the New York Bank for Savings took its first deposits in 1819, it was the first savings bank in New York. Customers—large depositors were turned away—received a passbook. Accounts between $5 and $49 earned 5 percent interest; $50 or more had a 6 percent annual rate. It would become the biggest bank of its kind and a significant investment force. After five years the bank had almost $1.5 million in deposits. More than thirty thousand customers had entrusted the bank with their scraped-together savings. In 1825, this one bank held 52 percent of the nation's savings deposits. After its opening and quick success, other savings banks, such as the Bowery Savings Bank and the Seamen's Bank for Savings, were chartered in New York and around the country, catering to the new, and less affluent, clientele. By 1860 savings banks around the country held $150 million in assets. With its rising assets, the New York Bank for Savings went on an aggressive buying spree. The bank's charter limited its investments to government securities issued by the United States, New York State, or

New York City. So the bank became the largest stakeholder in the Erie Canal. By 1828, it held roughly half of New York City's debt. In 1830, the state legislature amended the bank's charter to allow the purchase of bonds from any state.

The New York Bank for Savings performed much the same role as a lottery did, financing large public projects by amassing small amounts from thousands of depositors. In theory, it was a perfect replacement—the customer got interest on his deposit, and the government raised money without resorting to taxes. Because the Bank for Savings was restricted to buying government debt issuances or bonds, the state was able to broker better terms than would have been possible with private banks. The Erie Canal was built more cheaply because of the Bank for Savings. New York State was desperate to build the canal but had little means to raise the capital. Investors were hard to come by. The gargantuan infrastructure project, labeled Clinton's Folly, was considered too ambitious. Raising or creating new taxes to pay for it was a political death sentence. The legislature might have authorized an Erie Canal Lottery, but the lottery market was crowded. Too many lottery tickets were for sale, so that any one lottery could easily get lost in the crowd of schemes vying for the customers' attention. Sales would be too unpredictable.

Some wealthy individuals, such as John Jacob Astor, provided financing for the canal, but the bulk of the money came from the Bank for Savings. For a decade, it was the single largest holder of canal stock, easily beating private banks, which had fewer restrictions on investments, but were wary. The New York Bank for Savings' success with Erie Canal purchases inspired confidence among foreign and private investors in the once-questionable market of American state debt issuances. It created a groundswell of optimism in other states hoping to finance large capital projects. At a critical period in

America's financial development, the Bank for Savings funded massive public works projects necessary to the growth of cities and their businesses.

In the 1830s the Bank for Savings was also a major investor in New York City's ambitious plan to build the upstate Croton Reservoir and bring clean water to its populace, which was suffering a cholera epidemic. If anything the project was more ambitious than the Erie Canal and struggled to find financing until the bank bought $400,000 of its initial $1 million debt issuance.

The Bank for Savings was strong competition for the lotteries when state governments went looking for capital. The bank proved that public projects could be financed across state lines in a more stable manner than by selling lottery tickets. In some ways, it was the exact opposite of a lottery. It too depended on salesmanship and the dreams of the public for a better future, but its foundation was the wisdom and patience of savings, not a fevered dream of fortune. Lotteries had already proven that the pennies and dollars of the mass population could be tapped as a funding resource; savings banks demonstrated a way that benefited all sides. By their success, savings banks proved that people were willing to save money if given the opportunity. Just how many turned their money over to banks instead of buying lottery tickets is not known, but the death of the lotteries coincided with the creation of the banks. More important, the banks coincided with a shift in opinions against the lotteries.

The Civil War inspired a few states in search of money to cast aside their old oppositions to lotteries, but not in significant numbers. During Reconstruction some states, particularly in the South, debated renewing lotteries to fund government, but without much success. While most states did not get back into the lottery business, lottery operators stayed open after the Civil War in a new form, using storefronts to sell tickets through the mail, skirting state bans. Games continued in such places as Baltimore, Philadelphia, Boston, and New York. When Congress made an attempt to bar lotteries from the mail, it sparked lawsuits from the lottery companies. Barring them from federal posts was an infringement of free speech, they argued. The response from Alfred A. Freeman, the assistant attorney general for the Post Office Department, was passionate and illustrated how lotteries had reinvented themselves by 1880:

"The proportion that the lottery business has assumed within the last few years, invokes the serious consideration of the court and the country," Freeman argued in a Kentucky case. "Take, for example, the State of New York, where the organization of lottery companies or even the sale of lottery tickets is prohibited by statute. There are today in the city of New York alone 33 lottery agencies, receiving weekly, on an average 7,661 ordinary, and 1,933 registered letters. Millions of dollars are flowing annually into their coffers. They are huge financial vampires sucking the life-blood of legitimate business enterprises, inflicting upon society a species of distempered mental leprosy, which will require years to remove. This gigantic work of undermining the best interests of society is being accomplished by a monster that seeks to hide behind the mask of a State charter a visage more hideous than that of the veiled prophet."

There was no shortage of outrage. Perhaps Freeman's was the popular attitude. Horatio Alger wrote of the lotteries with similar disgust in novels such as *Do and Dare*, with parables about wasteful young men who play the lottery and try to tempt others into ruin. But not everyone was putting their money in savings banks. Freeman's contemporaries gave similar accounts of the widespread presence of lottery offices in New York and other cities. The life of thrift, so popular among the Puritans, Quakers, and social reformers, may have become the nation's popular ideal, but the siren song of lotteries was stiff competition for the consumer's attention. As historian Ann Fabian writes in *Card Sharps, Dream Books, and Bucket Shops*, "The savings bank might have offered him ownership and the right to work for himself, but it never offered him the right not to work and the right not to spend." This dream of riches and a life of ease, of escaping the daily grind, was enough enticement to keep lotteries going even when outlawed by government. Crackdowns removed many offenders. In the end, only one state openly embraced the lottery, and its game was bigger than any of those that came before it.

THE LOUISIANA LOTTERY was known as the Octopus because its arms reached into every state and city. As the only standing lottery left in the United States, the Louisiana Lottery was a byword for fraud and vice. Conducting its business through the mail, it capitalized on the death of other state lotteries, effectively forming a monopoly and demonstrating just how far the business could be taken. The Octopus was a massive, bullying operation with deep pockets. It seemed that everywhere the Louisiana Lottery went, bribery of public officials and the press went with it. With an army of lobbyists and money at its disposal, it bought Louisiana's legislature and courts as a weapon. The millions in bribes were easily covered by sales. It would ultimately require federal intervention to shut the operation down.

Montgomery Ward is often credited with starting the first nationwide mail-order business in the country, but the Louisiana Lottery came first. Taking advantage of improved roads and mail service, the Louisiana Lottery reached its customers through tens of thousands of circulars, tickets, and prize charts sent out every month.

Its postal costs accounted for nearly half the revenue of the Louisiana postal service. By some estimates, the envelopes sent out by the Octopus brought in as much as $30 million a year from customers, more than 90 percent of whom lived in other states. But the company was secretive about its income. The only tax it paid was the $40,000 it was chartered by the state to supply each year to the Charity Hospital of New Orleans. Other expenses, such as prizes, totaled $3 million a year during the heyday of the game. Winners lived in cities across America. In one 1879 drawing, the top prizes went to residents of New York, Louisville, Washington, D.C., and St. Louis. No one, however, in its twenty-four years of operation ever grabbed the trumpeted $600,000 grand prize. Operating costs, which often took the form of bribes or public relations–inspired acts of generosity, also took a portion of revenue. The profits of its owners may have ranged up to $15 million a year. At its zenith, company stock was worth more than twice the capital in Louisiana's banks.

A group of New York gamblers conceived this behemoth. They set up shop in New Orleans, where in 1868 they bribed the Reconstruction legislature to hand them a twenty-five-year grant to run a lottery to benefit schools. Hidden in the legislation's fine print was a monopoly that prohibited any other lottery from being established in the state. The company's point man was Charles T. Howard, who had been a lottery agent for Alabama and Kentucky. But a week after the law was passed the list of incorporators was changed. Ownership, it turned out, was really in the hands of the company's principal moneymen, John A. Morris and Charles Murray, and their group of New York gambling men. Born into an established American family that counted a prominent revolutionary, Gouverneur Morris, as a member, John Morris married the daughter of a Louisiana judge after graduating from Harvard. His money and local connections helped pave the way for the company's charter. Its original investors included John Morrissey, known as Old Smoke, who had a much rougher résumé than Morris. A former gang leader and heavyweight champion in New York, Morrissey had battled William "Bill the Butcher" Poole. Morrissey gave up fighting for gambling houses and, in search of greater respectability, opened a casino and racetrack in Saratoga Springs, New York, for well-heeled vacationers. He was also a congressman and power player in New York's notorious Tammany Hall political machine who later testified against Boss Tweed. Another man in on the ground floor was Zachariah Simmons, who, in alliance with Tammany Hall, controlled the policy games that flourished in New York after the Civil War. Benjamin Wood, owner of the *New York Daily News* and brother to the city's pro-Confederate mayor, Fernando Wood, also invested.

The brains behind the operation is said to have been an Austrian physician, Dr. Maximilian Dauphin. He realized the far-reaching potential for sales. He also attempted to win over the public, not just the politicians, by civic generosity, such as donations to victims of a terrible flood in 1890.

In an attempt to publicize an image of integrity, the company hired two distinguished Confederate generals, P. G. T. Beauregard and Jubal Early, to conduct the public drawings amid fanfare. Boys from a local orphan asylum were blindfolded and drew the tickets. In some drawings for great prizes the tickets cost as much as $40, but could be purchased in fractions for less. Daily drawings, introduced by Dauphin, were held at four o'clock and had two options. One could buy a cheap ticket or play the policy game and make a guess at what numbers would be drawn. The policy game cost just a few pennies to play.

The venture's ridiculous charter terms and outsize profits were so brazen that in its first decade it fought off several attempts by the legislature to abolish it or charter competing lotteries. It aggressively defended its monopoly by prosecuting small-time lottery operators. In 1878, the local outcry against it was so loud that the company trotted out General Early, armed with talking points, to calm the public: "As to the objection that the Louisiana State Lottery Company is a monopoly, we do not see that it is a very serious one, but are of the opinion that it is for the better that the charter confers a monopoly. If lotteries are all great evils, then it is better that they should exist as monopolies than that the right to conduct them should be general."

The company's money was said to have made its way into the pockets of the legislature, the courts, and the press. The company won both state and federal lawsuits that attempted to shut it down.

Charles Howard, who presided over the lottery until his death, tried to put a reputable face on the business and his personal wealth through local philanthropy and grand public works. He failed, but his stamp is still on New Orleans. His tomb lies at the heart of the city's famous Metairie Cemetery, which he founded on the former site of the Metairie Race Course. The story goes that Howard, angered that the Metairie Jockey Club refused him membership, drove the racetrack out of business by opening a competing track now known as the Fair Grounds. He bought the Metairie Race Course and, as his first order of business, marked the center of the outfield grass for his mausoleum. When he died in 1885, he was buried there. His daughter hired a renowned architect to build the Howard Memorial Library. It is now part of the Ogden Museum of Southern Art. One of his sons paid for Confederate Memorial Hall. "He aspired to be a leader of society, but was repeatedly foiled," the *New York Times* wrote in his obituary. "The Old Creole families refused to receive him, and this rankled in his mind."

The company's greater concern, however, was not social revulsion but political. As the Octopus grew, opponents spoke against it in nearly every state. With residents of New York and Boston spending about $50,000 a month on tickets, the lottery was impossible to ignore. Because it owned the politicians and judges of Louisiana and conducted its business through the mail, it was difficult to bring down. In 1890, as local and national pressure on Louisiana grew, the company sought to renew its charter, which was due to expire in four years. To secure another quarter century, the company offered to raise its contribution to the state treasury from $40,000 to $1 million. The state had just recovered from a disastrous flood in 1890 and the money was badly needed. The deal would put $450,000 toward levees on the Mississippi River and drainage systems for New Orleans. Another $350,000 would go to schools, and $50,000 to Confederate army pensions. When the governor refused to sign the renewal, the state's supreme court ruled it did not require the governor's signature. The fight over its charter made national headlines.

As corrupt as it was, its profits were so great that other states were tempted to copy the formula. North Dakota began to look at starting its own version. Dozens of outfits with mail-order lotteries opened on the Mexican border and elsewhere outside the state laws that advertised and sold tickets through the mail. Reformers were always afraid of the corrupting influence of lottery money, but now they were also afraid of its adaptability and its audacity at evading states' laws. The Louisiana Lottery, with its urgent warning to "Let Not a Moment Escape You or You May Be Too Late," was the leader of the pack. To kill the beast, President Benjamin Harrison sent a message to the House and Senate: "The people of all the States are debauched and defrauded. The vast sums of money offered to the States for charters are drawn from the people of the United States, and the General Government through its mail system is made the effective and profitable medium of intercourse between the lottery company and its victims."

Two months later Congress passed a bill outlawing the use of the postal service for sending any lottery-related materials. Lotteries joined obscene materials and information on contraception, which had been banned from the federal mail system under the Comstock Act in 1873. The antilottery laws were enforced by arrests in Boston, Sioux Falls, San Antonio, and New Orleans. The Louisiana Lottery Company bought its charter renewal from the legislature, but its dream of another twenty-five-year run was dashed by a popular vote that went against it, 157,422 to 4,225. The voters of Louisiana exiled the Octopus.

When the company's charter expired in 1894, it was nearly crippled. The company pulled stakes for Honduras, renaming itself the Honduras National Lottery. The business continued printing and distributing tickets in the United States, using private mail couriers. Congress responded in 1895 by making the interstate trafficking of lottery materials a crime. For a number of years the company operated outside the law, until raids on these operations finally killed the Octopus in 1907.

The Louisiana Lottery's barely concealed bribery and corruption of government and courts made lotteries a pariah in most state legislatures. Over the next seventy years the games would sporadically be suggested in times of fiscal need, but no state dared to adopt one. In this fallow period of state-authorized lotteries, the policy game would take hold in cities as an underworld phenomenon, franchised around the country through organized crime. The outlawed policy game with its player involvement and popular dream books became the format on which the states would model lotteries when they revived them, starting in 1964.

CHAPTER 3

GOING LEGIT

AUGUST 13, 2001, a Monday, was a lucky day—suddenly breezy and cool in the middle of what had until then been a sweltering month in Chicago. Sterling Plumpp left his apartment that morning, walked down the front steps, and headed down West Chicago Avenue to the liquor store.

He bought the *Sun-Times* and the *Tribune*. As he stepped up to the counter, he saw the display of scratch tickets. He put down $20 for two $10 scratch games called Vegas. He didn't buy scratch tickets often, but when he did he had a rule: always scratch with a dime. A nickel was too clumsy. He walked the six blocks back home. Another rule: never scratch tickets in the store. He sat down in his living room and scratched. He had won $15.

You're down five, Plumpp thought. He read the papers for a while, then walked back to the liquor store. He collected his $15, bought two more tickets, and headed home again. This time he won $25. He was even—$40 gambled and $40 won. There's no joy in even. Only a fool gambles to break even, his father had always said. If you're going to gamble, gamble to win. Now Plumpp was annoyed. He preferred to pick his numbers in the regular state-lottery jackpots. Cheap scratch tickets with small jackpots such as $2,000 were pointless. He only bought the expensive cards; the million-dollar prizes caught his eye. A million dollars—that could change your life, that was worth gambling on. He walked back to the store.

Helen looked up from the counter as he entered for the third time. Sterling Plumpp, acclaimed poet of the blues, literature professor approaching retirement, and winner of the Carl Sandburg Literary Award, was determined to beat the odds. He collected his $25 from Helen and put down $10. "Give me that Beat the Dealer card," he said. He liked the name. Beat the Dealer. It summed up how he felt.

Plumpp has the flattened nose and drooping eyelids of a boxer. It's hard to imagine him ever having the face of a child. He was born January 30, 1940, in Clinton, an unincorporated town outside Jackson, Mississippi. His grandparents raised him in their home, little more than a shack with no electricity or running water. He worked in the surrounding fields from an early age. School was an option, but not until he was eight years old—the eight-mile walk was too much. From an early age people commented on his intelligence, but Plumpp was on a fast track to being a cotton field hand, like his father and grandfather. In 1958, his aunt Carrie intervened. She and her husband, Aaron Jefferson, ran a saloon called the Big House. Aunt Carrie used some of her money to send him to the elite Holy Ghost High School in Jackson.

He felt like a foreigner among the other students there. They were younger and, from their perspective, from a better class. They grew up in Jackson. They lived in houses. Their parents owned funeral parlors and hotels, and worked in professions, not fields. They rode bicycles. He ran barefoot around Clinton every summer, switching to his Sunday shoes in the fall.

At Holy Ghost, the nuns in blue habits lashed out at the children for infractions of rituals that Plumpp didn't understand. As an out-sider, he internalized the experience, saving it up until he let it out in the poems he would soon write:

> *I am lost,*
> *Keeping somebody else's seven sacraments.*
> *Worshipping fear. Running from everything real.*

He became attached to the blues in these years. The blues was as real as the prayers he heard his grandfather Victor Emmanuel say at bedtime. " 'Take care of Seal, the workhorse that's sick. Drive the bo'weevils away. Put some softness in white folks' hearts so they won't cheat so badly this time.' "

Plumpp graduated as valedictorian, but he never felt at ease in school. In 1962, after two years of college in Kansas, he left and joined the last remnants of the Great Migration in Chicago, where relatives had moved decades earlier.

> *"Look, grandpa, old old man,*
> *I knows what I is doing.*
> *I is going to the city*
> *Where opportunity hides under*
> *Concrete like sweet taters.*
> *I knows I can dig what*
> *I digs up from the ground.*
> *I ain't, ain't going back*
> *Down to mister Mississippi."*
> *Will the circle be unbroken*
> *Bye and bye, yall, bye and bye . . .*

The job he found in the post office was not much better than sharecropping. He worked ten hours a day, watched as black men trying to climb the short ladder to a higher position fought each other and yessir'ed their younger, white supervisors. He turned to Howlin' Wolf and Muddy Waters in West Side clubs for an antidote to the grind. When Muddy Waters sang about his virility, Plumpp heard a song for men like himself, men who could be fired on a whim.

He began to write poetry. His first attempts came in his downstairs room at the home of his mother's sister, Aunt Mattie, and her husband, Jesse Dixon. The Dixons were his only relatives in Chicago who owned their own home. They had bought a two-family house with money they won playing policy, the widespread, illegal game that had outlived the lotteries. The Dixons won $1,000 playing policy numbers they picked off a receipt. The policy raised the Dixons into the middle class. Their success was legend in the Plumpp family, proof that there were no odds that couldn't be beat.

In the intervening years, the Illinois Lottery had been created in 1974. It was one of the largest in the country, eventually becoming so expansive that it had to create a program for people who wanted to voluntarily ban themselves from playing. Participants told lottery administrators to refuse them any prize greater than $600, and to not send any direct-mail or e-mail advertisements. Such were the problems of a successful lottery.

But this breezy August morning, Sterling Plumpp, an occasional player, stood at the liquor-store counter determined to beat the odds. Plumpp walked back home from the liquor store and found another dime to scratch off the ticket.

He shredded the wax, brushed it away, and saw the dealer had a two. He scratched again. He discovered that the prize at stake was a million dollars. He scratched a third time. He had a six against the dealer's two.

Six beats two. But he didn't believe it. He inspected the card and read the rules of play. The high cards wins the amount shown, it said. But that would mean he had just won a million dollars.

He called to find out where the nearest claim office was. There was no mistake. He had beaten the dealer. He had beaten the odds.

Sterling Plumpp had beaten the odds long before this ticket. He had risen from sharecropping to a master's degree and published volumes of his own poetry. But this was different. Now he was wealthy. What does a rich poet write about? he wondered.

He had always been independent, but he began to think that the money might also set him free. Not long after he won, he was invited to give a reading in New York. A few weeks earlier, he wouldn't have hesitated to fly across the country to collect the $500 speaking fee. It was decent pay for a poet. But now Plumpp found himself raising his price, setting a higher amount that seemed worth his time. The man on the other end of the phone hesitated. So Plumpp told him:

"Maybe you should find another poet."

THE POLICY GAME, later known as the numbers, did more than just survive the death of the lotteries. By the 1950s and 1960s it seemed as if everyone in big cities such as Chicago and New York played at least occasionally. It was a cheap game—just a few cents to play—and simple. There were variations over time, but in the original policy game, players picked a combination of numbers from a field, usually 1 to 78, and won if their numbers hit. In the late nineteenth century some policy games simply used the winning numbers from the last remaining legitimate lotteries: telegraph wires brought the results of the Kentucky or Louisiana lotteries, which were announced in illicit policy shops. Or the games were played with their own illegal "policy wheel": like the lottery wheels in use for centuries it was a drum filled with numbers on slips of paper that was spun until the slips were well mixed and ready to be plucked out.

A two-number combination was a *saddle*, three was a *gig*, and four a *horse*. The game kept the language of the track. The odds were long, but the payouts were high. From its inception in the 1800s the game quickly proved profitable because it allowed players to pick their own numbers and, above all, it cost so little to play. As states banned lotteries, the game carried on, mostly in cities, by going underground.

Policy lent itself to surreptitious operation. Unlike the "secret" gambling halls that flourished in the second half of the nineteenth century and through Prohibition, policy required no card or dice tables, no roulette wheel, or other paraphernalia. It was strictly low-rent. The lucky pick of numbers needed only some scraps of paper and a pencil. It was advertised through word of mouth. It had always been associated with the poorer classes, and often with blacks. Their penny gambles were barely worth cracking down on. Policy easily receded from public view; players were often on the margin of city life, and few of them wanted to be discovered. Inquisitive police were often bribed.

"The room where the game is played is, like those of other cheap gambling-dens, usually at the rear of a cigar-store, barroom, or other place where it does not rouse suspicion if many persons are seen entering," journalist Thomas Knox wrote in 1892. "A long counter extends the entire length of the room, and behind this counter, near its center, sits the man who keeps the game and is called the 'writer.' He is not the proprietor, but simply a clerk on a salary, and his duties are to copy the slips handed up by the players, mark them with the amount of money paid, and watch to see that no fraud is practiced."

Knox described his visit to a policy room in *Darkness and Daylight; Or, Lights and Shadows of New York Life*, one of several accounts, including Jacob Riis's *How the Other Half Lives*, that included policy shops on their tours of the city's "underbelly." The accounts invariably described players gathering in large crowds: men, women, and children, paupers, laborers, and clerks, immigrants, whites, and blacks. These crowds piled in en masse only to lose their money, according to Knox. In these descriptions, the mixture of races was proof of the immoral nature of the games. Young clerks were a favorite subject of nineteenth-century lottery opponents. It seemed that apprentices and clerks were always at risk of losing their desire for hard work by wasting their money and lives on dreams of lottery fortunes. Invariably, they ended up penniless and in the gutter in the morality tales of the era.

Like the stories about nineteenth-century lotteries, descriptions of policy were often followed by salacious accounts of suicides or madness brought on by either losing or winning fortunes. Choosing numbers was popularized as a mania among players who assigned number values from images in dreams. It was a long-shot game, but that only added to the mystery and excitement. The odds were long, but the advertised rewards were high.

"But a man stands as good a chance of being struck by lightning as he does of winning at this rate," Knox wrote after his policy-shop visits. "Nevertheless the game is full of seductiveness on account of its possibilities and also on account of its cheapness. Some of the shops have telephone connections, and a customer who is known to the establishment can play policy without leaving his office, by simply telephoning his guesses. That a large amount of money may be lost at policy is shown by the circumstance that quite recently the cashier of an important law firm in New York City embezzled $125,000 of the money of his employers. 'When the defalcation was discovered and investigated it was found that this enormous sum had been spent in playing policy in a notorious shop on Broadway.'"

Policy didn't explode until after World War I. By then business had grown to the point that there were recognized "policy kings." Midsize and small cities had policy or numbers games, but the two empires of the business were in Harlem and Chicago's South Side. John "Mushmouth" Johnson was one of the first black policy operators in Chicago, having arrived in the 1870s. He controlled several gambling houses and policy wheels. Historians write that "Policy" Sam Young got his start under Patsy King, Johnson's white partner, who had abandoned a career as a riverboat gambler for Chicago. Another of Johnson's early partners was an Asian man known as King Foo.

"Policy" Sam Young, often credited as the father of policy, ran wheels called the Interstate Springfield Policy Company, and the Frankfort, Henry, and Kentucky. The wheels often took their name from the Kentucky lotteries that had been the last legal games prior to the Louisiana Lottery. The Kentucky lotteries had in their final years supplied policy numbers to illegal wheels in New York and elsewhere. In South Side Chicago, policy drawings were held as often as three times a day.

Another major Chicago policy operator was "Big Ed" Jones. A graduate of Howard University, Jones migrated to Chicago from Mississippi and ran a cab stand with his brother. Jones expanded his profits quickly by hiring beautiful women to work in his policy shops and an "army" of runners.

In New York's Harlem policy world, Casper Holstein is said to have started the numbers game at the turn of the century. Holstein ran the numbers games alongside Stephanie St. Clair and her protégé Ellsworth Raymond "Bumpy" Johnson.

Policy and numbers operations were often left alone, in part, because they were seen as a problem confined to ghettos. But some exchange of money always occurred between operators and officials as protection to keep the games running. In New York, when the Republican Party took control of the legislature, it created the Lexow Commission to investigate the New York City Police Department, an arm of Tammany Hall's corrupt Democratic administration. The commission concluded in 1895 that the city had six hundred policy shops, and that policy kings divided their territory "largely for the benefit of the police, insuring a more rapid and easier collection of the tribute to be paid the 'policy king' to whom a particular district had been assigned, paying in bulk at the rate of $15 per shop for all the shops running in such district or districts."

The Lexow Commission heard dramatic testimony from a policy writer, J. Lawrence Carny. Everyone played, he testified: "Go down around Eldridge and Stanton streets, they play penny and two- cent gigs; you go uptown and they play from fifteen to twenty-five cents, and sometimes a dollar, and you go to Little Italy, and they play all sorts; and you come down where the brokers play, they put down a hundred dollars or fifty dollars, and they play according to their means; just the same as any other men do their gambling."

The Wall Street brokers might bet $100 on a combination, but the real money came from Harlem and policy shops in other poor neighborhoods, Carny said. "They are best districts; the very best," he testified. "They do not play such big amounts, but the quantity more than covers that."

Established operators in the South Side and Harlem reached an understanding with authorities that included the voting power of their districts. When things were running smoothly between the policy kings, the police, and the politicians, signs hung in windows announcing the daily draws. Some policy kings even advertised their big winners. Depending on the vagaries of the municipal administrations, policy operators were occasionally interrupted and arrested through the 1930s. Most of the time, though, too much money was at stake for elected officials to attempt true reform. Black policy kings could be tremendously helpful in delivering votes to campaigning politicians.

Entire South Side wards switched from Republican to Democratic in the mayoral election of 1923 on the promise that gambling and vice protection would continue under the Democratic candidate. It was the first time that Chicago's black community had ever voted Democratic. Policy had become a very profitable business, with many people interested in its continued operation. In 1938, the *Chicago Daily News* reported that the city's policy players gambled $18 million a year.

Through the 1920s and 1930s policy grew into a significant industry within the black communities of Chicago and Harlem. It employed thousands of people as runners, writers, managers, and "square squawks," who bribed gamblers' unhappy spouses to keep them from going to the police. The profits allowed blacks to buy businesses and homes within their own communities, at a time when they faced insurmountable economic and social barriers outside their districts. "Nineteen policy wheel operators owned at least twenty-nine different businesses in the black community," Robert Lombardo writes in "The Black Mafia: African-American Organized Crime in Chicago, 1890– 1960." Among the businesses were a department store and a Ford dealership. Other cities, such as Philadelphia, had policy games, but Chicago's South Side and New York's Harlem operated like autonomous cities, insulated against neighboring districts by racism and their own massive, semiautonomous populations. They were the two largest black communities in the country. Black lawyers, doctors, teachers, shopkeepers, and reverends lived inside each community, but there were also policy kings. And the relative generosity or cheapness of the policy kings was noticed. Some were viewed as beloved urban philanthropists. These kings, such as Sam Young who died in 1937, received lavish public funerals. Even when they lost their pennies and dimes to the wheel, players felt that some portion would go back to the neighborhood schools, churches, and arts in the form of the kings' largesse. Conversely, a policy king who gave nothing back to the community might find people in the neighborhood more likely to inform on him or at least show little loyalty to his policy shops. It paid to be a generous king.

Besides policy, a handful of illegal lotteries were based on the old-fashioned games, complete with printed, prenumbered tickets. One of the most popular was the Irish Sweepstakes. It started in 1930 by selling $2.50 tickets illegally through the mail in the United States. The federal antilottery laws were never enforced against it. The winning numbers, for prizes up to $200,000, came from the results of racetracks in Europe. Other illegal lotteries were based on a similar formula, with the winning tickets matching the payout at the racetrack. Many games were frauds, however.

In the eyes of the government, gambling was still a vice, if a

minor one. It came under occasional attacks when municipal administrations were shaken up or local ministers rallied opposition from
within the community. In the late 1930s, the *Chicago Daily News*
blamed numbers gambling for poverty, public corruption, and the
waste of the relief funds from President Roosevelt's New Deal. The
complaint was that in poorer sections of the city so many people
played, numbers bets could be placed anywhere people gathered—bars
and restaurants, barbershops and beauty parlors, elevators, and street
corners. Policy men made house calls to the homes of their regular
players to take bets, recording them in their policy book, and handing the players a receipt. The twice-daily drawings were part of neighborhood life. One innovation that expanded the games in this period
was using the numbers from a public and incorruptible source. "I
played on Clearing House, couldn't make the grade / Lord, think of
the money that I should have made," bluesman Blind Blake sang, re-
ferring to one of Chicago's policy games that took its winning numbers from the daily Federal Reserve Clearing House Report. Official
numbers assured an honest game. Other policy operators backed up
their games by using the daily amount wagered at local racetracks,
the dollars traded on the New York Stock Exchange, and the price of
cotton.

Picking the numbers was a mania among players. Players could
pick numbers of importance to them—their daughter's birthday or
their street number—or they could play the numbers tweezed from
their dreams or the sights from their waking life. According to one
established system of interpretation, if you saw an elephant—either in
life or in your dreams—you bet the numbers 7-6-1. The three-digit
gig was popular in dream books. As Ann Fabian recounts, there were
"policemen's gigs, beer gigs, washer women's gigs, dead gigs, Irish

gigs, sick gigs, money gigs, working gigs, 'Negro gigs,' and gigs for various days of the week and for famous criminals."

Dreams books, the keys to connecting the subconscious and waking worlds with their corresponding numbers, had been around since the eighteenth century. Their authorship was usually attributed to an older, wise woman—*Aunt Sally's Policy Player's Dream Book* and *Old Aunt Dinah's Policy Dream Book*—or to a mysterious "professor" with an exotic continental or oriental last name. Some gig superstitions changed from neighborhood to neighborhood. Others were set in stone. One of the most popular numbers was 4-11-44, repeatedly mentioned in blues songs, lampooned by blackface performers, and known to some as the "washerwoman's gig" and to others as the "Negro gig." The individual numbers each supposedly referred to a sign of good fortune (11, for instance, corresponded to a ladder permitting the player to reach greater heights). Another interpretation held that it was the combination to play when someone important died. The gig 4-11-44 hit once in 1886 and twice in two days in 1898 in Chicago. Players celebrated, the policy shops paid dearly, and the *Chicago Daily News* reported on the unlikely event. The combination remained popular until at least the mid-twentieth century.

Policy became so profitable that it attracted more powerful criminal interests. When Prohibition was repealed in 1933, white organized-crime figures such as Dutch Schultz in New York and Tony Accardo—Frank Nitti's successor in Chicago's "Outfit"—saw the numbers rackets in the black communities as a way to boost their dwindling income. Through the late 1930s and into the 1950s the Outfit's enforcers made offers to encourage South Side policy-wheel owners to hand over their businesses. If policy owners accepted the offers, they were put on payroll. They could manage the games and continue selling tickets to their neighborhood customers. If they refused, the Outfit used threats and violence and took over the operation anyway. Attempts, successful and unsuccessful, were made on the lives of other policy operators. Teddy Roe, the last holdout against the Chicago Mafia, was shotgunned in 1952.

There was local resentment as Chicago's Italian Mafia took over the South Side's homegrown and profitable policy industry. South Side congressman William Dawson said, "If anyone is going to make money out of the frailties of my people . . . it's going to be my people." Dawson later admitted that he took money from gambling, but said it was only for "political purposes."

By the 1950s a new policy era had begun, largely under Mafia control, which brought its own contacts among the police and politicians. Increasingly, it was referred to as the numbers racket. The game grew exponentially. As it grew, it attracted attention from state and federal governments in fits and starts. Raids and crackdowns came as the game grew through the first half of the twentieth century. Most were local-police affairs. Occasionally, there was a high-profile attempt at reform. Thomas Dewey, a New York district attorney, became governor and a presidential candidate based on his early reputation as, according to *Time* magazine, "a righteous combination of St. George and Charlie Chan." Dewey's target was Jimmy Hines, the powerful Tammany Hall and Democratic district leader, who gave the Harlem numbers racket protection from the law and the courts. Hines was convicted in 1939.

Hines was just one man, however, and criminal rackets, including numbers, continued to grow. The real interest began in 1950, with the creation of the Kefauver Committee. Inspired by municipal requests for federal help, the committee was named for its chairman, Tennessee Democrat Senator Estes Kefauver. The panel set out to expose organized crime. It succeeded. The hearings were televised and some thirty million Americans watched. "Never before had the attention of the nation been riveted so completely on a single matter," *Life* magazine reported.

New York crime bosses Frank Costello and Joey Adonis, and the late Bugsy Siegel's mistress and former moll to the Chicago Outfit, Virginia Hill, were subpoenaed to testify. Only Costello's fidgeting hands appeared on TV sets, at the insistence of his lawyer. If the government wanted to stop gambling, Costello told the senators, they needed to "burn the stables and shoot the horses." Hill said she knew nothing about any rackets. Her money was the result of gifts from her boyfriends. She told the court that she was skilled at pleasing them, elaborating in some detail. More than eight hundred witnesses appeared at hearings in more than a dozen cities. The hearings put the American Mafia on the map and prodded J. Edgar Hoover into admitting that a web of organized crime was strung across the country. The committee's final report, released in 1951, argued that the policy and numbers players' pocket change financed the larger enterprises of organized crime. And because many numbers operators shrugged off the fines they paid, the committee urged stiffer justice, the revocation of the license of any business harboring a backroom numbers game.

Under public pressure, dozens of cities created their own local crime commissions. Several states that were moving to legalize gambling stopped dead in their tracks. The numbers racket was just one part of the committee's interest, which included sports gambling, labor racketeering, and prostitution. The Senate soon instituted a Permanent Subcommittee on Investigations, known colloquially as the rackets committee.

Although the hearings brought Kefauver national recognition, the senator surprised many by stepping down from the committee in 1951. Author Curt Gentry points out in *J. Edgar Hoover: The Man and*

His Secrets that a few weeks earlier Kefauver's friend and campaign donor Herbert Brody had been arrested. Brody ran Nashville's numbers games.

The hearings established organized crime in the public eye. The *New York Post* estimated that $250 million was gambled each year on the policy games in New York City. In 1959, Harlem representative Adam Clayton Powell railed in Congress against the numbers rackets that were "preying on the poor" of his district. But worse to Powell was that police were focusing on Harlem numbers and not the Italian Mafia, whose gangsters took, in his estimation, $50 million from Harlem numbers players each year. The *New York Times* quoted him speaking to supporters: "Until the day when the numbers is wiped out in Harlem, I am going to fight for the Negro to having the same chance as an Italian."

In 1964, the *New York Times Magazine* reported, "There is hardly a factory, office building, or a large store in the city that does not have its resident numbers collector, usually a cheerful fellow who is known to everyone by his first name." The bets were still placed in nickels, dimes, and quarters, though most bets ranged from fifty cents to a dollar. The payout was 600 to 1, with the collector taking a 10 percent commission.

In 1965, President Lyndon Johnson declared "war on crime" and created the President's Commission on Law Enforcement and the Administration of Justice, better known as the President's Crime Commission. It conducted hearings, surveys, and field studies, which were pulled together into a report, *The Challenge of Crime in a Free Society*. The commission estimated that organized crime took in $20 billion a year from gambling, of which it kept $6 or $7 billion as profit.

Estimating criminal profits is guesswork, but whatever the true revenue of illegal gambling. Nevertheless, $20 billion was accepted as the size of the problem. In 1969, President Nixon upped the ante to as much as $50 billion in illegal gambling in an address to Congress on organized crime. As economists Lawrence J. Kaplan and James M. Maher wrote in their 1970 article, "The Economics of the Numbers Game," "The underworld is gradually finding its way into the upperworld."

In 1970, Congress authorized the Organized Crime Control Act, better known as RICO. The law would allow prosecutors to combine various criminal acts—such as bribery, extortion, murder, and numbers racketeering—committed by separate parties into a larger organized-crime conspiracy with serious penalities. The relatively small penalties for illegal gambling operations became much more severe.

AS GOVERNMENT AND law enforcement sought to solve the illegal gambling problem, someone always argued that the best way to control was to own it. After all, the government had approved lotteries in the past. And the public clearly wanted the games, even when they were outlawed. Maybe prohibition wasn't the answer to lotteries, just as it wasn't for alcohol.

As crime commissions tried to solve the problems of cities overrun by illegal rackets, some officials saw the answer in legalized gambling. Lotteries were offered as revenue streams on federal and state levels. They would meet the public appetite and be controlled by government, not racketeers, proponents argued. Someone could always be counted on to suggest a lottery in times of need. During World War I, the Great Depression, and World War II, lottery proposals were submitted to Congress. More than half of the participants in a 1942 Gallup poll approved of a national lottery to fund the war. A number of the proposals were offered to use a lottery to fund the Veterans Administration. Chicago Democratic representative Adolph J. Sabath was behind two of the several lottery bills introduced in Congress. "People have a lot of money," Representative Sabath explained to the Associated Press in 1943. "They can't spend it because many of the things they want aren't available, and if we can siphon some of it off into the Treasury in an honest gambling proposition, nobody will suffer." No bill ever passed.

In 1964, after fighting off lottery bills for more than two decades, New Hampshire became the first state to legalize lottery tickets since Louisiana. Having no income or sales tax, New Hampshire leaned heavily on so-called sin taxes—on beer and liquor sales, tobacco, and horse racing—for more than half of its revenue. A lottery seemed a reasonable way to skirt a looming deficit and improve schools without resorting to an unpopular sales tax. New Hampshire came in last among the fifty states in funds for education. Lottery boosters said the game would do $8–10 million in sales, much of it from out-of-state players, and net $4 million for education. Opponents saw a moral quagmire and wondered when the Granite State had gone soft. Newspapers disinterred the Louisiana Lottery and the Continental Congress lottery as evidence in support of both sides of the lottery fight. The Justice Department said that New Hampshire might be in violation of the 1890 and 1895 laws that banned lotteries from the mail. Everyone worried the lottery would attract organized crime. Superintendent of Schools Harlan E. Atherton told the *New York Times* that he didn't think lotteries would lead to a statewide gambling problem, but did not like the thought of depending on the whims of gamblers to pay for schools. "I really am quite liberal in many respects, but I take a dim view of government by wager, and subjecting education to the vagaries of volunteer contributions."

In a 1964 referendum, 73 percent of voters approved the lottery. They called it a sweepstakes, after the Irish Sweepstakes on which it was modeled. They hoped that a "sweepstakes" would not violate federal antilottery laws. Tickets cost $3. Drawings were held twice a year with winning numbers based on horse-race results from Rockingham Park. Top prize was $100,000 for every $1 million sold, then $50,000 and $25,000. Governor John King, the state's first Democratic executive in forty years, bought ticket No. 000001. The former head of the FBI's Boston office, Edward J. Powers, was hired to run the lottery at a salary of $20,000—the highest of any official in the state.

It was a rocky start. In retrospect, the New Hampshire game was ridiculously complicated. Not only were tickets expensive, but players had to fill out forms with their names and addresses—or contact information for the person they were buying tickets for. Once players filled out the form, they fed it into a metal machine a little larger than a breadbox and pulled a lever that cut the form in half. Their bet and personal information was locked inside the machine, and their receipt was shot to a slot at the bottom. It was not unlike voting. Tickets were only available at the forty-nine state-controlled liquor stores or the two racetracks. Powers was surprised that 75 percent of the sales came from liquor stores. The state had expected the game to attract mostly track enthusiasts. Organized crime didn't show up, but private enterprise did: a company offered to buy tickets for people unable to get to New Hampshire to buy their own. The company charged a $4 service fee.

The drawings were held during the summer of 1964 in advance of the September mile race of three-year-old Thoroughbreds. One Plexiglas drum held the names of the 332 horses nominated, including Northern Dancer, winner of the Kentucky Derby and Preakness Stakes. Only fifteen horses ran, but each horse nominated would result in a prize. As officials drew each horse's name, they pulled a corresponding player's ticket from other Plexiglas drums, which were massive—six feet in diameter and four feet wide, holding three hundred thousand tickets each. Six drawings were held under the watchful eyes of state troopers. Tickets were drawn by New Hampshire women, both young college students and mothers.

One of the tickets pulled bore the name of Stevie Bakula, age three. "He's a smart boy and with this he's going to get an education," his hopeful mother told the *New York Times*.

Everyone whose ticket was drawn won something. Players who pulled a horse that was nominated but not running in the race got a consolation prize. The win, place, and show horses paid out the top three prizes—$100,000, $50,000, and $25,000.

The sweepstakes lottery grossed $5.73 million from 1.9 million tickets sold in its first year. Prizes accounted for $1.8 million. The state's take for education was about $2.7 million, although some money was siphoned off to cut local real estate taxes. The lottery fell short of the $4 million promised for education. New Hampshire's property taxes went up anyway.

Sales dropped over the next several years until they bottomed out at $2 million in 1969, with $868,358 going toward state coffers and education. The lottery held to a rough formula that put 30–40 percent of sales toward prizes, with the state taking 40–50 percent. The problem was that operating costs gobbled up about 20 percent of the revenue.

As New Hampshire sales plummeted, six states rejected lottery bills. In 1967, the next state in the lottery game was New York, the first state to ban lotteries in 1833. New York went through the same debates over morality and fiscal need and, in the end, voted to amend its constitution to allow lotteries. The move was approved by

61 percent of voters in 1966. Tickets cost $1 and $2, and drawings were once a month.

Like New Hampshire, New York faced fiscal belt-tightening. In 1963, New York City braced for mass protests over a proposed increase of the sales tax from 3 percent to 4 percent. The Brooklyn Chamber of Commerce called for the borough to secede from the city. Democrats had submitted twelve lottery proposals to the state legislature that year, but Republicans, who controlled both sides of the state legislature, refused to let them pass. By 1966, the composition of the legislature had changed, new taxes were still unpopular, and the lottery passed.

New York's lottery had trouble in its first years as well. The first drawing was held on June 17, 1967, with a top prize of $100,000. Some four thousand hotels, motels, and bank branches sold the $1 tickets. The state was eager to appear legitimate and avoid the taint of gambling. Players found themselves in the ironic position of filling out gambling slips on counters where savings-deposit slips were on hand. Western Union backed away from selling tickets because five cents for every dollar was too low a commission. The state advertised on billboards and posters because federal law prohibited radio, newspaper, or television ads for lotteries. The marketing campaign stressed that the money would go to education. Television stations didn't know how to report on the drawings without risking violating federal law. The American Broadcasting Corporation would "broadcast no information concerning the lotteries, in conformance with the statutes," an executive told the *New York Times*. Supporters estimated first year sales at $360 million, with $198 million going to education. The *Times* had endorsed the lottery until it became clear that the money would simply replace existing state funds for education and not result in an overall increase to the education budget as a whole.

New York's drawing was even more complicated than New Hampshire's. As reporter Sydney Schanberg explained the rules in the *Times*: "First the raw list of winners will be picked. Then they will be divided into grand prizes and consolation prizes, with each ticket assigned a race track post position number of 1 through 15. The final step will be to pick the sweepstakes race from a fishbowl containing 12 slips of paper designating 12 races run in the state during the previous week. The order of finish will determine the order and size of prizes."

One of the $100,000 prizewinners, Aston Lewis, took a break from his $75-a-week job in a Brooklyn knitting factory to watch a drawing in Pennsylvania Station. Shortly after learning of his new wealth he left, telling a reporter in a West Indian accent, "Okay, I've got to get back to work."

Phone lines were available to reporters at the drawings, and more reporters were dispatched to the homes of the top winners to get their stories. This eclectic group included a salesman, a police detective, a college student, and a housewife. None had any immediate plans to quit what they were doing because of the windfall.

Despite long lines for tickets on the first day, sales were disappointing. The first full year of sales brought in $62.4 million, not the estimated $360 million. Education received 55 percent of that, about $34.3 million, not the promised $198 million. As monthly sales lagged in the first year, the state blamed banks' halfhearted promotion of the tickets. To boost sales the state started to promote a "get-rich-quick" theme in signs and posters, instead of funding for education. Sales only got worse. In 1968, the state took in less than $30 million for the treasury, far below the anticipated $45 million.

New Jersey came next. Voters in New Jersey went to the polling booths on November 4, 1969, to decide whether to approve a state lottery. By the day's end, voters had narrowly elected their first Republican governor in sixteen years and had shot down a referendum to lower the voting age to eighteen. But the lottery referendum was a runaway winner with 82 percent approval. The New Jersey lottery understood what New Hampshire and New York did not—the lottery was in competition with the numbers rackets for gamblers. Casinos in Atlantic City were still seven years away. Tickets cost just fifty cents and were sold at nearly two thousand newsstands, bars, and supermarkets—not in banks. "Whoever heard of placing a bet in a bank?" State Senator William Musto asked a *New York Times* reporter. Musto, who also served as mayor of Union City for sixteen years, was one of the lottery's earliest and stongest proponents.

Drawings were weekly. Twice a year there was a million-dollar drawing for $2.50. More important, the state began an aggressive marketing campaign, unabashedly based on the dream of luck and overnight riches. The state put its new logo—a four-leaf clover—everywhere tickets were sold. "Let's face it, the instinct for greed is more powerful than social concern," one unnamed New Jersey official told the *New York Times*.

Instead of trying to avoid looking like the illegal numbers game, the New Jersey lottery copied them. Players picked their own numbers and got a slip in return. There were no forms to fill out and process, and there was no connection to the racetrack. "People want to buy a number, not a horse," Musto said. Years later, in 1982, Musto was convicted in a racketeering trial and sent to prison for diverting education funds to mobsters.

On December 16, 1970, the newly elected governor, William T. Cahill, a former FBI agent and fiery liberal Republican, bought the first ticket. He would end his first and only term under a cloud of scandal that swallowed other members of his administration. Despite the lottery revenue the state enacted an income tax in 1976.

New Jersey projected $25 million in sales. In its first full year the state grossed more than $137 million. About half went to education. It was a runaway success that set the standard for every state lottery that would follow. Connecticut, Massachusetts, Pennsylvania, and Michigan climbed on board in 1972.

The new state numbers games received major attention from the media and the public. On January 28, 1971, Walter Cronkite led the *CBS Evening News* with a report on the U.S. bombing of Cambodia and toward the end of the broadcast gave thirty seconds to the story of a man who won $1 million in the New York Lottery. It was the same amount of time CBS gave to a federal judge's order to destroy the Kent State incident report. Only five years earlier, ABC had been afraid to broadcast stories about lottery drawings because of federal bans. "Can anyone doubt that the winner of a lottery is prime news by our press standards?" Supreme Court justice William O. Douglas wrote in 1975.

On its Web site the North American Association of State and Provincial Lotteries lists the highlights of this early period. In 1973, instant tickets hit the market and lottery sales broke $500 million. Massachusetts unveiled the scratch ticket the next year. No one had to wait for a drawing anymore. Playing was a transaction of brief anticipation and quick satisfaction. In 1975, the lottery, like the old-fashioned policy man, came right into your home to encourage you to play when the federal government allowed states' lotteries to advertise on radio and television. By 1977, the entire Northeast was selling lottery tickets. In 1978, New York and Massachusetts offered lotto, the European-style lottery in which players pick six numbers from a field of 1 to 30. The game proved popular. Another seventeen states initiated lotteries in the 1980s.

Money was still being made in the illegal numbers game. In February of 1971, the FBI ended a yearlong investigation into illegal gambling with raids in seven states. The combined take of the bookmaking and numbers operations was more than $60 million a year, J. Edgar Hoover said. Faced with competition from lotteries and such crackdowns, the numbers racket was diminished.

Leonard Minuto, who ran a Bronx numbers ring for the Gambino crime family during the rise of lotteries, complained about the state-run games. During his testimony at the 2006 federal trial of mobster Greg DePalma, Minuto described how business was so battered by the new lottery that he got the head of the family, Paul Castellano, to chop his weekly protection from $4,000 to $2,000. It was a shame, he said, because the illegal numbers games gave better payouts. "The state pays five hundred to one and the numbers give six hundred to one," he told the court.

The policy games were willing to take a smaller profit than the states. In the beginning, state lotteries insisted on keeping 50 percent of the take, giving back about 30 percent of sales to players after operating costs. The numbers kept roughly 15 to 30 percent. So illegal numbers players often had better payouts than they could get in the state-run games.

"I know a little bit about the numbers business," Ralph Natale, the Philadelphia mob boss, told jurors in 2001. "No matter what, there is a ten to thirteen percent profit margin from the numbers business at the end of the year."

Today, most state lotteries keep about 35 percent of sales and return about 50 percent to players. The illegal numbers game is still around. One can play numbers for as little as fifty cents. And no one has to pay taxes if he wins. The winning numbers still come from various racetrack returns, the stock exchange, and other legitimate sources. And in a logical move, they also use the state lotteries' winning numbers. In the 1980s the Chicago police took down a numbers ring that took its winning combinations from the Illinois Lottery's drawings. The operation was run on the South Side and was independent of the mafia, just as policy games had been eighty years earlier. But policy is now the property of the government. The states copied the illegal formula almost verbatim. New games have been introduced, such as scratch tickets, but nearly all are based on the same basic idea: a cheap game that relies on the player's imagination and the excitement of beating long odds, the dream of luck with a quick result.

When Sterling Plumpp beat the dealer to win a million dollars, one of the first thing he learned was that he hadn't actually won a million dollars. Like a lot of lottery winners he was quick to mention the tax on his winnings. He took home about $600,000 when all was said and done. He gave $10,000 to a gravely ill friend for medical bills. He paid off his credit cards. He set up a trust for his daughter. She later took him to Marshall Field's and picked out $10,000 worth of clothes for him.

And he bought a new car, a Mazda 626, a sedate, midsize sedan for a man accustomed to walking.

His purchases were modest compared to those of many dreams of lottery winning. But what Plumpp really won was time. He could now afford to be an artist without worry. He could travel, see the country, and gather material. "It freed me," he said. "I write about lived experiences. They're the most reliable reality."

The reality of lottery winners—their stories—are one of the greatest marketing tools the industry has. Better than any ad campaign about luck or the importance of believing in good fortune is testimony from a winner. As the newly established lotteries sought to market their games, they often focused on the luxury that winning could buy. No one was a better salesman, a better example of the suddenly wealthy, than Curtis Sharp. In the 1980s, Curtis had an all-or-nothing personality that matched the temper of the exploding lottery industry. Lines went around the block for jackpots of a few million. Curtis Sharp was proof that it was all worthwhile.

CHAPTER 4

THE BOOM YEARS

THE CLUMSY FIRST steps taken by government lotteries gave no hint at the frenzy they were about to unleash. As 1981 came to a close there were fifteen state lotteries. It was a three-billion-dollar-a-year industry that was growing faster every month, outpacing any other revenue source government and most private business had ever seen. New York reported a 70 percent sales increase in one year. By 1984 lotteries were an eight-billion-dollar-a-year industry. By the end of the decade there were lotteries in thirty states and Washington, D.C.

Lotteries held an easy answer for cash-strapped state governments as the 1980s began. Tax hikes were hardly an option for funding local budgets. Through the 1970s, rising taxes had taken increasingly bigger bites from people's incomes. Government could no longer grab at voters' wallets—the public was too busy struggling to balance their own household budgets against soaring gasoline prices and inflation that sent consumer goods through the roof. Lotteries, on the other hand, could be sold to the public as entertainment. That they happened to fund government programs, such as public schools, made them a win-win option. They were popular and profitable.

After their early, failed lottery experiments states found the right formula. It was much like Alexander Hamilton's ideas for a successful lottery: a simple numbers game with cheap tickets, long odds, and a big grand prize. Cheap tickets meant everyone could play and take a chance at the fairy tale of riches. Easy access meant high volume sales, which fed larger jackpots, which in turn drove sales upward. As bettors flocked to buy tickets, jackpots rose exponentially. First came the $1 million winners. By the 1980s there were $5 million jackpots and soon it was $50 million. The game that marketed dreams of overnight millions was in tune with popular attitudes of a decade that reveled in showy luxury.

Jackpots were supported by breathless coverage of lottery millionaires in newpapers and on television. The state lotteries put them in commercials, lined them up for interviews. They were regular people who could describe what the miraculous experience of sudden riches felt like. And everybody listened as they described what they were going to do with the money. They were the most powerful proof lotteries could trot out to show people that that, yes, it could happen to you.

In 1982, Curtis Sharp's marriage was dying. Not that it was unexpected. He always had a large appetite, and he loved women almost as much as food. At forty-five, he could look at his expanding belly and the state of his marriage and see that both his appetites were catching up to him.

Little was left at home, besides arguments. Sharp wanted a divorce but Barbara didn't. Still, they managed to get along. Their three children were all grown, and they knew each other too well to be hateful. They had dated in high school in Maysville, North Carolina, where she had been a year behind him. She was resigned to his ways. If she could put up with his fathering a child by another woman fourteen years earlier, she could handle his new beautician. Decades later, they remain friendly. He borrows money from her occasionally. "I always run out," he says.

At the time, though, Sharp had decided to move on. He had already proposed to Jackie Bernabela, a mother of four, a beautician ten years his junior. He may have liked to live large but he was stable. And that's what Jackie wanted for her and her kids. Within a decade of starting as a dishwasher in the cafeteria at Bell Laboratories in Murray Hill, New Jersey, he had been promoted to plant watch operator. He made sure the heating and air-conditioning were working. He had worked on farms in the summers in North Carolina, and his $30,000-a-year job at Bell was not something he messed around with.

On Friday, November 26, 1982, Sharp's friend Melvin "Big Man" Bedford started in about the New York Lottery drawing coming up that weekend. "I ain't playing no numbers," Sharp told him. "I ain't going to win nothing no way. I don't think this stuff is real." But Big Man wouldn't quit, so Curtis filled out the card. He picked four sets of six numbers from thin air. He went to work on Monday and joked around with co-workers about the lottery. He called Barbara.

"Barbara, what would you do if you won the lottery? Would you buy me a car?" he asked her.

"Yeah, I'd buy you a car because you've never had a new car," she said.

"Would you buy me a house?"

"Naw, I ain't going to buy you no house for you and some other bitch to live in." They both laughed.

On Tuesday a co-worker handed Sharp a slip of paper with the winning numbers: 1, 2, 9, 16, 34, and 40. He'd hit them all. His first thought was that it was too good to be true. (Then his stomach clenched at the thought that Big Man had not put in his numbers.) "Sweat started coming off of me," Sharp says.

He called Big Man, who was racing to work, holding on to the ticket for dear life. Another worker called the state lottery office because Sharp was too emotional. His next thought was to call Jackie. The line was busy. He called Barbara. She thought he was pulling her leg, continuing the joke from the day before. Not in the mood for his jokes, she handed the phone off to their daughter.

"Do you know how much the lottery was in New York?" she asked.

"About twenty thousand dollars."

"No, it's five million dollars."

Just then Sharp's co-worker, who was on the phone to the state lottery office, started shouting: "You're a millionaire! You're a millionaire! You won five million dollars!"

The next thing Sharp remembers is waking up on the floor with workers fanning him and cheering. Bell Laboratories gave him the day off. What happened next made Sharp a New York tabloid legend.

The New York State Lottery held a press conference at the World Trade Center to celebrate their new winner, who had beat 2,000,000-to-1 odds. When they offered to send a limousine to pick him up, Sharp said, "Well, you better send two."

Sharp stepped out of the limo they had sent for him in a pin-striped, three-piece suit and a tan bowler. Jackie was on his arm. Barbara, who arrived in the second limo, met them inside.

He stepped to the microphone and introduced the two women: "My wife, Barbara, and my wife-to-be."

He told the press, "As you can see, I've got a problem."

The newspapers had a field day. Sharp had a sharp wit, a quick tongue, and said whatever was on his mind. "The media just played that up, and I just went right along with it," he recalls, laughing.

"The media, they was dumbfounded because they was asking me questions and I was popping off just like that, and they just sat there looking at me. I said, 'Any more questions?' They said, 'Mr. Sharp, we don't know what to ask you.' It was really something."

New York Lottery officials were stunned, too, but they realized that Sharp was not an embarrassment to the lottery's image; he was a natural pitchman. The New York Lottery was nationally recognized for its cutting edge marketing campaigns, and its greatest salesman had just made his debut.

He soon received the first of his checks for $190,956, after 20 percent taken in taxes. The checks would keep coming until 2002.

He kept his job at Bell, but with his new riches Sharp bought a $38,000 brown Cadillac Fleetwood. He had it customized with a Rolls-Royce grille, a "fuzz buster," and a phone. He parked his other car, an eleven-year-old, green station wagon nicknamed the Dirty Dog, in the garage of a $550,000, six-bedroom home in West Orange, New Jersey, where he moved with Jackie and her kids. Barbara got a house and more than a million dollars paid out in installments of $50,000 a year for twenty years. Sharp had trust funds set up for their three children. Big Man got $10,000 in cash.

The year after he won the lottery, Sharp married Jackie Berna-bela. He bought her a $10,000, 2.5-carat marquise diamond and a blowout wedding that cost $100,000. The bride wore a $13,000 wedding dress and left the church with her dapper groom in a horse-drawn carriage, while the thirty-one members of the wedding party stepped into a fleet of a dozen limos. The nineteen hundred guests at the reception were joined by a hundred gate-crashers who wanted to be near the Five Million Dollar Man. Sharp saw no reason they shouldn't join the party.

A year into the marriage he met Marynell "Cookie" Moody, one of many women to come into his married life. His marriage to Jackie lasted five years. Despite the fancy house they bought together, the two lived as if they were single throughout the marriage.

"During that time I had women sticking their phone numbers in my pocket everywhere I'd go. It was like that. And a lot of them I did mess around with."

Neither of them was particularly faithful to the marriage, he says. He moved out. "We became friends. I have no animosity against her. I've been back there."

James Nolan, the New York City regional lottery director and spokesman, whom Sharp refers to as his "buddy," squired Sharp to promotional events during his celebrity period. "I was promoting the lottery, so he used to love walking with me down the streets of New York," Sharp recalls of his outings with Nolan. Crowds on the street would stop and chant Sharp's name. They called him the "Five Million Dollar Man." Once Sharp got recognized at Yankee Stadium—his distinctive bowler hat made him stand out in the crowd.

"Curtis! Curtis!" the fans chanted.

Finally, Dave Winfield, who was in the field, got so distracted that he called for time to see what the noise was all about. "He had just stopped and looked. A lot of people were wondering what was going on. The ushers ran up and said, 'Mr. Sharp, we've got to sit you down. You've gone and stopped the ball game.'

"Those were the days," Sharp says. "They were always taking us somewhere."

Sharp joined Lou Eisenberg, the 1981 winner, who, prior to being a millionaire, had changed lightbulbs in the subway. The two did numerous commercials for the lottery and became its regular pitchmen. To this day, veteran lottery officials around the country remember the impact Sharp and Eisenberg had on lottery marketing. "The commissioner, he used to say we couldn't pay you enough for what you do for the lottery."

But it was Sharp, with his unabashed flamboyance, who caught New York's eye more than Eisenberg. "Don't be chintzy with the mustard," he chastised a hot dog vendor in one television spot. It became a catch phrase. Sharp resonated with New Yorkers.

The lottery did not pay them for their first-class promotional outings, but took care of all their expenses. When they did the commercials, the lottery arranged to get them Screen Actors Guild cards.

Backstage at a fund-raiser for the United Negro College Fund, Lou Rawls asked to borrow money. "He said, 'Hey, Curt, let me hold two till Lou comes through.'" Sharp tells the story with laughter, clearly cherishing it.

"I went a lot of places I never would have went. Everywhere I went people treated me so nice," Sharp says. "In Italy and Germany people already heard about me. My face went all over the world."

It was a big stage and Sharp took to it as if he were born in the spotlight. Women threw themselves at him; and so did people looking for handouts. But Sharp loved the attention. His father was the kind of man who would get his paycheck and buy everyone a round of drinks. Sharp wasn't so different.

It was the right time for Curtis Sharp. Lotteries were popping up all over. They made too much money for a state not to start one. Ticket sales increased by double-digit percentages every year. It was easy money.

Some voices called them a swindle or destructive or addictive, but states lined up for the games. In 1985, a study based on Maryland, which had started its lottery in 1973, found that households in the lowest-third income bracket accounted for half of all the weekly-lotto-drawing tickets and 60 percent of the daily-drawing sales. In 1970, nationwide lottery sales were less than $50 million. By 1979, national sales topped $2 billion. Expansion in the 1980s moved even faster, and by 1990, lottery sales were $20 billion. State profits increased at unheard of rates. In one year in the early 1980s, nationwide revenue grew by 30 percent. New York had a single-year increase of 80 percent sales growth.

The economic recession in the early 1980s did nothing to slow sales. "People might take a chance on a dream by deciding not to buy a pack of cigarettes, or maybe put less gasoline into their gas tank for a pleasure trip and instead buy a lottery ticket," a Pennsylvania Department of Revenue spokesman told *U.S. News & World Report* in 1980.

When the decade began, New York stopped traffic by introducing $5 million lotto jackpots. In 1988, a woman in Florida won $55 million. The lottery seemed like it would grow forever.

Billions of dollars poured into state treasuries. Lottery campaigns ran full tilt, and Sharp was at the front of the pack, a regular on television.

He is one of the most famous lottery winners, in history and certainly in the New York area. He stills gets recognized around New York City, especially when he wears his trademark bowler. Twenty years after he won, he was walking past a group of construction workers on a picket line when they started chanting his name. But they were yelling at a different Curtis Sharp from the one who could stop traffic or a Yankees game and who could drink until dawn and go home with his pick of the women in the bar. That was the Sharp who hustled for the New York State Lottery.

Sharp, who once filled the tabloids as a flamboyant lottery winner, had become fodder for another standard tabloid story—the lottery winner who loses it all. But Curtis Sharp is still a busy man. On

Monday nights, twice a month, he goes to the Community Justice Center, a jail in Nashville, to preach. Tuesdays, in the afternoon and evening, he teaches a class entitled "Resisting Satan" at the Priest Lake Community Baptist Church, where he is an ordained deacon. On Wednesdays he's back at the church for Bible study. He's partial to Romans, Psalms, and Proverbs. The down-to-earth language appeals to him. He often draws from his own experiences when preaching.

His voice is reminiscent of Redd Foxx's. Sharp speaks in a wet rasp. When he starts to preach or gets worked up on a subject, which he does often, his voice breaks into a high-pitched bark.

"I give them the word of God," Sharp says, "that's all I can do. I look at it as God was leading me up to this. He let me win that lottery to show me regardless of the money you have, or I give you, still need Me. See, when I won that money, man, I thought I was on top of the world. I was like, 'Now I can do all kinds of strange,'" he says, laughing.

Thursday mornings, Sharp visits the minimum-security prisoners at the Correctional Work Center for Bible study. In the evening, he goes to the medium-security Hill Detention Center. On Friday nights, he's back to the church for an eschatological discussion of the end-time in the Bible. Early Saturday mornings there is a prayer group at the church, followed by Bible study at the CCA state prison in the evenings. On Sundays he attends services at seven forty-five and eleven A.M.

"You can burn your body, sacrifice your body, but if you ain't got the love of Christ in you, it don't mean nothing. You've got to put him first in your life. Just like Bill Gates, Oprah, and all them people. If they don't put Christ first in their life, bro, them riches ain't going to do them no good. Look at me, I'm drawing my pension and Social Security." Sharp breaks out laughing. "But God is blessing me, I still make it because of him. And I know he's going to bless me with something else. Bigger, way bigger. But I've got to wait on him. I've got to believe and trust in him."

In the downstairs den at his girlfriend Cookie's house there's an oil portrait of Sharp from the old days—in a sky blue suit with an open collar, and matching bowler—looking down from the wall. Sitting on a couch across from the painting, he's now built like a fireplug with a potbelly. An action figure of Oddjob, the Bond villain with the deadly bowler hat, perches on the mantel between Cookie's dog figurines.

"That's what they call me, Mr. Fuji." Sharp laughs. "They say I look like Mr. Fuji; they say I look like Fred Sanford. They call me a lot of things."

He still has a few bowler hats, but most of them—hundreds, he says—he gave away. Instead, he now wears a black leather baseball cap that has stitched on it JESUS IS MY BOSS. He is in the middle of a spontaneous discourse on sin. He jumps easily from a discussion of attaining God's forgiveness to the story of the Good Thief and the Bad Thief, who were crucified alongside Jesus, to the Bosom of Abraham, that place where the Old Testament faithful stayed until Jesus came to bring them up to heaven after his death. It's getting late, after ten o'clock, but he's energized now, his voice rising in emotion and taking on the cadence of a preacher's as he tells the story of man's loss of and reentry into paradise as if he were standing in front of a congregation, instead of sitting on Cookie's sofa.

"Man caused us to be sinful. So God had to send his son as a man to bring us back to the father. He called him his son Jesus. He came down as *man* because *man* had disobeyed *God*. Sin didn't *start* here on earth. It started in heaven with *Satan* and came *down* to earth.

"He told them don't eat from the tree of good and evil. He *warned* them. He told them in the beginning, *the tree of knowledge*, he said don't eat from that tree. He said the day you eat from that tree you will surely die. Now we know they didn't die physically, but they died spiritually. They were separated from *God*. God *told* them. But they listened to that Satan. That's the same thing we do today. We listen to that Satan, that's why we get in trouble. Listen to that Satan.

"When God said, 'Adam, where art thou,' God *knew* where Adam was. He wanted *Adam* to know where he was and what he'd done. But what did Adam *do*? He put it off on the woman, and the woman put it off on Satan." Sharp rocks back and forth laughing at the absurdity of Adam's and Eve's excuses.

The phone rings. It's a church secretary he had helped to move a piece of furniture earlier in the day. As a thank-you she bought him a Powerball ticket. The multistate game is up to $180 million.

"No, I haven't checked it yet," he tells her. "Did anybody win? I haven't checked mine. I don't even know what the number was . . . The Powerball was thirty? Lord. I don't know."

Two competing multistate games, Powerball and Mega Millions, are responsible for the headline-grabbing jackpots that get people to form lines out the door of the corner store and around the block. The large jackpots are built on sales of $1 tickets, pooled from several states, and dependent on successive drawings without winners. The games are traditional lotto—much like the old policy games— and allow players to pick a set of numbers from a field of fifty-five or so. Joining a multistate game has particular appeal to small state lotteries that don't have a large enough population to run their own in-state lotto.

Mega Millions is played in twelve states twice a week. It was called the "The Big Game" when it started in 1996. That year it held weekly drawings in six states. The odds of winning a Mega Millions jackpot are about 1-in-175 million. In 2007, a Mega Millions jackpot reached a worldwide record of $390 million. There were two winners: a truck driver from Georgia and a couple from southern New Jersey who were nearing retirement and put NO TRESPASSING and BEWARE OF DOG signs in their yard after winning.

Powerball is played in thirty states and Washington, D.C., and also held twice weekly. Powerball is managed by the Multi-State Lottery Association, a non-profit consortium of state lotteries based in Iowa that share in three other lotto games and the Ca$hola video lottery game. Powerball was called "Lotto America" when it started in 1992. In 2009, its jackpot odds changed from 1-in-146 million to 1-in-195 million when Florida joined and the game increased its field of numbers to fifty-nine. The largest Powerball jackpot was $365 million, which was won by eight employees of a meatpacking plant in Nebraska in 2006.

Tennessee sold its first Powerball tickets on March 21, 2004. Six months earlier, lotteries had still been illegal under the Tennessee state constitution.

When he came to Nashville in 1993, one of the first things Sharp did was to buy a bar called the Hole. It's located in Bordeaux, a suburb of Nashville. Sharp treated the bar like his personal club house. The spot served as a condensed version of all his nights out around New York and New Jersey.

"You own a bar, you know you've got women coming and going," he says. "I was messing around, too, then."

Cookie didn't know about the other women, but his drinking was impossible to miss. At the Hole, Sharp held sway over a liquor-addled audience, staggering to his car in the early-morning hours for the drive home.

"Man, I used to get so drunk. I'd pull up in front of the house there and Cookie would come out to get me out of the car, and she'd say I'd cuss her out. And I would never cuss a woman. And she said I used to call her a bitch or a whore.

"And I don't remember it." He sounds as if he's pleading. "I'd be so drunk I couldn't even get out of the car. And when she'd come down there, she'd take the keys out of the car, you know, and she said she couldn't get me out, so she just locked the door. Locked me in. I woke up in there many mornings with the sun shining."

One night in 1996 Sharp was driving home in a haze of alcohol and hit what could have been a dog or a pig or maybe a man. He still doesn't know for sure. He kept driving. "I hit *something*. That scared me 'cause I didn't know if I hit a person or not. I was looking in the papers for a couple days there and saw there wasn't nobody hit. So I said I know this is not what the Lord wants me to be. That's when I said, 'Well, this is it for me.'"

Through all the years of carousing he still sometimes made it to church on Sundays. But he had never let Sunday church get in the way of his Saturday nights. In Antioch, Tennessee, he had asked around and was told there was a preacher who was good at Bible study at Priest Lake Community Baptist Church. He had never noticed the church, less than a mile from his home.

Newly reborn, Sharp announced to friends at the bar that he had given himself over to Jesus Christ. "This is it," he told them. "I'm not doing this anymore."

He recalls, "They laughed at me. Yeah, they laughed at me. I was a big old mess."

He gave the bar away to a man who had been interested in buying it. "He said, 'How much you want for it?' I said, 'I don't want nothing for it, you can take it,' and I walked out. I didn't take not one dime. I walked out of there and I didn't look back."

At home, he told Cookie about his plans to change his life, to stop drinking and serve Jesus. He also announced that he would remain celibate until they had married. He moved into a room downstairs and soon after moved to an apartment a few miles away. He recorded a message on his answering machine that announced, "The Lord has come into my life."

He says, "Me and her ain't had sex in nine years now." Sex outside of marriage would not only be unseemly, it would break the seventh commandment, against adultery. Sharp and Jackie Bernabela never got a divorce after they separated in 1988. After he left, he gave her the house and continued to make the mortgage payments. After borrowing heavily against it, Jackie lost the house and moved to an apartment in New Jersey, Sharp says. When he asked for a divorce, she asked for $50,000, he says. He hopes to save up the money through restoring and flipping houses around Nashville. But business has not been great.

He gets up to check on the trays of pulled pork he's reheating for tonight. There is a pork shoulder for the pastor's house, and two trays for a church deacon, and a tray for the house we're headed to for a Super Bowl party. "They don't know how to barbecue around here," he grumbles. The pork is marinated in apple-cider vinegar, a recipe he grew up with in Maysville, a tiny crossroads town in eastern North Carolina.

"I saw where I was headed and I said, 'Lord don't want me to be like this,'" he continues. "See, I gave my life to the Lord since I was twelve years old. He just stayed with me while I was out there being a mess. He kept me. I always had me a church to go to."

Later, I ask Cookie about Sharp's sudden vow of chastity and sobriety. "I thought the world was coming to an end," she says. "I was really happy though. I feel like God must have really been with him. I mean he was so drunk I don't know how he drove to Antioch. I think the Lord wanted to use him for something, because, if not, he should have been killed a long time ago."

THE EXCESSES OF the eighties led to something different in the 1990s and into the twenty-first century. Jackpots grew to unimaginable amounts in the hundreds of millions, but the winners didn't seem to luxuriate so publicly the way Sharp did. Constance Laverty O'Connor, chief marketing officer for GTECH, says that for lottery winners and for state marketing the experience of winning is not about big boats or fur coats anymore: "A lot of the research we do proves that it's not just about the money anymore, it's about the quality of life."

The jackpot winner as an icon is a more complicated figure. Stories about winners, such as Sharp, who have had a rough time after winning have dampened some of the revelry. A moral note has crept back into the culture. Many lottery winners now talk about what they're going to give to charity. Whether the words are for public relations effect, who can say, but that's the state of many of the latest jackpot winners.

Most big lottery winners buy a new home or a boat, take a long vacation, maybe even retire early, or are otherwise never heard from again. There are those, however, whose lives are so altered by the large sum of money that they can't stay out of the news. The idea of a lottery "curse" (as one television program called it) nicely sums up the skewed perception that tragedy dogs lottery winners.

Lottery winners lose their privacy. Overnight, they become public figures, often encouraged to participate in publicity by the state lottery that is paying them. Even when the publicity is brief, winners are approached through letters, phone calls, and knocks on the door from strangers asking for money. Wealth, won or earned, attracts outstretched hands. Sometimes there is either a sorrowful story, a surefire invention, or a real estate deal attached to the request. Many times the ones asking are family, friends, and neighbors. Though there are joys and regrets in giving, there is also resentment from those who feel slighted or jealous. And there are the temptations that come with having what seems like unlimited cash for life. The publicized amount of money promised by jackpots is quickly depleted by taxes, while a divorce can cut them in half, and, not to mention, new houses are expensive. The money can disappear fast. Millions of dollars require managing just as a small household budget does.

Someone who earns a salary of a few hundred thousand or even a few million dollars a year doesn't find his or her personal life being reported in the media. But when a big lottery winner divorces, drinks and drives, or commits a misdemeanor crime, it rates as news in a way that a well-paid attorney or executive would not.

The greatest of all the so-called lottery curses fell on Jack Whittaker of West Virginia. He has received, perhaps, more publicity than any lottery winner to date, nearly all of it tracking his foibles and tragedies. When he won $314.9 million in Powerball, he already had money from his contracting business doing sewer work. He announced that he was going to give 10 percent of his $113,386,407 lump-sum payout to his church, and, in January of 2003, he said that even more of the winnings would go to the creation of the Jack Whittaker Foundation to help charitable causes in West Virginia. Ten months later, the foundation had given out some $4 million and was fielding a thousand calls per week. But his behavior, now public, seemed hypocritical. It made headlines. He flashed his money. He said he was robbed at a strip club and that his house was broken into. He was mobbed with requests for money. The Jack Whittaker Foundation was so inundated with requests that it was temporarily suspended. It eventually gave away tens of millions. His granddaughter's ex-boyfriend was found dead of an overdose in Whittaker's house. Less than two years after Whittaker won the lottery, his granddaughter was found dead, wrapped in tarpaulin.

Sudden wealth has an impact on people. Lotteries market their product as a chance at life-changing money. There are psychologists who make a living counseling people who've found themselves suddenly—and uncomfortably—rich. These days, winners are advised to get a lawyer and a financial planner before they call the lottery office. Some hire publicists.

Even after years of lottery winners and their crash-and-burn stories, not everyone knows how to react. In 2008, a man who won $14 million in New York was so nervous about exposure that he arrived to get his first check in disguise. The unemployed Bronx resident tried to avoid the waiting photographers and reporters by wearing a baseball hat and sunglasses and drawing a fake beard on his face with a marker. He was afraid someone would rob him, he said.

Occasionally, a feel-good winner story arrives like that of Debi Faris-Cifelli. She won $27 million in the California Lottery in 2004. For years before winning, she and her husband, Steve, had been activists for abandoned babies. They established the Garden of Angels cemetery for abandoned newborns and pushed for the 2001 Safe Arms for Newborns Act that allowed mothers to leave their unwanted babies at hospitals and other sites without criminal prosecution. The money, $9 million in lump-sum payout, would fund her foundation, she said. This time, instead of calling it the lottery curse or even just luck, her win was attributed by some to karma.

When Sharp won, the math was simple. Win the jackpot and you can have a yacht, a mansion, and a Rolls-Royce.

"Slow this buggy down," Cookie calls out from the back of the van speeding to the Super Bowl party. The kickoff was at five P.M., but someone told Cookie it was at seven P.M. so they're late. The speedometer pushes eighty-five as Sharp approaches the exit to Smyrna, Tennessee.

They met at the Terrace Ballroom on Broad Street in downtown Newark. It was a party for a bartenders' ball that Cookie remembers being dubbed the Cork and Screw. Everyone turned out dressed to the nines. None as well as Sharp though. When he walked in, a ripple went through the crowd.

"I said, 'There's the Five Million Dollar Man,'" Cookie says. "And all those ladies were running over there and I went with them. His wife wasn't with him that night," Cookie says, laughing. "We said, 'Where's Jackie?' He said she was in the hospital for something."

He put his arm around her for a photo, and later, as he went around greeting people, he stopped by her table. "I said when are they going to give you another birthday party," she recalls. "I knew they used to roll out the red carpet on his birthday. He said, 'give me your number, I'll invite you.' It was an honor to hear that.

"So one day he went to one of my friends' clubs. My girlfriend called me and said, 'Guess who's in the club? The Five Million Dollar Man.' I said, 'I don't believe you, girl.' When he got on the phone, I thought it was somebody cracking a joke. I said, 'You remember me?' He said he remembered me. Finally, I invited him over to my house.

"We were friends at first. Just friends. Because he was married.

He started having problems at home. The friendship turned into something else. That was in 1984."

Three years after he and his wife split up, Sharp and Cookie moved in together. In 1993, they moved to Nashville.

Just then his financial problems came at him like a hurricane.

In 1997 Sharp's answering machine message of redemption was silenced. Instead, a recorded operator's voice came on the line to announce that the phone had temporarily been disconnected. Shortly after he'd won the lottery, an attorney told him about a great tax shelter—an investment in an oil company. The company turned out to be a fraud, he says, and the Internal Revenue Service demanded payment of back taxes.

"When they came to me and said you owe $207,000 in taxes, man, I said, 'No way.' But I did. And everybody that got in that shelter had to pay."

It turned out that the IRS had sent him a letter, years earlier, to the house in West Orange advising him that he could eliminate his tax debt if he paid $40,000. The letter never got to him, he says. In the end he paid nearly a decade's worth of fines on top of everything else. The IRS took his entire 1997 lottery check and then some. He was quickly plunged deep into debt. To keep his head above water he decided to borrow against his lottery winnings.

He turned to the companies that look for lottery winners to offer them high-interest loans against future checks. From the time he won his $5 million, unsolicited offers from these companies had been arriving in the mail. He took loans through two companies. One company gave Sharp $100,000 in exchange for three annual $40,000 deductions from future checks. Creditors took bites from two of his last four lottery checks.

It wasn't just the IRS and high-interest loans that took his money. He gave a lot of it away. In an interview with *Reader's Digest* he said he would help anyone who needed it. Not surprisingly, requests for cash found their way to him from around the world. He hired a group of women to read his mail, and he says the phone company assigned an operator just to handle the thousands of calls that came.

"I had a guy who walked with a limp, and he wanted me to give him money for a house," Sharp says. "These girls that were on the job were investigating people, and we found out this man owned three houses. But here comes ol' softie Curtis. People just try to get to you when you are friendly, so you've got to be careful and start screening people, which I don't like doing."

He says he's not angry toward the people who tried to fleece him: "Money is not the root of all evil. It's the love of money that is the root of all evil. I always thought, 'Easy come, easy go.' That's why I'm broke now."

He is good-natured and easygoing, and if others aren't, it doesn't ruin his mood, he says. The ride was worth it. What he didn't give away or lose in bad business ideas, he spent. He gave $50,000 toward famine relief in Ethiopia and traveled there with Senator Edward Kennedy and activist Dick Gregory. But much of the money went toward luxury. He bought houses, cars, and clothes, and showered women with gifts. Cookie was one of the recipients of his generosity. The white Cadillac in her garage was a gift from Sharp. So was the three-bedroom house with vinyl siding on a cul-de-sac where she lives and he spends much of his time.

"He was kind of stingy at first," she says, continuing the story of their courtship. "I guess he was trying to figure where I was coming from. Then later on he started buying me things—fur coats, diamond rings, cars, the house. You know, all those little things that ladies like. He should buy me the Empire State Building after twenty-two years."

In the 1980s she shared the frenzy around Sharp, going to movie premieres and nightclubs. "We'd get out of the car and walk down the street. People would bump into each other shouting, 'There goes the Five Million Dollar Man.'"

When I ask her why she was drawn to him, she says, "I guess it was because he was a celebrity. I have a thing for celebrities. I had a chance to meet a lot of celebrities through him. He stopped the ball game one time. He used to like that, too. That attention."

Sharp, who's been quiet for a time and driving, says, "Well, you might as well enjoy it while you got it."

"It's like people say what they would have done if it actually happened to you," Cookie says. "But if I had won, I know I would have some. Still have some of my money."

"How would you know?" I ask.

"That's it," Sharp says, laughing.

"I wouldn't be loaning out a lot of money. You know, some of the things he did, I would not do. I'd pay cash for my house, cash for my car, cash for my furniture."

"Well, you're just like the rest. Everybody says what they would do," Sharp replies.

When we reach his pastor's house, Sharp gets out of the van and a slip of paper falls from his pocket. It's a lottery ticket he bought when he ducked into the gas station to get Cookie's Salems. "It's up to $210 million," he says, and chuckles. "No one won yesterday."

He turns and we walk down the long drive up to the house where a dozen cars are parked. It's crowded with church members every Sunday. "His house is always open," Sharp says. The brick mini-mansion looks more like the home of a prosperous orthodontist or a city lawyer than the home of a Baptist pastor.

Inside, Sharp's still clutching the ticket. He shows it to another deacon, a large man who is in charge of food service at the church. "We all have a cross to bear," the man says, smiling and shaking his head.

"We're gonna pray," Brother Sharp calls out. The people on the sofa in the living room watching the game on a big-screen TV don't take notice; neither do those in the kitchen.

"We're gonna pray," he calls out louder.

"Turn that down," the big man says to those in front of the TV.

"Again?" says a young woman's voice in a mix of humor and exasperation.

After a minute the kitchen and the TV room go silent. Brother Sharp asks the Lord to bless the house and all within. Each sentence gets some response: "Yes, Lord." "Amen."

It's a casual prayer. No one folds their hands, but all eyes are downcast. A child coming down the hall is gently hushed. "They're praying," an adult tells him. The child goes quiet. Then the prayer is over and everyone returns to what he or she was doing. The women go back to their conversation and pulling apart chicken. The volume on the Super Bowl goes back up.

Leaving the pastor's house, Sharp starts to talk about his latest investment—a plan that, if it works out, he says would make him more millions than he ever got from the lottery. He has invested in an invention that allows a battery to recharge itself. If put into a car, it would be a leap forward in eliminating dependence on gasoline. As a source of continuous electrical power, its applications are nearly limitless, Sharp says with excitement. He got in from the beginning about four years ago, buying twenty-one shares. He's put in $11,000 of his own money and convinced ten others to purchase shares in the company, Tilley Foundation, at $1,000 a share. All they need is someone to buy the technology and they will reap the windfall, he says.

Some other investors have sued Carl Tilley, the man behind the battery charging fraud. But everything is on the up-and-up, Sharp says.

"This ain't no fly-by-night. You know the electric cars they got now, you can drive them about one hundred miles and you've got to plug them in for eight hours. We ain't got none of that. This thing that he has invented can run your house and you never have to have electricity coming in."

They put the battery on a car, a DeLorean, and tested it on a racetrack. "It was the car of the future years ago, you know." The car reached 130 miles per hour and completed eighteen laps, but then the test was deemed invalid. Something about the DeLorean created its own high rate of speed, and the battery needed to be tested on another type of car, Sharp says. The story is hard to follow.

Sharp says the invention is worth billions and could return a million dollars per share. There are interested buyers, he says. "We're just waiting for them to get back to ask whether they want to buy it or not.

"We had scientists come down there. They knew it worked but they couldn't figure out how it works. Then we had a couple of scientists from one big company come up there and check it out. And they tried to tamper with it, right? But once you tamper with it, it collapses. So you can't know how it works."

He admits that he's been hoodwinked on bad investments a couple of times in the past. "I didn't know," he says, and laughs. "I just took a chance. I didn't know if it was good or not. This is just, I don't know, something just told me to get into this.

"I went out there to see this thing. I went out there and the first time I ain't know what I was looking at. But you had to buy five shares in the beginning, then after that you could buy one share, two shares, like that you know. I was trying to sell some shares around the church. Some people laughed at it you know. You know how people is, everybody think it's a fluke."

CHAPTER 5

ONE VOTE

THE NORTH CAROLINA Education Lottery had a difficult birth, like many in the Bible Belt. The states of the South have been among the last to adopt lotteries. South Carolina instituted the game in 2001, Tennessee in 2004, and in 2005, North Carolina became the forty-second state with a lottery.

Each state fought an internal battle over whether to overturn more than a century of bans on lotteries that in some cases were written into their constitutions. In each fight, lotteries had a polarizing effect. They were either a morally destructive and regressive tax on the poor or they were the saving grace of children's education. There was no middle ground.

The North Carolina Education Lottery nearly tore the state in two on its way to being passed. As it approached its one-year anniversary, the nation's newest lottery left scandals and recriminations in its wake, along with several hundred million dollars for education.

"It was far from painless," Dr. Charles Sanders, who chaired North Carolina's Lottery Commission in its first year, told me during a visit to Raleigh.

The seeds of North Carolina's lottery were sown years earlier in Kentucky by the political consultant James Carville. In 1988, he was working for a candidate who was behind in the polls, seemingly headed for defeat. Carville introduced a pro-lottery plank, and Wallace G. Wilkinson's campaign caught fire. The writing was on the wall: Regardless of the South's supposed family-values conservatism, people wanted a lottery. It was hardly considered gambling anymore. Kentucky voters were already driving north across the Ohio River to buy tickets. If playing the lottery was a sin, a good part of the state needed to hurry up and get saved.

The issue was so potent, Peter Beinart wrote in *Time*, that one of Wilkinson's last campaign ads showed a crowd of supporters chanting, "Taxes, no! Lottery, yes!"

Lottery tickets went on sale sixteen months after Governor Wilkinson took office.

Carville went on to Georgia, where he helped elect Zell Miller governor in 1990. That campaign used the lottery, with its tax-free revenue, as a battering ram against the Republican incumbent. The hallmark of the Georgia Lottery was that it strictly earmarked the dollars for education and vigorously promoted its HOPE scholarships for collegebound students. The Georgia Lottery was such a success that it quickly became a model for anyone in the South thinking of proposing a lottery for his or her state.

Not that either of the Carville-guided lotteries breezed through. Tempers got hot in both Kentucky and Georgia over state-sponsored gambling. Those with moral objections to the lottery may have been in the minority, but they were loud. Governor Miller still had to pass a referendum to amend the state's 1868 constitutional ban on lotteries. The referendum passed 52–48 percent.

The lottery entered the South as the spearhead of a Democratic party surge, tied to the promise of reforming and funding education. The political formula was simple—lotteries equal more schools, better schools, and college scholarships for the poor. More important, the new money did not require any tax increase. The Democrats had a winning platform in the fiscally conservative South.

In 1999, South Carolina Democrat James Hovis Hodges ended a twelve-year stretch of Republican governors with a campaign that called for a lottery to save education.

In 2000, Michael Francis Easley, a former state attorney general, won election as North Carolina's governor on a pro-lottery platform. It took him five years of failed attempts to bring the lottery to fruition.

Most states have had lotteries for so long that it can be hard to imagine that anyone would fight over them. In most states, the lottery is part of the furniture. But in North Carolina, antilottery sentiment was still strong among its opponents, and emotions were raw a year after tickets had gone on sale.

Politicians and the voting public have made the same passionate arguments for and against lotteries—that they are necessary supplements to the state treasury or are morally flawed social policy—for two hundred years. Nevertheless, one man, state senator John Garwood, is credited with instituting the North Carolina Lottery in 2005. The next year he was run out of office.

The politicians were supposed to be on their summer break. The Senate chamber was empty; the 2005 session was over. Over on the House side, the representatives were rushing to clear their desks of leftover bills and brewing up a small tempest over a half-cent increase in the sales tax to fund school construction.

A lottery would have brought in the money, but the Senate had just blocked it, 26–24. They arm-wrestled through dawn on Wednesday, August 24, but the lottery was blocked, again. After the twenty-one-hour session the exhausted senators went home.

George Reed, executive director of the N.C. Council of

Churches, was asked to comment on the victory over the lottery supporters. "Until they say, 'Adjourned until May 2006,' I will not be popping the cork on the champagne—or whatever it is that a member of a religious organization would pop open," he said.

His words were prophetic. On Friday, the Senate president, a onetime lottery foe now in favor of it, caught everyone by surprise. He told the members to report back after the weekend for one more day of work. He didn't say what kind of work, but many suspected the lottery wasn't dead yet.

Starting in 1983, bills to enact a state lottery had appeared in the state legislature every spring like dogwood blossoms. None lived long. Several cleared the Senate only to wither in the House of Representatives. Enough political and civic leaders opposed a lottery as immoral, and later, as bad economic and social policy, to keep it out of the largest state without one.

On Tuesday, August 30, the lottery finally won in North Carolina. In the Senate, the bill tied 24–24. The lieutenant governor cast the tie-breaking vote in favor of a lottery. Two senators were absent during the critical tie. One was away on his honeymoon. The other was John Garwood.

THE SENATOR'S ABSENCE ended North Carolina's stubborn resistance to lotteries. Depending on which legend you believe, North Carolina is called the Tar Heel State because (a) it was reluctant to join the rest of the Confederacy; (b) its soldiers refused to retreat in the Civil War; or (c) it exported a lot of tar. Excepting the third legend, the general idea is that North Carolinians are not the kind to follow the crowd. The state had lived up to its name for eighteen years as lotteries surrounded it on all sides in Virginia, Georgia, South Carolina, and Tennessee.

"I never thought it could happen," state representative Bill Owens told me in his Raleigh office. "I never thought we could get the votes to do it."

So how did it come to pass after twenty-two years of wrangling? For one, Virginia and South Carolina had been sucking money out of the state ever since they started selling scratch tickets and jackpot games. From his district on the Atlantic coast near the Virginia border, Owens had watched millions of dollars pouring across the border.

William Clarence Owens Jr. is a Democrat who had sponsored lottery bills nearly every year since taking office in 1994. A jowly man with a syrupy drawl, Owens could walk onto a Hollywood movie set and play the part of a Southern politico without stopping in makeup. He also has the bearing of leadership and someone who is comfortable and confident in his position.

There was no reason why dollars from wallets in his district should end up in Virginia never to be seen again. It was one of the strongest arguments in favor of a lottery.

It was undeniable that the Virginia gas stations and convenience stores on the North Carolina border were doing a booming business. The Virginia Lottery took in about $100 million a year in sales from North Carolina players. The convenience-store and gas-station owners along the border estimated that 80 percent of their customers were from North Carolina.

In any lottery state that neighbors a nonlottery state, the border always has brisk ticket sales. In his plan for a lottery in New Jersey, Alexander Hamilton had recognized the importance of cross-border sales. Not much had changed two centuries later. What can't be had on one side of the border becomes more desirable when it's for sale on the other. It is hard to accurately measure the amount of money a state government loses, in business sales and taxes, when its residents leave to spend their dollars on lottery tickets out of state, but the phenomenon has always been one of the arguments in the quiver of lottery supporters. The notion that millions are lost to the neighbors has helped propel many new lotteries into existence. After Mike Easley's election to governor, North Carolina's lottery supporters announced that the state lost $1 million every day to neighboring lottery states. The esimate included more than lottery tickets. Because they're sold in convenience stores and gas stations, the argument goes, chances are that customers also buy a tank of gas, a cup of coffee, and a hot dog with their scratch tickets. Which means more lost sales tax revenue from those purchases.

As a result, lotteries in the United States have often come in regional clumps. Once one state fell, its neighbors were sure to follow. During election season, candidates who pushed for lotteries reminded voters that neighboring lottery states profited from their hard-earned dollars. One of the most popular (or infamous) examples of this campaign strategy was seen in South Carolina's 1998 governor's race. Jim Hodges, a Democrat, running against the incumbent Republican, David Beasley, gave voters "Bubba."

Bubba was the hairy, redneck star of a series of campaign ads that targeted Beasley for his opposition to lotteries. Bubba owned a convenience store in Georgia where the lottery was legal. "Here in Georgia, we just luuuv David Beasley," Bubba told voters, because Beasley kept the lottery out of South Carolina, sending everyone there into Georgia to spend their money on lottery tickets. "The Georgia Lottery tickets y'all buy pay for computers in every one of our classrooms," Bubba said with a big smile. "Just reelect Beasley and keep buyin' our lottery tickets, won'tcha?"

The ads were so popular that Kerry Maher, the actor who played Bubba, became a local celebrity with hopes of parlaying the character into a movie like Jim Varney's "Ernest," who had pitched everything from used cars to pizza before hitting the big screen.

Hodges unseated Beasley. At the victory party, Maher, who attended in costume, got such applause that he nearly upstaged the governor-elect. Voters soon approved an amendment to the state's 1868 constitutional ban on lotteries. When tickets went on sale in 2001, residents in North Carolina could drive north or south to play the lottery. To those who wanted the game in North Carolina, it was as if thieves were coming in the front and back doors.

The strategist behind the Bubba ads was Hodges's campaign manager and public relations man, Kevin Geddings. "We don't want North Carolina to have a lottery," Geddings told reporters. "Heck no. We want North Carolinians to come to South Carolina and pay for our schools." Recalling the Bubba campaign years later, Hodges said to one newspaper, "That's a strength Kevin always showed—to take a concept like improving education and to put that in terms that people could understand. Kevin is one of the smartest people I've run across in politics."

Geddings served as chief of staff to the governor for a year, then went to work as a political consultant for hire in North Carolina, working on the push for a lottery to improve education. Like many others, Geddings was smart enough to see that North Carolina was the next lottery battleground. After the lottery passed the North Carolina state legislature, Geddings was appointed to the Lottery Commission that was choosing a vendor to run the games and oversee its operation. He sat on the commission for one month before it was revealed that he had been taking money from Scientific Games, one of the bidders to run the North Carolina Lottery. He was indicted on federal fraud charges soon after. But in the heady days of

2001, when lottery tickets went on sale in South Carolina, there was little forewarning of Geddings's future disgrace.

In 2004, Tennessee overcame twenty years of failed proposals and opened its lottery. It shared the border on North Carolina's western flank. North Carolina was now hemmed in on all sides by lottery states. Its residents were estimated to spend about $300 million a year on out-of-state lotteries. When everyone has it, supporters said, there's no sense in fighting it. You might as well keep those lost dollars in-house and put them to good use.

Besides the loss of money to other states, proponents relied on another argument: it's not gambling. This has always been the public relations angle on lotteries. Paying a dollar for the chance to win thousands or even millions on terrible odds is a lark. It's entertainment. People spend money in all manner of ways to occupy and enjoy themselves. Paying a buck for the fantasy of lottery winnings is no different, the argument goes. Most states had marketed lotteries in just that way for years. "No self-respecting gambler would play," one Raleigh pro-lottery lobbyist told reporters. "The lottery is purely chance. You can't win the lottery by skill."

The argument wins, in part, with increased exposure to lotteries. In North Carolina, where so many already played, over time the lottery became more acceptable. The Bible Belt's deep moral opposition to lotteries as gambling wore down over the years.

The state's newspapers, nearly unanimous in their opposition to a lottery, had printed the results of Virginia's lottery drawings for years. One local paper suggested buying yourself a lottery ticket in an article that gave advice on how to pamper yourself on Valentine's Day. It was, at the time, still illegal to possess a lottery ticket in North Carolina.

As North Carolina's moral opposition wore down and lottery proponents trumpeted the increased revenue a lottery would bring, new polls were conducted. In North Carolina, more than 50 percent of the people wanted a lottery. When it was tied to education, the poll numbers jumped to 60–70 percent in favor. The polls added another arrow to the pro-lottery quiver: why won't you give the people what they want? Opponents were seen as paternalistic, trying to protect people from themselves by outlawing a freedom that the vast majority of the country's citizens enjoyed.

Still, this was the Bible Belt. The moral argument against lotteries might have weakened (though the Christian right was making headway on other issues), but it was not dead. In Georgia and in South Carolina, proponents had discovered that by promoting the good that lotteries could do, they could trump both moral and political opposition. The revenue, after all, is free money for the government. There was no shortage of suggestions for what to do with lottery money in North Carolina. Crime is up? Lottery money will fund prisons and crime-prevention programs. Water is bad? Let's spend it on cleaner water and filtration. The Minnesota Twins are thinking of moving? Let's build them a stadium and bring them here. These suggestions were all put forward along with improving highways and building a NASCAR track and a symphony hall.

These ideas all had debatable value, but no one could argue against more money for education. Lotteries weren't about gambling, the campaigns argued, they paid for schools, textbooks, and college educations—and North Carolina was missing out. Don Siegelman spoke right to the heart of the Bible Belt's moral conflict with lotteries when he ran for governor of Alabama as a pro-lottery Democrat. "Southern Baptists have children and they want the best for their kids," Siegelman said shortly before his victory. "Folks come up to me in the grocery store and whisper in my ear, 'Hey, I'm for this lottery, too.'"

Siegelman also proved that one should not underestimate the moral opposition to lotteries. He was elected governor but lost the battle over lotteries. Opponents turned out in large numbers and rejected by 54–46 percent a stand-alone ballot initiative that would have amended the state's 1901 constitutional ban on lotteries.

In June 2006, Siegelman was convicted of federal bribery, mail-fraud, and obstruction-of-justice charges. He was sentenced to more than seven years in prison, but released pending appeal in March 2008 after serving less than a year. One of the charges he was convicted on was taking a $500,000 donation to his pro-lottery campaign in return for appointing someone to a seat on the board that oversaw Alabama's hospital system. Siegelman maintained there was nothing illegal about the donation. Since his conviction, dozens of state attorneys general have called for a reexamination of his prosecution. Many have alleged that it was an unjust vendetta, engineered by Karl Rove, who has denied the accusations.

Siegelman's downfall aside, the lottery helped push him into office. On Southern campaign trails, Democrats who wanted lotteries had an ace in the hole. Branded for years as a tax-and-spend party, the Democrats could now offer a practical solution to budget shortfalls that promised to bring in hundreds of millions for beleaguered educational systems—without raising income, sales, or property taxes. The antilottery folks had few counterproposals to offer on Election Day.

"Why would you raise taxes when you could implement a lottery where seventy percent of the people were against raising taxes and seventy percent were in favor of a lottery?" Owens asked me.

Why indeed? Opponents tried a number of arguments to sway people against a North Carolina lottery. They accused lotteries of cynically attaching themselves to children's education; they argued that lotteries were financially unstable, preyed on the poor and gullible, opened the door to casinos, and otherwise were just a bad idea. But few viable alternatives could match the kind of money that a lottery generated.

"There is no more appreciated poll than on Election Day," a GTECH spokesman said after South Carolina elected pro-lottery James Hodges to governor.

After Governor Mike Easley started his first term in 2000 as the first governor to advocate for a lottery, North Carolina still had a tough fight ahead. He made an aggressive pitch to opponents in the legislature. The lottery, he and his supporters said, would be a conservative lottery. Half the money from the legal gambling would go to education—a much higher percentage than in any other state. Advertising would be restricted in tone, and its budget would be strictly limited.

Even with a Democratic majority, Easley, with the help of Owens and many others, had an uphill battle. They succeeded in bringing a lottery to North Carolina against a coalition that defied many common assumptions about politics. It was a rare alliance—a strange partnership of progressive liberals, conservative Republicans, and the Christian right. Some, tongue in cheek, dubbed it the "unholy alliance."

"It is the single most fascinating public policy issue I've ever been involved with," said Chuck Neely, who chaired the lead group, Citizens United Against the Lottery. "Everybody that was in this debate came at it from a different perspective."

The group formed after Easley's election and included prominent citizens such as Billy Graham; Dr. William Friday, former president of UNC; Harlan Boyles, a past treasurer of the state; and others who came from a broad political spectrum. It included those who thought that lotteries were a regressive tax on the poor, those who believed lotteries were an inefficient way to raise government revenue, and those who believed it was immoral for government to encourage gambling. There may be no other issue on which they could get together.

The arguments they have raised against lotteries in North Carolina and elsewhere—that they prey on the poor and gullible, are corruptible, and make little economic sense—were the same accusations that led to the banishment of lotteries in America more than two hundred years ago. "They're going to encourage people to gamble and spend money on a hope as opposed to teaching values of thrift and hard work," Neely said. "The lottery is, in my view, adverse to the whole ethic upon which our society is built."

A lot of money was at stake, but not just for education. With a population of eight million, three quarters of whom were of legal gambling age, North Carolina, the last state on the East Coast without a lottery, was a potential windfall. "This is the last of the big prizes, so to speak," one pro-lottery lobbyist told the *Herald-Sun* of Durham.

Both sides in the debate hired lobbyists to bring votes to their cause. The two companies with the most direct financial interest in the outcome had lobbyists working the hallways in Raleigh. Two giants virtually run the American lottery system, providing and operating the vast majority of state lottery games—GTECH and Scientific Games.

GTECH is the larger company, with $1.3 billion in annual revenue from contracts in most lottery states and several countries around the world. In 2006, the company was sold to the much smaller Lotto-matica, an Italian firm, for $4.65 billion. While GTECH dominates the online numbers games of daily and weekly drawings—it runs them in twenty-five states—its competitor Scientific Games has scratch tickets covered. Scientific Games takes in nearly $1 billion annually from scratch-ticket games in thirty-four states and online numbers games in fifteen states. Nearly half its business comes from overseas contracts.

Any state looking to start a lottery will likely be hiring one of the two companies. Not surprisingly, they are fierce competitors. How much the companies' lobbyists spent is unclear; North Carolina law protects the companies from having to disclose such information. But with such a big state at stake, and few other new accounts to chase, it is safe to assume the competition was stiff.

The forces arrayed against the lottery made their arguments in op-ed pieces, research papers, pamphlets, radio ads, and sermons over several years starting with Governor Mike Easley's election. But in the legislature, as the 2005 session drew to a close and the lottery was about to be shelved again, the dispute was a matter of twisting arms in hallways. "It is the most pressure I have seen in my twelve years down here being placed on legislators," said John Rustin, a lobbyist for the antilottery North Carolina Family Policy Council. "It was 'We need you to do this.'"

The North Carolina Family Policy Council is a research and lob-bying group that works to protect Judeo-Christian "family and tradi-tional family values." The group, founded in 1992, promotes teaching abstinence in schools, supports a constitutional ban on gay marriage, and opposes stem cell research and abortion. With the vote coming up, Rustin, the council's point man on the lottery, was busy.

The lottery bill had already passed the House in April, 61–59. "We picked up two votes on the floor of the House on the day of the vote," Representative Owens said. "We just told them that the majority of their constituents were in favor of it."

House Speaker Jim Black, a former lottery opponent, was the first leader of the House to approve of a lottery. Both supporters and opponents gave him much of the credit for driving the bill through. "I was never for the lottery when we were not surrounded by it, when our money was not flowing out of this state," Speaker Black said after the vote.

Democrats held the majority in both the House and Senate, but a handful had remained opposed. The morning of the vote, Black, who lived near the South Carolina border, gathered his caucus for an emotional speech—a last-minute push for the lottery. Education, he told his fellow Democrats, was desperately in need of increased funding. The welfare of the children of the state was at stake.

To move opponents to their side, lottery supporters made a late agreement adding severe restrictions to the bill. For example, the lottery could only advertise in the locations where tickets were sold—no TV, no radio, and no billboards. Lottery revenue would be earmarked for education only and could not supplant existing funds.

The physical limitations on advertising were later removed from the bill by language added to the budget bill. One concern with limiting ads to point of sale was that Powerball or other popular multistate games would not come to North Carolina under such a restriction.

The law still stated that "advertising may not target specific groups or economic classes; advertising cannot be misleading or deceptive and cannot present any lottery game as a means of relieving financial or personal difficulties; and advertising cannot have the primary purpose of inducing people to participate in the lottery." How the state was going to market the games without "inducing people to participate" left many scratching their heads.

Just as the House was reversing its antilottery trend, the Senate, which had passed lottery bills in the past, proved unexpectedly difficult. Although Democrats had a 29–21 majority, the outcome was uncertain. State Senate leader Marc Basnight, a Democrat, wanted a lottery, but five members of his party were against it. Proponents were two votes short.

The governor called the holdouts in an attempt to change their minds. Time was running out. There would be no lottery that year it seemed. On August 13, the Senate blocked the lottery by a vote of 26–24. As the legislature entered the final day of the 2005 session, on Tuesday, August 23, Basnight told the senators, "Prepare to stay tonight, and then go for good." There was some housekeeping to do, then the statehouse emptied. A few day later, on Friday, Basnight made his surprise call to return for one more day of work. When they reconvened on Tuesday morning, August 30, two Republicans were missing. Senator Harry Brown, a car dealer, had left on his honeymoon. He later said that he was unaware that Basnight had recalled the Senate.

"Yeah, but he got married in April," Representative Owens says, laughing. "He got married in April, but he had his honeymoon four months later."

John Garwood was at home in Wilkes County recuperating from a leg infection. All eyes were on Garwood to cast the deciding vote and block the lottery. He didn't. In fact, he didn't vote at all, although he could have used a house procedure to do so. Instead, the lottery tied, the lieutenant governor cast the winning vote, and the lottery squeaked through. "As squeaky as squeaky can be," Owens says.

The half-cent sales-tax increase to fund school construction, which counties would have had the option of enacting, was shelved. The *Raleigh News & Observer*, a consistent opponent of the lottery, ran a photo of Garwood's empty seat the day after the bill passed.

I FOUND JOHN Garwood's street in the darkness off the state highway where western North Carolina rises into the Blue Ridge Mountains. I was late—it was nearly nine P.M., which I assumed was past polite visiting hours. Still, Southern etiquette being what it is, he opened the door and invited me in to sit down. His wife made a brief offer of coffee or tea and disappeared, leaving us alone in the living room of the low-slung ranch house.

"There's times I regret the decision," Garwood says. "That's the reason I'm not in Raleigh now. I was pressured a hell of a lot to vote against it. Nobody pressured me to vote for it."

That's not entirely accurate. The N.C. Association of Educators targeted his district with radio ads that called for a lottery to increase education funds.

Garwood is as much a victim of the lottery as the tabloid tales we read about people who won it all only to watch their lives disintegrate around them. Their tragedies would be too mundane for a newspaper—divorce, substance abuse, reckless behavior, bankruptcy—if they hadn't been millionaires. Garwood destroyed his own political career by letting the lottery pass. The local Republican Party ran him out of office by pulling their primary-election support for him in favor of another candidate.

"They told the people in these mountains that I as sure as voted for it," he says. "I did not vote for the lottery."

To his former colleagues, caught in a debate with no middle ground, not voting was the same thing as a yes. Particularly galling to opponents of the lottery, who had thought he was on their side, was the way he tried to straddle the fence. "I'm opposed to gambling, but I won't block its way into town" was how they interpreted his lack of resolve. Others had been taken to task for trying to have it both ways in the lottery feud. A *Chapel Hill Herald* editorial had called the position "butt-romping" a few years earlier in reference to a former governor. Butt-romping, as defined in the paper, is that moment when "your butt is on one side of the fence and you are eating out of a trough on another person's property."

The paper had targeted then governor Jim Hunt as a butt romper. Once a stalwart lottery hater, Hunt had spoken in favor of a popular referendum on the issue, though he said he was personally opposed to lotteries. Because polls showed most people wanted a lottery, backing a referendum was tantamount to backing the lottery. The *News & Observer* ran a cartoon showing Governor Hunt preaching a sermon against lotteries as a lotto machine next to him picked the hymns.

Garwood should have known that trying to have it both ways would only bring him enemies. He knew that voting for the lottery would anger voters in his district. But in a rural county that was solidly Republican, he never thought his own people would come after him for standing on the sidelines.

He had returned home for the weekend, shortly after Basnight had asked the Senate to reconvene on Tuesday. With the second vote looming, Garwood was at home in North Wilkesboro, his infected leg elevated. He had cellulitis, a serious infection that had briefly hospitalized him. When it became clear in Raleigh that he was not going to make it back for the recalled session on Tuesday, the phone started ringing.

Under the rules of the North Carolina legislature a vote can be paired with an opposing vote and the two simply cancel each other out. His colleagues had found someone, a Democrat, who would pair his vote with Garwood's. All Garwood had to do was agree to the pairing over the phone.

"I want this thing behind me and behind everybody," he told a reporter from the *Winston-Salem Journal*. "I just feel like, 'Let it do what it'll do.' If it passes, that's fine with me. And if it doesn't, that's fine, too."

It wasn't much of an answer. His indecision was a mystery and a shock to other Republicans. "I even had a Baptist preacher from Raleigh show up at my door on Tuesday," says Garwood, who is Methodist. "He came in the house and drank a cup of coffee. I still had not made up my mind one hundred percent. He left and went back to Raleigh." Garwood decided to stand aside because it meant more money for education, he tells me.

After the honeymoon, Senator Brown returned to North Carolina. He said that he would have voted against the lottery if he had been able, but he didn't know the Senate had been called back. Senator Brown won reelection. Garwood, without a decent excuse such as a honeymoon, became a lightning rod for attacks. The newspapers went first.

"North Carolina Democrats and the gambling industry have finally won the right to con people into throwing away money on an 'education lottery,'" read an editorial in the *Wilmington Star-News*. The editors then lashed out at Garwood and Brown. "It will be fascinating to see how he and Sen. John Garwood of North Wilkesboro are rewarded for their cooperation."

The *News & Observer*'s editorial said, "Republican state Sens. John Garwood of North Wilkesboro and Harry Brown of Jacksonville may have a little trouble filling out a foursome for golf from among their GOP colleagues when they return to Raleigh next spring."

Garwood says that when the political attack came it caught him unprepared. "It was like I was taking a payoff or something," he says. "It was like I was in bed with the Democrats."

Former allies in his remote backyard came out swinging. U.S. representative Virginia Foxx, whom Garwood supported in her run for Congress, spoke out against him, he said: "She hit all the Baptist churches. These mountains are full of them." Foxx, whom the *National Journal* called the most conservative member of the North Carolina delegation and who scores 100 percent with the American Conservative Union, told voters that Garwood was not a true conservative. "I'm not saying we're lily-white," he says. "But her speaking to a Republican organization against somebody who's an incumbent is unheard of."

Garwood lost the Republican primary to Watauga County commissioner David Blust, who blamed him for two things: bringing the lottery into North Carolina and not doing enough to restrict access to abortion. Blust declared that he had decided to run after Garwood had suggested that Blust was "too far to the right to serve in Raleigh."

"Since I am of the same fabric of moral and ethical conscience as Ronald Reagan, Jesse Helms, and Virginia Foxx, I will wear this comment as a badge of honor and thus consider it a compliment," Blust told reporters. "I will make a stand, you will know how I stand, and I will not bend to criticism or praise."

The decision to attack one of their own may have backfired on the Republicans, who ultimately lost the seat in the general election to a Democrat, Steve Goss. "No way he would have won if people didn't have the opinion that I got hoodooed," Garwood says. "Every time I see him he thanks me."

Now that it's over, Garwood says, at least more money is going to education. "If people were going to blame me, they were also going to have to give me credit for money in four counties."

But the battle over the lottery has not ended with its passage into law. Down the hall from Representative Owens I found the glorified broom closet of Representative Paul Stam, who continues to fight against the lottery a year after the tickets went on sale. A former marine and all-county fullback with a crew cut, he keeps a piece of flag from the USS *Braine* above his desk. His father served on the destroyer, which was hit by two kamikazes during the battle for Iwo Jima. It's not hard to see where Stam stands on the political spectrum—conservative Republican.

For Stam, and many others, the lottery's numbers are not what they appear to be. He hands me a two-week-old article about the first millionaire from an in-state game, Jackie Alston. The article breathlessly reported that Alston had just stepped forward to claim a $74 million Powerball jackpot. She didn't win $74 million, Stam says. She won $36 million, or to be precise, about $24 million after taxes, he adds. I point out that she took the lump-sum payout. It is an increasingly popular choice and, as a standard practice, is a lower amount. Lotteries don't keep the jackpot money on hand. The jackpot is the value of the money as it accrues interest over twenty or twenty-five years in a conservative investment such as Treasury bonds. The lump-sum payout is the cash that would have been invested.

"They're doubling the stated benefits while you're betting," Stam says. He wrote a letter to the editor of the paper who said that he understood Stam's point but that the amount had been clarified in the article. "The meaning of the word *jackpot*. It's all the jacks in the pot. But there's only half the number of jacks in the pot. There's only thirty-six million jacks in the pot."

She would have received $74 million if she took the money over twenty years, I say.

"Did she buy her ticket over twenty years?" he asks. "It's one of the oldest scams comparing apples and oranges, something with a present value to something with a nominal value. No interest until 2009 or whatever. It's fraud. They're giving true information that is completely misleading."

It's a complaint I've heard before, but it seems so literal-minded as to be pointless. We all understand that the lump-sum buyout is less, that's just the way it works. I can see his point that the hoopla raised over, say, a $74 million jackpot is not exactly what it claims to be, but it's still more money than Jackie Alston would ever have seen in her life.

Then he hits me with a stumper: "We actually lose more money in a state with a lottery than without one," he says matter-of-factly.

Pardon? He points out that lottery winners pay a hefty 28 percent in federal taxes. That money is, theoretically, returned to the states in services. So federal taxes siphon money from lottery states to nonlottery states. "We are donor states to states that don't have lotteries," he says. By Stam's math, North Carolina's lottery winners would pay $210 million more into the federal treasury through gambling taxes than they would if they only played the lottery in neighboring states.

Then there's the inefficiency argument that economists have

raised. No other "tax" costs so much money to collect. The state government spends a lot of money on running lotteries. North Carolina spends about 13 percent of its lottery revenue on the private-sector salaries, commissions to retailers, bonuses to sales staff, marketing, and general operation and upkeep of its Education Lottery. The expense of operating a lottery, and keeping up public interest, has been a concern in government-approved lotteries since the eighteenth century in America.

In 2001, the Raleigh-based John Locke Foundation, a conservative think tank that fought against the lottery, compared state revenue raised through a lottery to the usual tax route. The year before, the state had collected $13.2 billion in taxes through the Department of Revenue, which operated on a $75 million budget. The state spent about a half cent in administrative costs (the Department of Revenue's budget) for every dollar it raised. By contrast, the governor estimated the lottery would cost about $180 million in administrative costs and put $450 million toward public education. In other words, as a tax, the lottery would spend about twenty-nine cents for every dollar it put back into public use.

Stam estimated that a 0.75% increase on the state sales tax could bring in a comparable amount of money. He estimates such an increase would raise the price of a gallon of milk from $3.50 to about $3.53. Stam is a lawyer known locally for his thorough research into the law and the minutiae of policy. He is not particularly popular with Democrats because of his conservative stances on social issues such as abortion and has irritated some in his own party with the minutely detailed reports he puts out on certain subjects. The lottery was one of those.

A group of antilottery citizens, angry at paying money into the state treasury, filed suit against the state, accusing it of enacting an illegal tax. Lotteries operate like a tax, by putting aside money from consumers into the treasury, but they are technically not taxes because players send in the revenue voluntarily. Several legislative hurdles have to be jumped before the state can enact a tax. The lottery bill skipped them, the case argues. It would be an understatement to call the case a long shot. The court quickly dismissed it. Stam, who is a plaintiff in the suit, reminded me that the case was still before the Court of Appeals.

Another complaint Stam raises—and one that is true in nearly every state—is that after all the hoopla, lottery proceeds don't really bring much to the state budget. For all the promised revenue—and $425 million is a lot—it amounts to a "rounding error" in the state's roughly $20 billion budget, Stam said. In its first year the lottery was about 2 percent of the state budget and about 4 percent of the governor's proposed education budget. "It is less than the annual cost-of-living increase in education spending," Stam said.

In Stam's analysis, Easley was blind to the effect that an increase in lottery sales would have. In his annual budget, the governor had just proposed setting aside $150 million for tax-funded programs for the poor. He also proposed changing the lottery formula to increase sales. New sales alone "take $150 million from one group of poor people and give it to another group of poor people," Stam said.

Another opponent, the liberal North Carolina Budget and Tax Center, argued that the lottery acts as a regressive tax. The center estimated that poor taxpayers, as a percentage of their income, would pay forty times more into the lottery than the top 1 percent of wage earners. This matter has been hotly debated since the early nineteenth century, when people worried that their servants were stealing from them to buy lottery tickets. Do the poor play more than other people? Or, from the social, paternalistic perspective, are the poor more susceptible to the fantasies that lotteries advertise? And should the state be encouraging them?

"They're all regressive," Duke University professor Charles Clotfelter had told me earlier on the day I met with Stam. "Some are more regressive than others. They take a higher percentage on average of the income of a low-income person than a high-income person." Clotfelter, one of the leading economists on the finance and structure of state lotteries, is quick to point out that regressive taxation can be a misleading argument. In absolute terms someone with a lower income spends a higher percentage of his or her income on most things, whether it's barbecue or toilet paper, than a person with higher income. As an economist he has no moral bone to pick with lotteries. "To make illegal this thing and not to make illegal smoking and drinking seems ridiculous," he said.

For Clotfelter, regressive taxation is not the major problem—it's the taxation, period. There may be no other consumer product in the country that is taxed so heavily as a lottery ticket. Clotfelter and Philip Cook, who coauthored *Selling Hope: State Lotteries in America* in 1989, calculated that on each $1 ticket, the State of North Carolina takes 35 cents for itself and uses another 15 cents to cover administrative costs. Players are given back just 35 cents of every dollar they spend, while the state takes the lion's share as an unspoken tax. "We take the lottery and we just tax the hell out of it," Clotfelter said with wonder.

The Budget and Tax Center also argued that lottery sales took money that consumers would spend on other items. The center estimated that if the lottery took in a total of $900 million, the state would lose $23.6 million in sales tax revenue, and counties would lose $12.7 million in local sales taxes.

But fiscal debate aside, Stam also had a moral opposition to the lottery. The biography on his personal Web site mentions his family's work in their local Baptist church. When asked, he told me that he can only conceive of a theoretical situation in which gambling is morally acceptable: If two rich people who have set up trusts for their dependents want to gamble to while away a half hour, that might be acceptable. "Almost always when it's used, it harms other people who are unsuspecting, foolish, or improvident," he quickly added.

The moral argument against lotteries does not play as well as it did in, say, the nineteenth century. As an elected official, Stam does not invoke God to argue against the lottery; he brings out numbers. Later, at my request, he e-mailed me a selection of Bible passages, mostly from Proverbs, that his church put out as a warning against gambling. But, when addressing the general public, members of the Baptist Convention and other religious opponents of lotteries, rather than quoting the Bible and its condemnation of gambling, are more likely to adopt the arguments of liberal progressives: lotteries hurt the poor; are a regressive tax; and are an inefficient way for government to collect revenue.

While there's no reason both arguments can't simultaneously be held, I suspected that much of the stated economic opposition was cover for a deeper, unstated moral opposition. Emotions were too high for opposition to be based on a policy dispute. So where had moral outrage gone? Moral opposition to lotteries had been common enough in the early days of the lottery. In the 1970s, opponents in New York City churches argued that it was immoral for the government to profit from gambling. Moral outrage, mixed with social reform, had run lotteries out of the states in the nineteenth century. Clearly, times have changed. Moral disgust was still there, but it was hidden by some Bible Belt opponents under fiscal-policy arguments. The moral component was still clearly there because no one could remain so emotionally strident in their refusal to accept the lottery, a year after it had passed, over a question of inefficient revenue collection.

I sought out the Reverend Chester Debnam because a local newspaper profile had called him the "Conscience of Raleigh." His antilottery letters to the editor that ran in the *News & Observer* quoted Scripture on the perils of greed, not tax rates. Over the phone the Reverend Debnam offered to take me on a tour of the places where he says the devil resides.

Those lottery opponents who knew of him seemed as if they wanted to keep their distance. Many of those leading the fight against the lottery muffled their religious and moral views on the lottery, even when they were strong, in favor of economic and social-policy arguments. When it came to the lottery, moral suasion seemed almost a bygone thing, even in Bible Belt. I was interested in why, and even more curious that someone was still shouting down gambling as evil. More than one person I interviewed told me that the Reverend Chester Debnam was "eccentric." I quickly learned he has some extreme views. On the phone, for example, he told me that the earth is about seven thousand years old.

I found him in his backyard, under the spreading branches of towering trees, where he invited me to sit down on a bench. The yard was overrun with green in the early evening and birds were singing.

"You belong to a false religion" was maybe the third thing he said to me. Really. It was the first thing out of his mouth when I told him I was Catholic. He didn't say it to offend me but matter-of-factly.

He said it to inform me. "The Sistine Chapel and all—perishable things. It's wicked and corrupt."

He says he refused to join the antilottery coalition because "I don't go to war with people of strange religions. Eliminate the Catholics off of the stuff and I'll join. I couldn't let them fight with me in the name of Jesus."

A short distance from his home, in a mostly black neighborhood near downtown Raleigh, we pull into a full-service gas station where Satan's temptation is thick, the Reverend Debnam said. Inside, the whole front of the counter was taken up with an enormous display of brightly colored scratch tickets. A dozen people in the store were cheerfully chatting in line, waiting to buy lottery scratch tickets, numbers tickets, and Powerball tickets. I saw fives and twenties go into the cash register. The customers were on their way home at the end of the day.

A sign at the curb out front read DREAM BOOKS FOR SALE. The woman behind the counter pointed me to two shelves of books. They were the same books sold throughout the heyday of the policy game in the nineteenth and twentieth centuries. I bought *Grandma's*, a slim $2 pocket book, from among the ten or so on the rack behind the counter. The book offered lucky numbers based on whether it was hot or cold, sunny or rainy; numbers based on birth signs; and a "very special page" of combinations that Grandma insisted could only be used if winners gave 10 percent of their prizes to the needy. "Winning makes you feel very good, but not as good as you will feel when you have helped someone poor or old. Love, Grandma."

"Does it work?" I ask. The woman behind the counter assures me that it does.

Back in the car Debnam tells me that temptation, even if it comes in our dreams, is a sign of Satan's presence. "If you dream about a lover, it's not of God, it's of Satan," he says. "So God ain't going to give you no number to dream."

He's no stranger to gambling. Years before, when he was "out there in the world—I'm talking in sin," he resided in Washington, D.C. He was an inveterate poker player and made regular drives to Maryland to play the lottery. "I would be dreaming of numbers, man."

The gas station does a lot of business, especially at the end of the day. "This is the real world out here, man," Debnam says. "You get home from work: 'Hey, man, I want me a cigarette, I want me a cup of coffee, and I got to play my number.' *My number.* That's when you're hooked. You internalize it. My number is different from your number. My number is unique. *My number.* That's a key word right there. I have to go play my number."

He drove past a place where he said an illegal numbers game operates. He later asks me not to reveal the location. I did not see much more than a small huddle of men standing by the back door of a mechanic's shop. "You don't mess with these boys here," he says, nodding discreetly toward them. "They're going to play their number for tomorrow."

At the end of our tour we stop at a gas station where I buy a few scratch tickets. I watch a woman put down $5 for tickets and scratch them off without leaving the counter. I ask her casually if she won. Just $1, she says. She immediately put her winning $1 into another ticket.

Tickets in hand I turn to walk out the door when she stops me. "No, you've got to scratch it now," she says. I do and lose. I look at the counterman and grimace. He says he doesn't believe anyone can win.

I ask the Reverend Debnam about the good the lottery does for education and why someone such as Jackie Alston can't do good with the money she won. He is quiet for a few moments, then replies, "Don't offer an unclean gift to the Lord. Love the Lord first, raise taxes fairly, and the money will be there."

ACROSS JONES STREET from the state legislature, in the North Carolina Museum of History, in a section devoted to highlights of state achievement, are the first lottery tickets printed. On opening day, March 30, 2006, North Carolinians spent $8 million on lottery tickets. By the end of its first year the North Carolina Education Lottery had collected $895 million. About $300 million went to pre-K programs for at-risk children, class-size reduction, school construction, and need-based college scholarships.

The John Locke Foundation released a report on county-by-county sales for the year. The highest per capita sales were in the counties along the eastern edge of the state. These also were the counties with the highest poverty rates and property taxes. Nash County came in first, spending $227 per adult on tickets.

GTECH, which was awarded contracts for both the online numbers games—Pick 3, Cash 5—and the scratch tickets, took 1.6 percent of sales or about $14 million. It was a rough year.

"Here was an opportunity to start a billion-dollar business from scratch, to set it up right, to put all the appropriate ethical standards in place," Charles Sanders says as a deep chuckle rises in his throat. Sanders's laugh was rueful. For the last year North Carolina has been discussing its lottery scandals. One of the leading criminals was Kevin Geddings, the man behind Bubba. But Geddings wasn't the only one in trouble. The scandal went all the way to House Speaker Black's office.

The feathers had started flying about a month after the governor had signed the bill into law with the creation of the Lottery Commission. The commission was charged with the responsibility for choosing either Scientific Games or GTECH for the vendor contracts. It was to hire a director to run the lottery and oversee its operation. House Speaker Black appointed Kevin Geddings to the commission. Geddings knew lotteries and had worked to promote the lottery legislation through his public relations firm. He was the fox in the henhouse.

In October 2005, one week after the Lottery Commission held its first meeting, the *News & Observer* reported that Scientific Games had been paying Geddings. He knew Scientific Games well—it held the contracts for both scratch tickets and online numbers games in South Carolina. Scientific Games paid Geddings $250,000 between 2000 and 2005. He neglected to mention this massive conflict of interest on the ethics questionnaire he was required to submit before joining the commission.

Governor Easley, Speaker Black, and Senate president Tony Rand testified during Geddings's three-week trial. The jury deliberated for six hours. He was sentenced to four years in prison on federal corruption charges.

Another commission member stepped down a month after Geddings because he owned stock in a chain of supermarkets that would be selling lottery tickets.

Geddings, who had been mulling a run for mayor of Charlotte before the scandal broke, did participate in one important decision during his brief time on the commission. He helped name it the North Carolina Education Lottery.

"Geddings is a talented man," Sanders says. "Somehow or another, I mean the switch was off in his ethical code."

More skeletons popped out of the closet. Meredith Norris, a former legislative aide to Speaker Black, secretly worked as a lobbyist for Scientific Games even as she continued to act as his unpaid political adviser. She never registered as a lobbyist, however. She used Black's laptop, e-mail, and his staff to help her. She got Black's permission to sit in on a legislative meeting in which the lottery bill was being drafted and Scientific Games' proposals were discussed.

In a 2005 e-mail to Speaker Black's press handler, she wrote about her future with the lottery vendor: "I think when my contract is written I will be listed as a consultant, not as a lobbyist, and therefore I will not be registering as a lobbyist until after the lottery passes and they are vying for the state contract as the lottery vendor. I just tell you this as a FYI and not to share with anyone. So, as far as anyone knows, I am not the lobbyist for Scientific Games, though I may be in the future."

Norris was working with Alan Middleton, Scientific Games' registered lobbyist and one of its vice presidents. "I think we made some progress last night at dinner in that we kept an on-the-fence Member on the fence instead of going to a 'no,' and another 'no' came back to on-the-fence," Norris wrote Middleton in another e-mail during the campaign for the lottery.

Norris pleaded no contest to a misdemeanor charge of violating state lobbying laws. She was banned from lobbying in North Carolina for two years. Alan Middleton, who prosecutors said worked with Norris to get Geddings appointed to the commission, was convicted of violating lobbying laws. He was sentenced to one year of probation and banned from lobbying in North Carolina for two years. Scientific Games fired him.

Speaker Black was never charged with any crimes related to the lottery, but he took the hardest fall. Federal agents had been looking at the Speaker's activities for years as an outgrowth of their investigation into North Carolina's video-poker industry. Code-named Double Black Diamond, the investigation discovered that Black had paid a Republican member of the House $50,000 in 2003 to switch parties and help him keep his hold on the speakership, and had violated campaign laws, taking cash from chiropractors as he supported legislation that benefited their industry.

Before he was indicted, however, and just after he won a close reelection, the embattled Black stepped down from his position as Speaker of the House. That night he told the news to a gathering of Democrats at Vinnie's Steak House & Tavern in North Raleigh. Black held court in a private dining room at the back of the restaurant, while another group from the Senate Republicans met in another private room to say good-bye to John Garwood. Describing the odd scene, a reporter from the *Raleigh News & Observer* noted that in a third dining room prominent lobbyists were holding their annual Christmas party. Their room had a door that connected to the Democrats' room.

The next year Black pleaded guilty to taking money in return for legislative action and was sentenced to five years in federal prison. He was fined $1 million on state corruption charges of bribing a House colleague.

Prosecutors also alleged that in 2000 he had taken $500,000 from a video-poker lobbyist, put the money into his campaign war chest as a "loan," then paid the cash back to his personal wealth. The accusation has not been followed by charges. Black supported legalizing video poker in North Carolina at the time the payment was reportedly made, in 2000, before the lottery was approved. The video-poker industry wanted to install the machines in North Carolina because neighboring South Carolina had banned the gambling devices after Governor Hodges was elected on a pro-lottery platform. Black favored bringing the games into North Carolina until the lottery was approved. Shortly after the lottery started, North Carolina phased out video poker.

The Lottery Commission weathered all of these storms. A lot of eyebrows were raised when Governor Easley tapped Charles Sanders to chair the Lottery Commission. He had been one of biggest guns in the antilottery coalition. A Harvard-trained cardiologist, former director of the Harvard Hospital, former CEO of pharma giant Glaxo Inc., chairman of the Foundation for the National Institutes of Health, and a member of too many corporate boards to count, including Merrill Lynch and Reynolds Metals, Sanders was preceded by his glowing reputation.

About the only thing Sanders seems to have ever failed at is politics. He spent $1.7 million of his own money in a bid for the Democratic nomination to challenge Jesse Helms in 1996. Helms won his fifth term. "My skin got pretty thick," Sanders says.

He agreed to take the position for one year, saying it was hard to turn down a governor. As we sat down in his office, he quickly made it clear that he has no moral objection to the lottery. He thinks it's just bad business, a lousy, ineffective way for the government to raise money. "It's basically a politician's dream because they can raise money without having the *tax* word put on it," he says.

Looking at other state lotteries, he saw that, over time, the revenue supplants money the state had previously used for a given purpose such as education. His opinions have not changed, but once the lottery became law, he stopped fighting and turned his attention to making it work, like a business, he said. "Once we crossed that bridge, the mind-set now is how much money we can make from it. What has passed is past, now let's make as much of a success out of it as we possibly can."

If the lottery has a silver lining, it's that it will probably cut down on illegal numbers gambling as it did in the Northeast, he says. He then tells me a story from his early days as a doctor at Boston City Hospital, when he was still new to the city. A patient had been in a coma for two weeks, completely unresponsive, when one day he roared, "Four! Three! Two!" and lapsed back into silence. "At which point everybody that was employed there on the floor ran to the elevator operator and placed a bet of four-three-two." Sanders laughs. "That doesn't happen anymore. Those days are gone."

Easley gave the lottery a strong start by choosing Sanders, who was unflappable as the lottery kept on taking hits. It was the fastest lottery start-up in the country at three months and twenty-five days. Sanders and the commission hired the man responsible for the quickness of the start-up, lottery director Tom Shaheen.

I am about to end our interview when Sanders volunteers, "I should tell you about Shaheen. Shaheen is a very interesting guy. He wears his heart on his sleeve, he's very open. He's got very thin skin."

"Forewarned," I say.

Shaheen was hired in the midst of the lottery lobbying scandal at the private-sector salary of $235,000. He took some knocks for this. High salaries are common practice in state lotteries, but since the governor makes only $125,000, it stuck in some throats. It's a far distance from where Shaheen started, cleaning toilets on Eastern Airlines planes.

"I don't think I can personally be under any more pressure than I am today, and I have been for the last year," he tells me. "As far as I'm concerned, it's just business as usual."

He looked like someone under pressure until he warmed up to the conversation. *Prickly* seemed like a better description than *thin-skinned*. When he gets warmed up, he answers questions with a crouching intensity. The ends of his sentences have sharp points and sometimes sarcasm, like a jab.

The governor's controversial proposal to lower the percentage that the state takes from lottery sales in order to raise the prize payout rate and a projected shortfall in revenue were on Shaheen's plate that day, and he had been dealing with the press. "Anybody who is opposed to the lottery no matter which way it goes will have a win-win story in their mind," he says. "Because if we're not successful, it's going to be 'See, we told you they couldn't do it.' And if we are successful, they're going to revert to 'They're preying on the poor and those who can't afford it.'" He was optimistic about the governor's suggestion that with the new plan the lottery could bring in $1.5 billion in the second year, but Shaheen would not endorse it as a prediction.

A television reporter and a cameraman interrupt our conversation to interview Shaheen for the local evening news. I watch from a polite distance as he and the reporter joked about the $300 million shortfall as a "never-ending story" about an amount of money that is a blade of grass in the just-released $20 billion budget plan. "You guys," Shaheen said, "you guys keep the story going."

"The critics out there are thinking, 'Gosh, raising the goals by fifty percent—it's Pollyannish," the reporter says as the interview starts.

Shaheen quickly shoots back that Texas did a booming $42 million a week in sales in the 1990s, prompting the legislature to slash the payout rate and increase the state's take from sales. The golden goose nearly died: Sales fell to $20-plus million a week, and it took four years for Texas to get back to its previous levels. Shaheen delivers the information rapid-fire. Clearly, he knows his business and is impatient with being questioned on it. Shaheen was director of the New Mexico Lottery for more than five years, was part of the Georgia Lottery start-up, and has worked for lotteries in Florida and Texas. He had obviously been challenged and questioned since he came to town, like a newly elected politician with no honeymoon.

"This is not a government job," he tells me after the television reporter left. Shaheen runs a business with annual sales of a billion dollars. A comparable job in the private sector might be a vice president of marketing at a major corporation such as Coca-Cola, he says. "Lottery directors still are underpaid for what is required of them."

Yet his business operates under the strictures of a government agency, a government agency created with some strong reluctance. Shaheen professes to be dumbfounded by the political hand-wringing. The polls showed that more than 60 percent of the state wanted to play the lottery. "What I don't understand is, when it goes to vote in the legislature, how that correlates into a tiebreaker," he says. "See, that's where my political background is lacking. From my ignorant, tunnel-vision world, as a normal citizen, why is there a debate in the legislature over this?" He laughs.

He is hampered because the legislation squeaked through. He can't do certain things that would automatically increase sales. One limitation is advertising, which some states have limited to salve the anger of lottery opponents and supporters. "You're expected to go out and sell lottery tickets and make money, and you're expected to market them," Shaheen says. "And they're basically, in some cases, throwing handcuffs on you, tossing you in the lake, and saying, 'Let's see you swim.'"

Shaheen is not allowed to spend more than 1 percent of revenue on marketing and may not, by law, engage in marketing that has "the primary purpose of inducing people to participate in the lottery."

"I think it could be a little bit more, not enticing, but more leading than we're allowed to do," he says haltingly. This is a touchy subject. "I think we should be able to show people having a good time because they won the lottery or celebrating a little bit because they won the lottery, and we can't even do that. I think we ought to be able to show somebody buying lottery tickets and maybe the next shot of them is on a sailboat somewhere or even a cruise. Even a cruise is not a huge investment. We're not even allowed to do anything like that."

Shaheen made perfect business sense, but he had run up against the problem that nearly all lottery officials find—as much as the states want lotteries to make money, they fear some of the business practices that will guarantee greater profits. Most states don't truly maximize their lottery's profit potential. But North Carolina was still young, still experiencing growing pains. As has happened in many other states, there would be time to expand the game once people had grown accustomed to its presence and the hurt feelings of lottery opponents had faded. But at this time, as much as the war for the lottery seemed over, battles were still taking place.

On the day of my meeting with Stam, Governor Easley was under attack. The governor's prediction that the lottery would sell $1.2 billion in tickets and send about $425 million to education was wrong. Sales were falling short. Revised estimates put sales at about $900 million with about $350 million for education. In bottom-line terms, the $75 million difference for education was negligible. The real issue was that the shortfall gave ammunition to newspapers and those citizens who had been against the idea. The governor and the legislature had sold the public on something that wasn't what it had been cracked up to be.

Easley's proposed solution brought more heat. Easley wanted to change the lottery's formula. Easley wanted to cut the percentage for education and increase the amount that goes to prizes. He correctly reasoned that people buy more lottery tickets when there's more money to be won. It's a tried-and-true method performed in many new state lotteries to increase sales. He estimated sales would sky-rocket from a first-year gross of $900 million to $1.5 billion the next year. Education would get a smaller slice of the pie—29 percent instead of 35 percent—but the pie would be much larger. Education would win.

Lottery opponents raised a public outcry about a bait and switch. The "conservative" lottery had not reached its first birthday and was already starting to look like lotteries everywhere else. But more sales meant more state revenue. The public was learning that lotteries, at least technically, exist to maximize sales.

CHAPTER 6

GTECH: LOTTERY GIANT

LOTTERIES SEEM AN odd fit for a government operation because they are. In fact, much of the work is handed out in contracts to private companies that specialize in running lotteries. The two biggest in the United States are GTECH and Scientific Games. GTECH dominates the lotto and number-picking games by supplying software and computer terminals and management expertise to states. Scientific Games controls the scratch-ticket market in most states. But as aggressively as the two compete for state contracts, GTECH is, easily, the bigger of the two. And it is growing bigger. It accurately calls itself the worldwide lottery leader.

On October 17, 2006, GTECH Holdings Corporation cut the ribbon on their new glass-and-steel headquarters in downtown Providence. The company's vice president for government relations, Donald Sweitzer, served as the master of ceremonies, introducing one of Rhode Island's U.S. senators, its governor, and the city's mayor, and finally the company's CEO, from a podium in the plaza out front. Ten stories above them, GTECH's name stood out against the shining façade in six-foot-high letters.

It was an important day for Providence. With Election Day coming up, much had been made of the blue-collar city's economic struggles, with 25 percent of the city's residents living below the poverty line. While a few critics complained that the ten-story, glass-and-steel structure was too boxy and modern, it was hard to argue with an $80 million investment and the first high-rise to go up in downtown Providence in more than a decade. Providence was looking for an economic comeback, and GTECH, with nearly $1 billion in annual sales, was helping lead the way.

By setting up headquarters in Providence, GTECH was moving back from the suburbs to where it had begun, almost thirty years earlier, in an office above an Italian restaurant. The opening celebration was a bit sentimental: the once local, now big and global business, putting down roots in style. Not that GTECH didn't make some demands before it agreed to stay in Rhode Island.

The move to the glass tower from a suburban office park in West Greenwich began in 2002, when GTECH began to grumble, publicly, about its need to expand. There was talk of relocating to Massachusetts—a slap in the face to Rhode Islanders, who have an inferiority complex when it comes to their neighbors in the Bay State. The workforce in Massachusetts was better trained and more tech savvy, and Massachusetts, coveting GTECH's technology jobs, would probably offer the company incentives to move. State officials in Rhode Island panicked. GTECH was one of the state's largest employers. Its departure would mean the loss of more than nine hundred jobs, along with a steady source of tax revenue for the state. Before long, GTECH executives were invited to sit down with the governor and the leaders of the legislature.

They came up with an agreement. GTECH would get a twenty-year no-bid contract to run the Rhode Island Lottery, get a bigger percentage of lottery sales, and take control of the state's slot machines, including any new ones allowed. The deal had an estimated value of $770 million. It also flouted the 1975 order by Governor Philip Noel, who signed the state lottery into law, that lottery contracts must be awarded by competitive bid.

In return, the company agreed to build its headquarters in downtown Providence—free of local property taxes and sales taxes on construction materials, furnishings, and computers. It would add another eighty or so jobs to bring its employee count to one thousand. Both sides announced that they were thrilled. In truth, GTECH had Rhode Island over a barrel. The state's political leaders were dealing with a company that was well practiced in take-no-prisoners negotiating.

Sweitzer, the emcee of the happy ribbon-cutting, was an example of the company's political acumen. He was just the latest and most impressive of the company's hires. He joined the company in 2006 as chief of government relations, following a long career in politics: adviser to the failed 1984 Mondale-Ferraro campaign; finance director of the Democratic National Committee; fund-raiser for Bill Clinton's first presidential campaign; political director of the DNC; and all-around political consultant known for his close ties to labor. It's hard to imagine a stronger résumé for political experience and access. Access to political decision-makers was extremely important to GTECH, which is the world heavyweight champion in an industry based on winning government contracts.

Since the company's creation, it has consistently hired people for their political muscle. After all, the lottery business is as much about negotiating the intricacies of state bylaws and access to those with control over contracts as it is about gambling and new technologies. GTECH executives knew not to be stingy about it, spending millions on lobbying whenever it counted. Everywhere GTECH went it seemed to absorb politicians, their staff members, and state lottery employees onto its payroll. A few months after the ribbon cutting, the company hired the former chief of staff to Providence's Mayor David Cicilline to work under Sweitzer in government affairs. On the other side of the political fence, the company has also hired lobbyist Charlie Black, a Republican Party insider and adviser to John McCain's 2008 campaign.

GTECH dominates that part of the lottery that is rooted in computer technology. Early on, its computer whizzes developed random-number generators and programs to link thousands of terminals to central computers to record lotto ticket numbers. But just as important as the technical experts who built the company, if not more so, were the people who could find the shortest route to securing government contracts.

Today GTECH controls about 70 percent of global online lottery games, with 440,000 lottery ticket terminals. GTECH is no longer a domestic company, having sold itself to the much smaller Italian lottery and publishing firm, Lottomatica, for $4.65 billion in 2006. The sale firmly established GTECH in the growing European gaming market, which investment banks estimate is worth some $70 billion.

The company claims more than $1.25 billion in annual revenue and five thousand employees in fifty countries. Its numbers are impressive, as is the efficiency and skill with which it runs the online lotto games in twenty-five of the forty-two state lotteries.

The company dominates in "online" lottery systems, meaning lotto number-picking games such as New York's Pick 6 or Florida's Play 4—but it has a smaller share of instant games, which are primarily run by Scientific Games. It did not come by success without a fight. Over the last four decades, GTECH has earned a reputation not only as the leader of the worldwide lottery industry but as a politically wired company with one of the most aggressive, and on occasion illegal, lobbying operations in the country. Wherever GTECH sought contracts, public officials, and sometimes the company, seemed to get into trouble.

There may be no other company with so many government contacts that has such an extensive rap sheet of indictments, convictions, and accusations of fraud and abuse.

GUY SNOWDEN GREW up in Peekskill, a rural town in upstate New York, where he was classmates and friends with New York's future Republican governor George Pataki. He gave college a try at Syracuse University's forestry program, but soon dropped out. Later, he took a job with IBM, where he was drawn into the emerging world of computers.

As Snowden learned new technology, Victor Markowicz, a Polish émigré who had studied mathematics in Israel, arrived in America. The two met a few years later while they were working for Mathematica, a company created in the 1960s by Princeton University mathematicians. The company applied numerical models to financial markets, using the data to create software applications. It offered the technology to newly emerging lotteries. Snowden and Markowicz were Mathematica's point people for the lottery business. By the mid-1970s, the company boasted that it could set up a lottery in three months using a series of secure lines to transfer data. The software was based on mathematical-probability models that performed the complex task of running an honest numbers game, generating random four-digit or six-digit combinations.

As early as 1969, Mathematica had a contract to help New Jersey start its lottery. In 1973, the company had a contract to create an instant game for New Hampshire. By 1976, the two had started their own company, Gaming Dimensions, and won their first contract to assist the Rhode Island start-up. They worked under a company called Datatrol, which manufactured lottery terminals and systems. Datatrol was itself owned by Applied Devices, a defense contractor that made electronic weapons systems in addition to lottery terminals. In 1979, the company brought Gaming Dimensions into Datatrol to create a stronger lottery division, which they called Gaming Systems.

It was a small operation. They set up offices in Providence on the third floor of a downtown building above an Italian restaurant. "Our whole firm was on one floor that was smaller than the floor of my house," recalled Walter Szrek, a software engineer who joined the young company in 1979.

The real value and talent of the early lottery industry was not gambling, but distribution. Where the numbers racket had relied on slips of paper and hand-to-hand transactions, the new legal lottery used early technology that transferred data from thousands of retail stores to a central location. The cashier at a liquor store entered gamblers' numbers into a computer terminal that sent the bet to a central terminal. These hundreds and thousands of lotto ticket orders had to be lined up and processed in systems designed by early software developers, such as Szrek. If the software was good, no one's lottery numbers got lost or jammed together and clogged up the line. The lottery companies sought to build applications as cheaply as they could.

The technology of the network of terminals was borrowed from the systems being used to verify credit-card purchases. In fact, Datatrol made terminals that American Express used to authorize credit cards. One of the first systems had 192 kilobytes of memory, and a mainframe containing two fifty-megabyte hard disks. The systems had to be cheap because the profit margin in servicing state lotteries was low and there were so few customers—just a handful of states—that not many companies were in pursuit of lottery business. One had to amass a number of state contracts to be profitable. GTECH began to move, picking up contracts in Connecticut and Michigan to go with Rhode Island.

The competition included some major companies, such as General Instruments, whose AmTote division manufactured lottery games. GTECH later bought the division. "I don't think they were bad," Szrek says of the competition. "GTECH was maybe more aggressive, and whatever a client wanted, they would do. I know that when there were very complex environments, GTECH always said yes, and we were always trying to figure out how to fulfull it."

A couple of years later, Snowden and Markowicz, joined by Applied Devices executive Robert Stern, bought their division from Datatrol for $2 million. They had financial backing from the Texas Bass brothers Ed, Lee, and Sid. The three had taken the oil fortune their father had built and invested it wisely, aided by Richard Rainwater, a business school classmate of Sid Bass's. Ed Bass was friends with his Yale classmate, and fellow Texan, George W. Bush. The brothers became big backers of Bush both before and during his political career.

In 1981, the new company was renamed GTECH, short for Gaming Technology. It now had 116 employees and contracts in Quebec and Ontario to go with the three U.S. states. The company went public and joined NASDAQ in 1983. Their IPO took in $16.7 million and sold two million shares, according to *New England Business*. GTECH added superior technology with a new system built on the guts of a RadioShack TRS-80 computer. In 1984 they won their biggest contract to date, for the New Jersey Lottery. The company began to dominate the competition. Joan Zielinski, a professor of marketing at Northwestern University's Kellogg School of Management, who was New Jersey Lottery director from 1985 to 1987, recalls the company as "a very young, very nimble start-up business. They entered the industry with superior technology. They were all the things that you need to be when you are the new kid on the block. They squashed everybody else. They were like IBM in the early days."

To some, GTECH was creating a better product. Others saw the company's success as the result of bare-knuckle lobbying. The more successful the company became, and the more states adopted lotteries, the more business relationships mattered over technology. Once a state awarded a contract, it was not likely to switch to someone else with unsampled technology. "Unless you go with a well-established vendor, you're not going to change," Szrek says. It wasn't long before there simply weren't many established lottery providers. Not that many businesses had been vying for contracts to begin with. Lotteries were a fairly small, specialized field. And since profits were marginal, large companies were unwilling to devote much effort.

Early on, the companies vying for state business sought to outperform each other in a few different areas. The first goal of state lotteries was to sell an honest game that the public could play with confidence. The games had to be secure against fraud. In 1976, Ohio's lottery had been up and running for two years when it sold its first instant tickets. The contract was held by a Delaware company called Systems Operations Inc., a subsidiary of Mathematica Inc. Scientific Games, the losing bidder for the contract, discovered that the game could be cheated. Lightly scratching the surface of the tickets would reveal the numbers beneath. You had to look closely, but the numbers were visible through the card. Someone with access to the cards and time—a store employee, for example—could go through them and pick out the winners. The remaining cards could still be sold because a customer would likely not notice that someone had tampered with the card. The Ohio Lottery was made aware of the problem.

Not surprisingly, Systems Operations sued Scientific Games, which still wanted the Ohio contract. This, one of the earliest lawsuits in lottery history, was to become almost par for the course. Lawsuits are now almost an expected stage of the bidding process for lottery contracts.

Convenience was another cornerstone of the lottery competition. States learned a lesson from the failure of early complicated games based on prenumbered tickets that related to real-life horse races. Games had to be a quick and simple transaction at the nearest corner store. Ideally, the purchase should be as no more complicated than buying a candy bar. "The lottery in the United States was driven by convenience," says GTECH's Laverty O'Connor. "Retail expansion was a big part of that, and retail expansion was enabled by technology."

The technology was in the computer terminals that connected a network of stores, but behind the scenes at lottery headquarters, an old-fashioned machine still churned out the drawings. Before joining GTECH, Laverty O'Connor spent more than twenty years helping run two of the most successful lotteries, in Georgia and New York. "We would pick up receipts for lotto, take them to White Plains," she says, recalling the 1980s at the New York Lottery, "put them into a big batch, then go through them for forty-eight hours to make sure there weren't issues, then do a drawing on Channel 5 on live television."

The perils of failure were great. Breakdowns were unacceptable. Public trust in a clean game was central to the success of government's new lottery games, just as it had been for the illegal numbers operators. On October 22, 1975, Governor Hugh Carey was pulled away from dealing with the impending bankruptcy of New York City to attend to a misprinting of lottery tickets. A bad line of computer code had caused printers to spit out hundreds of identically numbered tickets for the $1.4 million Super Colossus jackpot drawing scheduled for Halloween. It was the first and last time that a governor shut down a state lottery. New York's lottery stayed out of operation for almost a year.

Within a week of the shutdown one of several reviews discovered that a July fourth jackpot drawing had been $500,000 short of the prize money it promised. Within a month, Carey ordered the dismissal or reassignment of all 324 lottery employees, including the director, a veteran of the presidential campaigns of both John F. Kennedy and Robert Kennedy. He didn't go quietly. "I get mail calling me a gyp, a thief, a racketeer," Jerry Bruno, New York's lottery director, told the *New York Times* in the midst of the shutdown. "I've never done anything wrong in my life."

An outside report found that the lottery was "riddled with mismanagement," vulnerable to fraud, and sloppy in record keeping. Two thirds of lottery employees were appointed by the government, rather than hired at large. In July 1976, after much reorganizing, planning, and political wrangling, the lottery reopened in New York. The state held a drawing to satisfy the customers who had purchased tickets for canceled games, but it was the last time anyone would see the weekly prenumbered, six-digit tickets selling for $2.50 a pop. The new lottery went on sale a few months later with $1 scratch tickets, with printed directions on how to scratch "using edge of coin gently." Scientific Games, based in Atlanta, had the contract for the game, which was backed by a $1.5 million ad campaign.

Players take it for granted that lotteries are run fairly, and they almost always are. The whiff of anything shifty is death to sales. But perfection is hard to create. For most of August 2007, Tennesseans were unwittingly barred from winning if they picked repeating numbers in the state lottery's Cash 3 and Cash 4 games. The lottery had replaced the familiar Ping-Pong-ball drawings with computerized random-number generators that refused to choose certain duplicates. Anyone who picked 7-7-7 or 1-3-1-3 was at odds with a bug in the software.

No one fixed the problem until three weeks after the switch in technology. More than $2 million was gambled on repeating combinations during that time.

Less than a year later, in search of pure random returns, Tennessee Lottery computers spitting out Cash 3 combinations seemed in love with zeros and sevens. For three days running, an increasingly disbelieving public watched 077, 707, and then 077 again come up as winners. The Tennessee Lottery checked and rechecked but could find no problems with its software. The coincidence seemed to defy belief, especially when people considered that a month earlier, the state's Cash 4 game had results over two days of 1-3-7-2, 1-7-2-3, and 2-3-7-1. Some state officials demanded that the lottery bring back the Ping-Pong balls.

But Ping-Pong balls, which held some kind of old-fashioned trustworthiness in Tennessee, have been fooled. That's what Nick Perry did on April 24, 1980. As emcee for the Pennsylvania Lottery drawings, Perry and a group of co-conspirators, including a state lottery official, rigged the drawing. A stagehand injected white paint into the Ping-Pong balls; an earlier experiment with baby powder had not worked. The balls, except the fours and sixes, were weighted. As

Perry introduced the daily televised event, the numbered balls, driven by circulating air, bounced like popcorn inside their transparent plastic canisters. Someone looking closely might have noticed that the balls acted funny, moving erratically and at different speeds. Also, the fours and sixes were lighter and stayed closer to the top.

At the climactic moment a trustworthy senior citizen—state lottery dollars benefited seniors—hit the switch that sucked the winning numbers into slots on top of each canister. Three numbers were pulled—6-6-6. The combination paid off $3.5 million. In Pittsburgh, the illegal numbers game's operators, who used the state drawings combinations, refused to pay out. Too much money had been placed on the winning numbers. They were certain the game was rigged. In the end the suspicions in the illegal world made their way to law enforcement.

Perry and the lottery official were sentenced to prison for a maximum of seven years each.

On the other end of the spectrum from Perry's low tech scam is that of computer whiz Richard Lee Knowlton, who oversaw the Kansas Lottery's computers. Knowlton programmed the computers to pay him $62,000 on scratch tickets over a year and a half. He was sentenced to sixty days in jail in 2001.

And in Washington, D.C., three technicians who serviced ticket terminals at convenience stores allegedly used access to the lottery's computer network and spare ticket terminals to print their own tickets. Sometime in 2005, the thieves were believed to have printed $86,000 worth of tickets and won $70,000 in prizes. The fraud was uncovered by the lottery when stores complained about being charged for ticket sales that they had never made. The fraud was only made public when the *Washington Post* uncovered it. But neither GTECH, which supplied the terminals, nor the lottery would answer the news-paper's questions. The three were fired but never charged. In September 2008, Washington, D.C., fined GTECH $1.4 million for the breach of security, a move the company described as "blantantly po-litical" and said it would appeal.

Despite these scandals lotteries have survived through player demand. And GTECH early on established confidence by delivering on the first contracts it won. Lotteries ran smoothly, and that's what mattered to state officials. During the 1980s, lotteries cropped up in seventeen states and the District of Columbia, winning over the West Coast, the Midwest, and border states such as Kentucky, West Virginia, and Virginia.

GTECH won the contracts in many of them, in addition to that for Texas, which joined the lottery industry in 1991. The company had a reputation for selling a better product, but also for aggressive pursuit of contracts. No discussion of GTECH's success in these formative years takes place without reference to J. David Smith, their star national sales director. When GTECH hired Smith in 1987, the company was one of a handful wrestling for government contracts to supply and operate the still-young state lottery games. From 1987 to 1994, Smith secured more contracts than anyone else in the lottery industry. It was well that he did. He joined the company just as GTECH's net revenue plummeted, from $10.5 million in 1987 to $4.6 million in 1988. The company was badly in need of new contracts to cover its expenses. Smith's successes in Idaho, Indiana, Kansas, Kentucky, and Wisconsin were integral to the company's growth. In his territory, GTECH's revenue rose from $22 million to $240 million. The company's overall revenue in 1987, the year Smith was hired, was $130 million. By 1994, GTECH's revenue had quadrupled to $632 million. Over the seven years, thirteen states adopted lotteries. The most significant new market was Southern states.

West Virginia adopted a lottery in 1986, then Virginia in 1988, Kentucky in 1989, Texas in 1991, and Georgia in 1993.

Smith was paid more than $1 million annually for his talents and ultimately negotiated a contract with the company that allowed him to do outside consulting work. Not surprisingly, though, Smith had enemies. One of GTECH's biggest competitors in the 1980s and early 1990s was Automated Wagering International. The two companies fought tooth and nail over state contracts, with GTECH winning nearly every time. Eventually, convinced that GTECH was playing dirty pool, AWI hired private investigators.

Two investigators began to look into Smith's work for GTECH in Kentucky. When the state's lottery director, a good friend of Smith's, got wind of their interest, he had his head of security look into it and, against his own organization's interests, report their findings back to GTECH. But his efforts weren't enough. The Kentucky Lottery director later took a job with GTECH in Texas. Before long, the FBI was looking into the company's practices in several states.

In 1994, Smith was indicted in Kentucky and New Jersey nearly simultaneously, on charges of defrauding GTECH. It was not his first brush with the law. In 1981, before GTECH hired him, Smith had been indicted for putting illegal video-poker machines in bars in his native Kentucky. The felony charges were reduced to a misdemeanor, to which he pleaded guilty. His criminal record occasionally proved inconvenient later as he lobbied for GTECH, but Kentucky governor Wallace Wilkinson—who won on a pro-lottery platform—pardoned Smith on his last day in office in 1991.

In 1994, in the lead-up to his trials, Smith resigned from GTECH but continued to be paid as a "consultant." And rather than turn on him as a crooked employee, the company declined to talk with prosecutors.

Luther Roger Wells was indicted in Kentucky along with Smith. The prosecution alleged that Wells, working with Smith, had used his paper company, Bluegrass Industrial Distributors, to submit fraudulent and inflated bills to GTECH. Smith and Wells were accused of splitting the fraudulent payments. Wells, a Kentucky native like Smith, had been the state's secretary of finance under Governor Wilkinson. At the time of the indictment he was the head of a lottery-ticket vending-machine company.

A Kentucky judge dismissed the charges three days after the trial started, saying that it was one of those rare instances where there is smoke, but no fire. GTECH said it was aware of the payments. Wells later described them as "goodwill" payments, an assertion the company denied.

The Kentucky case fizzled, but in New Jersey, the jury found fire. The U.S. attorney's office in New Jersey described a kickback scheme in which Smith hired Steven Dandrea, a former city councilman and member of a family that was well connected in Republican circles, and Joseph LaPorta, a cousin of Joseph Salema, the chief of staff to Governor Jim Florio. The two men arranged meetings between high-ranking state officials and GTECH, which was trying to convince New Jersey to expand its lottery to include keno. In return, Smith arranged for Dandrea and LaPorta to be paid $30,000 a month as consultants, but kept a cut for himself. As in Kentucky, the government alleged that Smith had defrauded GTECH.

The two "consultants" were paid more than $700,000; Smith took some $169,000. During the trial, GTECH acknowledged that it had spent more than $10 million a year in lobbying nationwide to defend its contracts and expand its business.

The jury took six hours to convict Smith on all twenty counts of fraud and money laundering. But the story didn't end there. In their presentencing report, prosecutors introduced secret grand jury testimony linking officials from other states to shady payments by Smith. Prosecutors put the presentencing report with the sealed grand jury testimony into the public case file, where it was picked up by reporters. The inference was that the information had been leaked in the hopes of broadening the case against Smith, but the prosecution claimed that putting the grand jury information into a public file was accidental.

Ben Barnes, the former lieutenant governor of Texas and Speaker of the House, was one of the people implicated. Barnes was supposedly instrumental in scoring the outsize Texas contract for the GTECH against Control Data, a Minneapolis company and parent of Automated Wagering. As a lobbyist, Barnes was well paid for his work. In one year, Barnes was reported to have been paid more than $3 million by GTECH.

The New Jersey presentencing report alleged that Barnes had paid more than $500,000 to Smith, and that William Fugazy, a New York limousine mogul, had paid $72,613 in kickbacks to Smith. Neither Barnes nor Fugazy was ever charged in connection with the allegations. The judge issued a harsh rebuke to the U.S. attorney's office for releasing the information into the public record. In 1996, Smith was sentenced to five years and three months in prison.

Despite the accusations it generated, the Texas contract put GTECH on the map. In a report to the SEC, the company noted, "The Texas Lottery contract is GTECH's largest, accounting for approximately 16% of GTECH's total revenues in fiscal 1997." By other reports the Texas contract turned into a free-for-all in which Texas officials doled out patronage jobs at GTECH, with Smith acting as the political "point man," making contact with many of the hires referred by state officials. One Kentucky Lottery official told investigators that

Smith had bragged about payments to Texas legislators—from $2,000 to $10,000—that helped secure favor for GTECH in that state.

For their efforts, Barnes and his partner Ricky Knox were given 4 percent of GTECH's revenue for as long as it held the Texas contract. In 1997, GTECH bought out the Barnes and Knox contract for $23 million. In 2001, Texas quietly added a new paragraph to its deal with GTECH that forbids the company or any of its employees from giving any donations or gifts to members of the legislature.

By the 1990s, GTECH was no longer a small company, and it had corporate toughness to spare. Indeed, all during the Smith trial, the company continued to battle for contracts in such places as Florida, Washington, and New York, where it hired six different firms to lobby the legislature to expand the lottery to include keno.

But the fallout from the Smith trial continued long after it was over. Luther Wells, who was acquitted in Kentucky alongside Smith, turned up a couple of years later in Georgia, where he was politically well connected. There, another of his companies, Integrated Strategies of Georgia, was paid $30,000 a month by GTECH as a "business consultant." Since the early 1990s, GTECH had paid the company more than $1 million. The state's lottery director, Rebecca Paul, told the *Atlanta Journal-Constitution* that she understood the company was a GTECH lobbyist. If that was the case, it was unregistered. It was revealed that GTECH had won the Georgia contract after it was quietly given an opportunity to lower its bid, which was tens of millions of dollars higher than the nearest competitor's.

In Florida, GTECH sought to take a contract away from Automated Wagering International. The contest became so personal and heated that in 1995 Representative Jim King told the *St. Petersburg*

Times, "The lottery wars are ugly wars because the companies in them are ugly companies."

GTECH's Florida lobbyist, Barry Horenbein, told the newspaper that in his thirty years "I've never seen anything dirtier than lottery stuff." He blamed the viciousness of the fight on the amount of money at stake and that "there's only one or two companies that can compete." Even since the eighties, the battleground had changed, with fewer competitors still standing. GTECH has often explained its troubles as part of the volatile territory that it occupies—government and gambling are tricky to mix.

In many instances, state lottery officials have made their own trouble. In 1994, former West Virginia Lottery director E. E. "Butch" Bryan was sentenced to four years and three months in prison for steering a $2.8 million marketing contract to a second-rate company. He also had planned to expand the state's video-lottery system in a no-bid contract. At the same time, the state lottery's attorney was sentenced to two years for insider trading after he bought stock in the Montana-based video-lottery company that was supposed to get the contract.

In December 2002, Oregon's lottery director, Chris Lyons, resigned after the lottery was accused of charging $800,000 in questionable expenses, such as first-class plane tickets to conferences, at a time the state was in a budget crisis. Lyons later went to work for GTECH.

That same month, Florida's lottery secretary, David Griffin, resigned, a few months before an investigation opened that eventually revealed that he and other lottery officials had accepted gifts from vendors. Four lottery executives were fired as a result. Griffin had left the lottery before the misdeeds of his executives came to light to become executive director of Governor Jeb Bush's reelection transition team.

In 2003, the Colorado Lottery director, Mark Zamarripa, re-signed in the midst of a probe into his expenses. He and other lottery officials were regularly wined, dined, and entertained by the vendors to whom they gave contracts.

In January 2004, the Minnesota Lottery director, George Ander-son, committed suicide when the agency's finances came under scrutiny. Prosecutors later reported that he had engaged in "self-dealing, favor-granting and contract-rigging" with an advertising company.

A few months later, Nebraska Lottery director James Quinn found himself in hot water for accepting a $5,000 plane ticket from the lottery company, Intralot, so that his wife could join him on the company's junket to its headquarters in Greece. Intralot had just beat out GTECH for the contract to run Nebraska's online lottery games. Quinn paid for the ticket after the trip was made public.

In 1992, a Democratic state senator from California was charged with taking a $13,500 bribe from a GTECH lobbyist in exchange for a lottery vote. The lawmaker pleaded guilty and the lobbyist was con-victed of several charges. GTECH was not aware of his actions, ac-cording to the trial record.

And as GTECH grew, its battles began to rage overseas. In Britain, GTECH was a stakeholder in Camelot. The company won the contract to run the massive British national lottery in 1994, after a bitter contest with Richard Branson, head of Virgin Atlantic. The next year Branson accused Guy Snowden of offering him a bribe to back away from the national lottery. Snowden called Branson a liar and found himself sued for libel. Snowden lost the case. The civil court ordered Snowden to pay $192,000 in damages and to reim-burse Branson his $1.6 million in legal costs. The next day Snowden resigned from GTECH, the company he helped create. There were few repercussions in the United States. Snowden was quickly replaced.

In 1998, with the dust still settling from downfalls of Smith and Snowden, GTECH's new chairman, William Y. O'Connor, tried to put a new face on the company and distance it from both embarassments. Waving a copy of the company's recently completed ethics handbook at a reporter from the *Providence Journal-Bulletin*, he announced, "The controversies are all past history."

It was wishful thinking.

In 2002, New York State's lobbying commission fined GTECH $90,000 for improper lobbying. As lobbying fines go, the number was tough to beat—neither the New York Yankees nor Philip Morris had earned such a steep penalty in the state.

A few years later scandal struck again. In 2006, Illinois governor Rod Blagojevich wanted to add keno to the Illinois Lottery's roster of games. The game was already controversial. Critics saw it as unseemly and having greater potential for addiction. The governor responded to critics with financial estimates supplied by GTECH, which said the game would bring in $80 million a year for school construction. A short time later a former aide to Blagojevich joined GTECH as a lobbyist. The governor tried to push forward under fire from critics and insisted the addition of keno was an executive decision that did not require legislative approval. John Wyma, the former aide turned lottery lobbyist, and GTECH denied any connection between his lobbying work and the contract, and Wyma said he had never mentioned keno to the governor. Blagojevich lost the battle and the keno plan was shelved.

Finally, in 2008, GTECH got some strong backing from a prospective client. GTECH was lobbying for keno approval in Ohio, as it had been for at least a half dozen years. This time, Governor Ted Strickland argued in favor of keno, saying it would bring in $73 million for state education in a time of belt-tightening. The estimate was familiar—it had come from GTECH's lobbyists. In fact, a member of his cabinet had once lobbied for GTECH. Ohio became the twelfth state with keno games. The money would be used to forestall a cut to education spending.

As controversial as fast-paced keno is in some states, the game is clunky when compared to the games offered by lotteries in Europe and elsewhere. The future of the lottery industry—its ability to increase sales—lies in the technological leaps that have helped lotteries to grow in other countries. So far, lotteries in the Unites States have come up against controversy with keno games and video lottery terminals. The new games that have succeeded overseas would draw much greater public concern in America.

LAVERTY O'CONNOR STEERS the strategy and marketing operations of GTECH. She also makes certain the message gets across: GTECH exists to serve its state customers. Helping maximize lottery profits means more state revenue and therefore more public benefits. GTECH helps states create new games, positions the states' portfolios of games, and prepares them for the future of lotteries.

It's the future that is the most interesting, but in the future, GTECH may be frustrated with the United States. "The industry really is at somewhat of a crossroads in this country," she says. Elsewhere, in Britain and Finland, for example, GTECH has already moved past lottery tickets and keno games and gone into online gambling. Worldwide, nations are moving into online gambling, but not the United States. Although a lot of gambling takes place here, Internet gambling by and large remains illegal.

Although an accurate figure may be impossible, Christiansen Capital has estimated that online gambling brought in $12 billion in 2005—some estimates say the United States accounts for half that amount—and will increase to $24 billion worldwide by 2010.

And gambling is not stopping at the Internet. In fact, Internet gambling is starting to look somewhat dated as a way of getting to the youth market, Laverty O'Connor says: "The PDA seems to have more of a compelling life to it for the younger generation." In 2008, as part of its nonstop market research, GTECH was conducting surveys into what type of games young people play, in what type of environment, and on what type of device.

The Internet, cell phones, and PDAs all remain viable devices, but the future of gambling lies in whatever technology provides the most direct and convenient link with the consumer. Just as the instant ticket won over customers in seventeenth-century London, and scratch tickets prevailed in twentieth-century America, the small color touch screen of a handheld entertainment device is where GTECH wants to position itself. The company could sell its customers games while it sells access to its customers. It now makes computer terminals and provides the link between states and their customers in convenience stores. The link could be more profitable if GTECH brokered connections to its gaming customers. But first its customers have to be willing to register.

Laverty O'Connor imagines a time when the customer could be the business with GTECH as the manager of the relationship. "And at that point, who knows, maybe all these folks will be registered," she says. "But that's not going to happen in the U.S. as long as there isn't an ability to provide value to the customers." By "value" she means rewards and givebacks to entice players to register. There have been fledgling attempts to link clients directly to players by inviting them to text-message entries into lottery contests, but nothing on the scale that Laverty O'Connor and others in the industry see as the future of gaming. What they see is a potential storehouse of willing players who can directly be reached by vendors electronically.

"The casino industry creates a direct relationship with the consumer," she says. Whenever gamblers go to a casino, they get free drinks, and if they go enough, they are e-mailed or sent coupons for all kinds of discounts and free merchandise and free chips. If given rewards for gambling, people gamble more. Casinos have proven it, and GTECH would like to apply the same tactics to U.S. lotteries.

Many lotteries make an effort at "gifting" customers with things such as coupons in newspapers. Mostly these are untargeted, clumsy attempts to encourage play, and they are expensive.

According to Laverty O'Connor, market research has shown GTECH that the only way to get players to overcome their desire for anonymity and to register their personal information with companies is to give them a reward. But state laws present a barrier. "There's no limit here to good ideas," she says. "Good ideas really have to be executed in an environment where reality is whatever the statute says."

As GTECH charts a course for the next five years, technology is front and center in coming up with interactive games for continents around the globe. The games currently produced by GTECH's international subsidiaries have little to do with the lottery as it's played in America. In 2007–8, GTECH went on a buying spree and acquired the Internet gambling companies Finsoft, which deals in online sports betting, and Boss Media and St Enodoc Holdings, which create online slots, bingo, poker, and casino games. They also make video games that include an element of wagering.

These are the kinds of gambling where GTECH sees future expansion, but are not likely in America soon. "Even if the actual games apply," Laverty O'Connor says, "it's very possible that the legislation will never get us there."

The Department of Justice interprets the Interstate Wire Act of 1961 as applying to all Internet wagering. The law was written to combat interstate bookmaking in sports and numbers gambling. But it is an awkward fit for the changing times. Interstate gambling is allowed on horse racing, for example. U.S. restrictions have been repudiated internationally. The World Trade Organization ruled in favor of Antigua when it sued the United States for blocking access to online gambling servers located there.

Although the United States has not complied with the WTO's decision, international disagreement with the U.S. barriers to Internet gambling is increasing. That the Department of Justice has declared Internet gambling illegal frustrates nations that don't have a problem with it. It's been suggested that the United States is motivated by economics rather than ethics. Besides the World Trade Organization, the European Commission is in favor of peeling back national barriers to Internet gambling. Instead of directly addressing the question of online gaming, President Bush signed the 2006 Safe Ports Act, which increased maritime security against terrorism, except for Section 803: "Internet gambling in or through foreign jurisdictions." The law made it illegal for credit-card companies to process online gambling transactions.

Some state lotteries have looked into online games, while others have chosen to play in the shallow end of the pool, using text messaging only for marketing purposes. One congressman from Washington

State estimated that the federal government could make anywhere from $8.7 billion to $42.8 billion in the first decade if it regulated Internet gambling.

Just as they did at the birth of modern American finance markets, lotteries are again starting to look clunky and inefficient—this time in a technological sense. The draw of increased profits from new gambling technology may prove irresistible to government, in the same way the paper lotteries first did hundreds of years ago.

Casinos have it easy. They generate more profit than lotteries, and all the government has to do is levy a general sin tax on them. A lottery ticket charges a sin tax, too, but it's paid directly by the player, and at the incredibly high rate of about 50 percent—the amount that goes to fund public programs and the lottery's administration. For lottery companies such as GTECH, the markets in Asia, Africa, and elsewhere are less burdened by regulation, and it can't just sit idly while it waits for the Department of Justice to come around on Internet gambling. GTECH's future is in emerging markets.

China, which started its first lottery in 1987, sold some $13.7 billion in tickets in 2007, up from $8.6 billion in 2005. Citigroup analysts estimated that China's sales will rise to $21 billion in 2008 and $34.5 billion by 2010, which would put the country second only to the United States in national lottery sales.

GTECH has a 50 percent stake in a venture to create a national keno game in China. In an earlier contract to supply instant tickets to Taiwan, the company had a setback when someone figured out how to use the bar code to determine which tickets were winners. Scientific Games has a similar stake in an instant-ticket company in China. China is just one of the emerging economies where GTECH, Scientific Games, and other companies are fighting to win contracts.

Compared with the bounties of these wide-open audiences and growing economies, America has little new growth to offer. The states that have no lotteries—particularly Alaska and Wyoming—barely have enough population to be worth the trouble. And a lot of effort, and money, is expended on the clawing and fighting that is needed to protect existing state contracts that come up for renewal. In 2003, GTECH finally beat out Automated Wagering for the $25 million annual contract to run the Florida Lottery. With Florida now added to New York, Texas, Georgia, and California, GTECH runs the top five state lotteries. The Florida victory was the culmination of a decade-long fight complete with lawsuits and tens of thousands of dollars in political donations. In 2006, GTECH beat the competition to run North Carolina's new lottery. And in 2008, it defended its contract in Kansas and almost took the Pennsylvania Lottery contract away from Scientific Games.

But the wars that take place year in and year out take their toll. In 2006, GTECH ran into trouble with the New Jersey contract it had held since 1984 because there was at least a perception that the company had an unfair advantage. GTECH and the state's Lottery Commission had hired the same lobbying firm. The state canceled GTECH's contract extension and sought to rebid it.

Added to the cost of doing business in the United States is what has become almost standard practice in the lottery industry—after a contract is awarded, the loser files suit. In 2008, GTECH lost the Ohio Lottery contract to Intralot. The contract was valued at about $30 million a year. GTECH argued that Intralot didn't have the experience to qualify as a bidder because it had never contracted for instant-ticket vending machines. The argument seemed silly considering GTECH began by making up technology to order.

The American market is lucrative for Lottomatica/GTECH, but it costs a lot of money and labor just to keep things running. Without some kind of direct-to-player gambling over cell phones, PDAs, and the Internet, or privatization that might loosen the state regulations on its practices, the only way for lotteries to expand in the United States is through existing retail sales. Having glutted gas stations, liquor stores, and corner convenience stores, the best barely touched opportunity is in chain stores such as Wal-Mart, Home Depot, Lowe's, and others.

"If you look at the ten biggest chains in the North American continent, eight of them do not sell the lottery," says Laverty O'Connor. The chains don't like lotteries because they are time-consuming low cost transactions. Someone has to enter the players' numbers into a computer and wait for a printed ticket. It takes a few minutes to process a purchase that is likely under $20. Big chains make their profits from bulk purchases processed quickly.

It's a stigma that the lottery is trying to overcome. The Delaware Lottery sponsored a contest among store clerks to see who could process tickets the fastest. The winner of the XFingers Challenge took one minute twenty seconds to enter a series of lottery purchases, a lifetime to some customers standing on line behind the lottery player waiting to buy a gallon of milk.

The future for GTECH is overseas. In America, the company is in a holding pattern—ready to provide gambling on iPhones or whatever device is popular tomorrow, but frustrated by American moral and legislative limitations. Europe, the company says, is more "progressive." If Europe is progressive, perhaps China will be downright radical in its embrace of instant gaming over the next few years. Left behind in America, GTECH's state operations seem to be an increasing burden if they can't expand. The only potential for the company to expand seems to be in video-lottery terminals or keno games, which come with political and social controversy. The controversies are dampened during fiscal downturns, however. The company will have to lobby for expansion of some of the most addictive games available.

CHAPTER 7

TICKET SCRATCH FEVER

ROBERT, A TALL, older man with a proud bearing, stepped into a convenience store on his way to work, said hello to the woman behind the register, put down $20 for four $5 scratch tickets, and offered her a bland smile. He hadn't won anything in a while and was feeling unambitious; otherwise he would have bought more tickets. He was just going through the motions as he stepped off to the side and scratched the silver off the cards. There was no rush of anticipation. When he uncovered a $10,000 prize, he didn't react. His insides cartwheeled, but he clamped down on the smile that pulled at his lips. I'll be damned if she shares in this, he thought. He put the ticket in his suit pocket, wiped his hands clean, brushed down the front of his pants, and walked out the door into the parking lot.

It was his win, not hers. The woman who'd sold him the ticket had nothing to do with it. He resented it when they acted as if they were a part of your luck, as if they made it possible. Every day they took his money, but they never accepted blame for his losses. She probably paid her kids' college tuition with the money he lost at this store. They make the payouts on small wins—under $600—and smile and act as if it's their gift to you. As if they brought you luck. But Robert—not his real name—knew better. The store gets a commission on winners. The store was the house, and all the house does is take. The real struggle was between him and the tickets. Everyone else was just a bystander.

For a few days Robert was elated. He had never won so much in the lottery. "Why can't I do that more often?" he thought. And he needed to. He was spending thirty grand a year on instant tickets.

Lottery players are a punch line in popular culture. Whether it's a character on *The Simpsons* or the protagonist in *My Name Is Earl*, a character that plays the lottery is usually a dope—a Big Gulp–swilling, trailer-park-living piece of trash or an urban dweller, ignorant and poor. The general depiction is someone who is just dumb enough to throw away their hard-earned money on hopeless odds. These patsies bank on hitting a million-to-one chance, instead of opening a savings account. By contrast, casino gamblers—with the exception of slot jockeys—who play poker and other games of supposed skill are viewed as crafty artists.

"You can tell by the way you're talked to that there's no respect," Robert says. "You're a loser and you're stupid. Even though we make money, we are the low end of the population. And you feel it. In my case, being a successful businessman and pretty proud of what I've accomplished and who I am, it was very, very disturbing and degrading. But not enough that it would stop me."

Robert was not the average lottery player. In a casino, Robert would have been a whale, a high roller who spent his $30,000 a year exclusively on $5 and $10 scratch tickets. Over a decade, he estimates he spent as much as $125,000 to $225,000.

"Would you believe if you play these enough, you start to see a pattern?" he asks. It's closing time in the back office of his store—a successful retail business in Massachusetts. He has a lot of nervous energy and twists a telephone cord between his fingers as he talks. He jumps every time someone comes to the office door. Robert came to

Massachusetts decades earlier, leaving his family behind in New York while he tried to build them a future with an investment of a few thousand dollars. If the business took off, he told his wife, he would send for them. If not, he would come home. He opened a store, lived in a rooming house, and took no salary. He worked nonstop, and a few months later he was able to send for his family. Over the years, he added more stores and built a mini-empire. By the time he was seventy years old, he had amassed a small fortune that provided for his wife and six children in luxury. He had a vacation home. He drove a luxury car. He and his wife took vacations when they wanted. He had achieved everything in life that he'd set out to do. Perhaps it was the awareness of approaching retirement, the satisfaction of accomplishment, but Robert decided to live a little and gamble a little more.

Gambling had always been second nature to Robert. On fishing trips, he would put money on who was going to catch the most fish. He was fiercely competitive, and a little money on the line made it more exciting. Still, as he approached retirement, he had made no more than a dozen trips to casinos. When he went, he played heavily, dropping $8,000 or $10,000, he says. He could afford it. And the casino trips were pleasant, social affairs. Robert liked to bring his family on his adventures to Las Vegas and the Caribbean.

In the early 1990s, he started buying $1 and $2 scratch tickets. He'd stop for gas or a gallon of milk and pick up a handful of tickets at the register. In 1992, the first $5 scratch ticket was introduced. Robert saw the $5 ticket with its bigger prizes and figured it was more of a real bet. The idea of playing for real money compounded the good feeling he got from scratching the tickets—a mix of anticipation, competition, and hope. He started to take the game seriously, buying large numbers of tickets to increase his odds. If you're going to gamble, he thought, you might as well play to win.

In 1999, the first $10 tickets came out. Robert switched back and forth between $5 and $10 tickets, depending on his mood, how his luck was running, and which games seemed due for a winner. He bought in bulk. Customers would stop to watch when the cashier unspooled a three-foot strip of $10 tickets from the dispenser; Robert would hand over a thick stack of twenties totaling $200 or $300. His big spending attracted attention, and that added to the good feeling. Within a short time of starting, Robert was spending $10,000 to $15,000 a year. In his last three years he spent $30,000 a year on scratch tickets.

Inside almost every grocery, gas station, and one-stop convenience store, rolls of scratch tickets line the walls behind the registers. Each roll usually has a hundred tickets, of which a random number are winners. In Massachusetts, the typical formula for a $10 scratch ticket runs like this: thirty million tickets are printed, ten of which have $1 million prizes. The prize values drop off steeply from there. There are perhaps a thousand second-place prizes worth about $10,000 each. Altogether, there are millions of prizes ranging from $5 to $1 million. The vast majority of the winners are at the low end; maybe two million of them are worth either $5 or $10. This glut of half-price and break-even prizes allows the lottery to proclaim on the face of the card that players have 1-in-4 odds of winning.

Robert was only interested in the top prizes, though. A $500 win felt good for a day, but Robert would quickly lose interest and move on to the next ticket. Money like that functioned as a bankroll to pay for a week or so worth of tickets. He became obsessed with finding a big winner.

Thousands, if not millions, of lottery-ticket scratchers around the country believe there's a method to improving their odds. Robert believes that he has won more than he should have because of his system. "It's a real pattern," he insists. He only talks about his system reluctantly and in sketchy terms. It comes down to knowing which rolls of tickets to play.

"If you know the owners, they're going to talk directly to you," he tells me. "Because you're a favored player. You're not a guy that comes in and bets five dollars. You're dropping several thousand, so if anybody gets a break, it's going to be you. That type of thing was prevalent in different convenience stores or gas stations. If they could throw you a bone, they would." The cashier might tell him that a lot of money had been spent on a particular roll without any winners showing up. "Or maybe the guy is pulling my leg," Robert says. "I don't know."

He participated in this gas-station drama most mornings on the way to work, during lunch depending on how the morning went, and often on the way home. He worked a rotation of stores, following a pattern in his head to mix it up. In the six-mile drive between home and work there were six different places to play the Massachusetts Lottery. Every visit was a chance to check in and see how the tickets were playing. Depending on the information from the owner and the depth of the available ticket rolls, Robert would play the beginning, middle, or end of a given roll.

"Let's say I was working one roll of tickets and I dropped three hundred dollars on it," he says. "And for one reason or another I'm not taking the next card. Maybe it's not available. Maybe the guy is taking care of somebody else. I can't get the next card. Somebody comes in and gets the next card and wins five hundred dollars. I get upset. I should have gotten it. I was planning to get the next card. By the luck of the draw he bought something, cigarettes and one card, and he gets five hundred dollars. You say that's the luck of the draw. I say that what I did allowed him to get that. It set the thing up. And don't put it past the guy that he wasn't observing me for twenty minutes to a half hour and said, 'The minute that man stops, I'm gonna buy at least one ticket.' That's the kind of atmosphere you're in."

Over time, as Robert lost more than he won, the emotional investment in the game took its toll. He got angry at his wife if she spent money on anything because it meant money he could not spend on lottery tickets. His mood changed depending on whether he was winning. He knew he couldn't control his gambling. He told the owner of one gas station never to sell him lottery tickets again.

"I was aware I was getting myself a reputation," Robert says. "It was getting worse." The owner didn't take him seriously. "He laughed at me," Robert recalls. "I said, 'Hey, I'm telling you something. Don't sell me lottery tickets.' So he didn't."

What shamed Robert more than losing self-control was that he had to reveal his weakness to a stranger. One morning he stopped to play on the way to work. After losing $250 on $10 scratch tickets, Robert became desperate for a win. He went back to the counter and asked the owner to cash a personal check. This particular convenience store knew Robert—he had spent thousands on scratch tickets over the years. But he'd never asked to cash a check. With the owner's quick assent, Robert wrote out a check for $65—he didn't want to go overboard—and bought another batch of scratch tickets. Two minutes later he was back at the counter with his checkbook in his hand. He knew he was crossing a line, but he had no choice—he was watching from outside himself. What mattered most was that he not leave the store a loser. He wrote out another check for $65 and bought more tickets. He lost again. He wrote a third $65 check, cashed it, and again, all his tickets were losers.

"If you scratch tickets, you get dirty, did you know that?" Robert says, pausing in his story of that day. "Your hands get filthy. Your nails get black."

In some convenience stores they let him use their employees-only bathroom to wash up. He was a good customer. Sometimes he kept wet wipes in his car. He never walked into work or his home with dirty hands. It was a point of pride. So after cashing the three checks, he made sure that his hands and fingernails were clean. He walked out the door twenty minutes after he had entered. He was miserable, completely disgusted with himself. While people around him were buying coffee and a newspaper, Robert had flushed $380 down the toilet. Worst of all, for the first time he had asked the house for credit. He went to his car and drove to work.

Robert is not alone in Massachusetts, where they love the lottery. On average, Massachusetts adults spend more than $700 each on lottery tickets each year. The nearest competition doesn't come close—the District of Columbia sales came to $470 per person and in Georgia $350 per capita in 2006. The lottery estimates that 70 percent of the Massachusetts adult population (roughly five million people) buy a lottery ticket at least once in a while. Players spend $4.5 billion a year, and almost three quarters of the money comes from scratch-ticket sales. The state returns nearly $1 billion from those sales to local towns, cities, and the state treasury. The rest goes back into the game to pay for prizes and operating expenses such as state salaries, commissions to convenience stores, and advertising. The Massachusetts State Lottery has brand appeal: People cross state lines to get tickets, even though the states bordering Massachusetts all have lotteries. People from New Hampshire and Connecticut will literally drive the extra mile to get a Massachusetts Lottery ticket. In many ways, Massachusetts has come to depend on this draw.

Just a stone's throw from the New Hampshire state line, on Route 28 in Methuen, is Ted's Stateline Mobil. For the last decade or more, Robert has perhaps been the Massachusetts Lottery's best customer; Tony Amico, the owner of Ted's Stateline Mobil, has been its biggest retailer over the same span. From the road, the three-pump station looks like almost any other, except it has more parking. Inside, it's obvious that the store exists to sell lottery tickets, not gasoline. The racks for chips, candy, and maps are an afterthought, shrunk down over time to make more room for lottery paraphernalia. If the state lottery makes it, Ted's Stateline Mobil sells it. It's like a casino for lottery players.

As you come in the front door, on the left-hand side are three employees who stand behind a long counter operating three computer terminals that print out lotto tickets. On the wall behind them are Lucite boxes that dispense rolls of different scratch tickets—more than fifty varieties. Past the front counter the store opens up into a back room adorned with keno screens. To the right, the room dead-ends at two cutout windows where young women sit like old-fashioned bank tellers waiting to sell keno, lotto, and an assortment of a hundred different scratch tickets arrayed behind them. One of the tellers, a young woman, got college credit for working in the store. It took some doing, but she convinced a professor at the University of New Hampshire that the store's booming lottery business counted as entertainment and therefore applied to her degree in hospitality management. The walls in back are covered with framed news clippings of people who've won here, posters with game rules, plastic holders for keno slips and pencils, and the claim forms that are required for anyone who wins more than $600. There is a long, thin counter for filling in keno slips and scratching tickets. If the window tellers in back and the registers up front are crowded, customers can use one of the three scratch-ticket vending machines. Lottery ads, handwritten charts of lotto drawings, and a regularly updated list of the scratch-ticket prizes—both claimed and unclaimed—fill any left-over space.

Out the back door there's a concrete patio with three picnic benches facing the seventh keno screen, which is securely mounted against the back of the building inside a Plexiglas-and-plywood box. This is where smokers play. In the cold or rain, they pull up and watch from their cars.

Amico took over the business seven years ago from his brother, who started it as a shack attached to three garage bays where he did oil changes and repairs. In the shack he had one lotto machine and space for a couple of different scratch tickets. Pretty soon, Tony's brother sold $1 million in lottery tickets. His customers decided his future for him. He focused on gambling instead of gasoline. Now, the Amico brothers are almost exclusively supported by the game. Tony's brother now lives in sunny Florida, and 80 percent of the store's income comes from the lottery. In 2005, Tony sold more than $13 million in lottery tickets. He kept a little more than 5 percent as profit—about $650,000. It's a volume business, and there are a lot of labor costs.

"It's a Tuesday afternoon and I've got five people working," Amico says over the electric whine of printers grinding out lotto tickets. The five employees are just enough to serve the store's customers, even in the middle of the workweek.

A dozen players sit on padded barstools, sharing the three small tables in back. There is no conversation as their eyes move from the screens to their cards and back again, checking their keno slips against the cartoon balls bouncing into the numbered grids on the flat-screen televisions mounted overhead. Two men are playing out back, but it's cold and they come inside between cigarettes.

"Some of them don't even know there's a store out front," Amico jokes.

It's the regular players who fuel Amico's sales. He sees the same faces every day. They play keno and scratch tickets and don't pay much attention to the lotto jackpot drawings. On this afternoon there is a mix of male and female players, most of whom look older than forty. Only one man is wearing a suit and tie.

Big lotto jackpot drawings pull in the office workers who share their tickets in groups. "When it gets to be $225 million, I see a lot of new faces. They don't even know what the game is," Amico says. "The media creates the frenzy. When the jackpot's $300 million, we've got a line out the door and a cop to do traffic."

Amico has a cynical note in his voice, but it is drowned out by his passion for his business. He sells more than everyone else, it seems, because he works harder and has invested more in the game. Turning his brother's garage into this oasis of lottery delights cost a lot of money, and it's all staked to a 5 percent commission on sales, plus a 1 percent bonus on winning prizes. But Amico wants to expand. The state lottery might wonder whether it's facing a saturated market with 70 percent of eligible gamblers playing and $700 per capita spending, but he sees more money to be made. The storage room to the right of the front door is the future home of a keno parlor. He points out where the players can sit at tables and watch keno screens in privacy, behind a closed door. "The lottery could be much bigger," he says.

After years of watching the players, Amico has learned some of their habits. Some rotate among the five different sales counters so as not to seem like heavy players. "They're embarrassed," he says. Others, just like Robert, move around to different stations because of their own system or superstition. If they win money buying from one cashier, they may return, or move to someone else if they lost. If someone has just won on a certain roll of scratch tickets, a seasoned player will move on, trying a roll at the back of the store. "Some like to play the end of the roll, some play the middle, some play the front," Amico says. "They think there's a system." But he has seen three winners successively pulled from the front, middle, and end of a roll. "It's so random there can't be a system."

Once a woman in his store won $500 on a $10 scratch ticket. While she was still dancing for joy, a regular player stepped to the counter and bought the next ticket on the roll. He won $4 million. "She almost dropped to her knees," Amico says, laughing at the memory.

Because Amico's store is so busy, a salesman from the lottery visits twice a week to keep him well supplied with tickets and promotional materials on upcoming games. "This only just started being a sales job," the sales agent says. In past years, he says, it felt like a brainless delivery job. The state was restrained in its approach to winning new customers. But now, under new leadership, the lottery is trying to bounce back from a bad year in 2007. They've loosened the reins and salespeople are allowed to start selling again.

But Amico thinks the lottery is still too timid to admit that it's in the gambling business. "They want the money, but they're all in the closet." What's particularly under his skin is that he can't sell one particular new lottery product—a keno-style game in which players bet on digitized horses and watch on television screens as they race around the track, kicking up realistic-looking puffs of dirt. The Daily Race Game is virtual horse racing, and the lottery is banking on it as a growth product. Amico wants it in his store. Historic Rockingham Park, the New Hampshire track that held its first Thoroughbred race in 1906, is a four-mile drive from Amico's parking lot, and it has long been the province of veteran bettors. With the Daily Race Game you don't need to know anything about horses or jockeys. The winning horses are selected at random. The odds are relative to your ambitions—1 in 12 on a first-place pick, 1 in 6 on second, 1 in 4 on third, and so on, all the way down to picking the top three virtual horses in correct order—better known as a trifecta in real horse racing—at odds of 1 in 1,320 and a payout of $900 on a $1 bet. Wagers range from 50¢ to $5.

The state lottery will only put the game in bars and restaurants. Massachusetts wants to brand the Daily Race Game as social entertainment, not solitary gambling. Keno, though played heavily in Massachusetts, has a bad rap among many for the hypnotized silence it spreads wherever it's played. The lottery wants to reach new players and expand sales, and Amico's store does not fit their marketing strategy. Without the new game, Amico feels vulnerable to competition. Someone could open up a bar on the vacant lot on the other side of Route 28 and offer the Daily Race Game alongside a few scratch tickets and cut into his business. As the state's biggest vendor, and therefore best customer, he feels that he deserves it. At a minimum, he's certainly earned the right to speak his mind.

"If they really wanted to increase sales, they'd put that game here," he says.

DESPITE HIS INSISTENCE that the state lottery should be more aggressive, Amico says that he doesn't see addicted players at his store. It's a change from his comments to a *Boston Globe* reporter in December 2004 when the state, flush with newly approved advertising funds, was running an upbeat campaign that promoted lottery tickets as Christmas gifts. "The ads show young people, winners who are going places," he said. "They don't show the old people who are picking through the trash looking for scratch tickets."

The Daily Race can be played in one nonbar establishment—the lobby of the state lottery headquarters in Braintree, Massachusetts. In keeping with its low overhead, the lottery headquarters is in an out-of-the-way, nondescript office park, well south of Boston. The lobby, where players come to collect any winnings of more than $600, offers plenty of opportunities to play. Besides the horse-racing game playing on a large flat-screen monitor, there are several scratch-ticket vending machines, keno screens, and keno number slips. A long line of winners is waiting to collect from two windows at the end of a three-day weekend.

The Daily Race Game is a departure from the Massachusetts Lottery's normal marketing scheme. The state has succeeded so far by eschewing games with bells and whistles. Other states try fancy ways to dazzle new players, but scratch tickets have been the heartbeat of the Massachusetts Lottery since it became the first state to sell them in 1974. Called the Instant Game, the ticket carried a top prize of $10,000 and could be entered into a drawing with a chance at $1,000 a week for life. The state printed twenty-five million tickets, which sold out, so they printed ten million more. Lottery officials have long understood that a cheap, instant transaction with good odds is the best motivation for players. Relative to other states, it doesn't hurt that Massachusetts is heavily Catholic—a denomination that out-gambles other religions. But the primary reason the Massachusetts formula works so well, and vendors such as Amico get repeat business, is that the state is generous with prizes. It pays out more than any other lottery. Massachusetts puts 76 percent of the money spent on scratch tickets back into ticket prizes. No other state comes close. The nearest are top-selling states such as New York, Georgia, or the District of Columbia, paying back a percentage in the high sixties. It means that Massachusetts has a small profit margin and must sell a boatload of tickets to turn a profit. But the formula works. Massachusetts sells more instant tickets per capita than any other lottery in the world. By the dollar, the state ranks third worldwide in instant ticket sales at more than $3 billion. They also keep operating costs down. The Massachusetts Lottery runs on a shoestring—less than 2 percent of revenue goes to overhead, the lowest rate in the country. It's yet another reason that the lottery relies heavily on scratch tickets.

The horse-racing game was an experiment, a departure from the fast, no-frills products that the lottery usually puts out. In the lottery's wildest dreams, it would get some of those 30 percent who never played the lottery to give it a try. And it would probably entice infrequent players to try something that looked active and fun. The lottery had to fulfill its mandate to maximize sales for the state. But it also had to recover from fiscal year 2007, which was rough. Sales dropped below projections for the year—about $60 million less. It was not a major loss, about 1.6 percent below expectations, but it was enough to elicit alarmist newspaper stories, announcing a shortfall in public funding, and to put public and political heat on the lottery. Mark Cavanagh, the lottery's executive director, was driving home one evening listening to the radio when a report came on that the lottery "was bleeding red."

"There are 351 cities and towns that rely on the revenue," Cavanagh says in his Braintree office. A gruff man, he has agreed to meet with some reluctance. Lottery officials have been conditioned to assume media coverage is going to be negative, if not uninformed, on how the lottery operates. In general, the only times lottery officials are happy with coverage is when it's an upbeat story about a lottery winner. "Cities' and towns' costs and expenses are going up, so they continually look to the revenue for an *increasing* source of funds. So when you have flat growth or no growth or 1.4 percent dip, you get a lot of people up in arms. People love to point fingers and say what the reason is and the sky is falling and it's all 'life is over as we know it.' "

In Massachusetts, there were several causes. For one, the market may be nearing saturation—$700 per person per year is a lot of money. Major lotto jackpot revenues were down, until a large Mega Millions jackpot suddenly drew in players and led to a sales spike. Also, the people who drew up the state budget in 2007 had burdened the lottery with a giddily optimistic projection for a sales increase.

The lottery turns a profit of just under $1 billion for the state, equivalent to 3 percent of the state budget—a greater percentage than that for nearly any other state lottery. New York has the nation's wealthiest lottery with total annual sales of around $7 billion and profits of $2.3 billion. But that amount is less than 2 percent of the total state budget. In most states, lottery revenue is around 2 percent or less of the budget. In Massachusetts, with so much money at stake, it is not surprising that the lottery can find itself caught up in political tugs-of-war. Former governor Mitt Romney and the state legislature helped alleviate a state budget deficit by capping the amount of lottery dollars that went to local towns and cities and siphoning off a portion—more than $100 million—for the state treasury. A few years later, Romney's cap remains in place, even though the lottery believes its popularity derives from its profits being given directly to the budgets of local towns and cities. When the money goes to a local town fire department, it has a greater populist appeal than when it is sucked into the state's general treasury, where it is soon lost from sight.

Besides elected officials, looking to fund the state's budget, the lottery has to contend with the misperceptions that plague the whole industry—state governments tend to think that lottery profits continually grow by leaps and bounds, as they did in the 1980s and 1990s. "People don't think it's ever going to fully mature," Cavanagh says. "In a finite state—Massachusetts—we've got our boundaries, we've got our population. We've got market penetration at about seventy percent, and I think you can only do so many things and achieve the kind of [growth] numbers that they achieved several years ago. I think we've averaged about two percent growth per year over the last five to eight years."

There is only so much room for growth, but government is always in need of more money. With total annual sales at $4.5 billion, the Massachusetts Lottery is a strong company, but toward the end of Romney's term in office, someone putting together the state budget must have decided it had superpowers—projecting a 6 or 7 percent profit increase for the year. It meant, at least on paper, a bigger budget for the state. The lottery protested—not loudly enough, to Cavanagh's regret—and did its best to meet the budget projection by trying to increase sales. They fell short.

"As we begin to, maybe, bump our head up against a certain ceiling with limited population in a pretty small state, we've got to work harder and harder to be more creative and find that next new edge," Cavanagh says. To boost sales after the slump in fiscal year 2007, they tried a raffle, but were left holding unsold tickets when the Fourth of July drawing came around. Players did buy almost 1.4 million Star Spangled Sweepstakes tickets for $20 each, however—about the same as much larger states such as New York had done with their raffles. But Massachusetts overplayed its hand with the raffle and left its customers, who were weaned on simple scratch tickets, confused by the complicated raffle drawing. Next came the video horse-racing experiment.

But true to precedent, what worked beyond expectation was the state's first $20 scratch ticket, which was rolled out in September 2007. "It's breaking all previous sales records," Cavanagh says. "That's something the players did take to. It was more of an instant gratification, which is more of their liking." The game offered players 10 instant prizes of $10 million and 130 prizes of $1 million. Total prizes totaled $1 billion, so someone in marketing or product development came up with the name Billion Dollar Blockbuster. There were nearly twenty-two million winning tickets in all, but more than fifteen million prizes were valued at $20 or $25. The vast majority of winners were going to break even or win $5. Because there were so many prizes, the state was able to advertise the odds of winning were 1 in 3. The state printed more than sixty-five million tickets.

The success should not have been a surprise. Every time the lottery has raised the price of scratch tickets, the players have followed. Robert was one of those players who led the charge when $5 and then $10 tickets were rolled out. Having previously moved up from $1 and $2 tickets, Robert and other ticket-scratchers had in turn been primed by the $5 tickets by the time the first $10 ticket came out in 1999. Called the Millennium Spectacular, it was obscenely generous. It paid back 80 percent in prizes and offered five $4 million prizes and five $2 million prizes. It sold faster than any previous product.

High-price scratch tickets were an experiment when they were first released. From a marketing point of view, the pricier scratch tickets were a good bet for the Massachusetts Lottery. People who hadn't been buying scratch tickets, the kind of people who might play the lotto when the jackpots get big, the kind who play for the chance at life-changing money, were drawn to the game. It had the added appeal of instant winning. In general, the new players were at a higher income level than the $1 and $2 scratch-ticket players. At the same time, some $1 and $2 players, such as Robert, who already liked the instant-win drama of scratch tickets, were willing to spend more.

If it worked, the increased price and the greater excitement of a bigger win would entice $1 and $2 scratch-ticket buyers to play more than they had previously. It was a smart idea. The lottery encourages players to choose a product that has a potential for a higher profit margin. Players can win instant jackpots of hundreds of thousands or a few million dollars at odds that are better than those for the astronomical jackpots in lotto games such as Mega Millions and Powerball. Instead of a 1-in-150-million chance, the player might have a 1-in-5-million chance of becoming a "millionaire." These "instant" top prizes are generally paid the same as lotto jackpots—in annual installments over twenty years. Customers, not just in Massachusetts, gladly paid more for scratch tickets. High-end scratch tickets are the fastest-growing lottery product in the country. Once experimental, the $20 tickets are now commonplace. Some states have released $50 scratch tickets.

AS SALES GREW, led by the new scratch tickets, more money went into the Massachusetts public treasury, but some evidence suggested that the increased sales were not entirely beneficial to the state. People were sifting through the garbage in hopes of scoring an overlooked prize. In 2007, the same year it released the Billion Dollar Blockbuster, the lottery canceled its Instant Replay Recycling Initiative. The recycling program offered a free $1 scratch ticket to anyone who turned in twenty-five used tickets. The stated goal was to encourage recycling. It helped counter the negative image people had that scratch tickets led to street litter. But the lottery was not prepared for just how many people were holding onto their losing tickets and were willing to go through the garbage for tickets. Some had tens of thousands of them. The program cost the Massachusetts Lottery about $1 million a year. They had only budgeted about $100,000 for it. After a few years they pulled the plug. People were pawing through trash for tickets, but what lottery officials may not previously have realized was that some of them had been looking through the trash for winners long before the recycling reward program started. Scratch tickets can be confusing to read and decipher, and it is not uncommon for winners to get tossed away. One of the "scroungers"—as they were dubbed in a *Boston Globe* column—was Ed Rader. When he heard that the lottery had canceled the program, he wrote a letter to the *Boston Globe*, discussing his addiction to lottery gambling, noting, "It is an addiction that has made and kept me poor, and that I struggle with every day."

On the phone, Rader says that the recycling program upset him because it encouraged people who were desperately hooked on scratch tickets. "It's like your neighborhood pusher giving you a free shot. It's one on the house. The people who are going through the garbage are not going to be your casual users."

Rader says he scrounged in part because it once paid off. He found a $10,000 winner in a garbage can outside a newsstand in the Back Bay train station. A couple of weeks later Rader bought a ticket that hit for another $10,000. He paid off some of his debts, but not all. He decided to keep some money to gamble.

Rader started playing the lottery around 1992. Quickly, he was spending more than he could afford. He never played for millions, just for the rush of anticipation and the exhilaration of free money.

"If I just scratch a little fucking number, I might have five hundred bucks in my pockets," he says. "It was about validation. I didn't feel great about myself, so that little victory was a form of power." He's intelligent, has a college degree, and is very self-aware, all of which makes him more frustrated at his periodic inability to control his addiction to scratch-ticket gambling. He buys the $1 and $2 tickets. If he's won some money, he moves up the ladder to the $5 and $10 tickets.

Some years after the addiction began, Rader got divorced. He didn't date anyone for three years afterward because all of his spare money, and more, went to lottery tickets. At his lowest point he shoplifted food for about six months, forged checks, and missed weekends with his daughter because he had no money to take her anywhere or feed her. On a half dozen occasions he's begun sobbing in the middle of a convenience store, overcome with his inability to control himself. And, like Robert, he knows how people look at lottery players. "But you go to the card table and you're James freaking Bond," he says.

For some time now, he's been able to control his spending on scratch tickets, limiting himself to $5 or $10 every once in a while. The desperate need to play, the uncontrollable compulsion, is gone. Occasional GA meetings help. He's started dating again, which he says is huge. And he almost never goes through the garbage anymore. "I still occasionally do look over, and if there's a clean ticket, I might dip in and take a look at it," he says. "The lottery should be abolished, period."

Those who study and offer counseling for gambling addiction look at the problem as existing within the individual's relationship to the game he or she plays, not the game itself. Gambling is not "evil" or inherently addictive. But a significant portion of the national adult population—about 4 percent or eight million people—has a gambling problem. Most people think of casinos when they think about gambling addiction. The obvious difference with lotteries as opposed to casinos is that the games are created, marketed, and encouraged by state government. Why would the state produce and market a product that does such damage to its citizens?

Because it needs the money. Government makes a big show every time it cuts taxes, but no state has ever said it should reduce the money it takes in from lotteries. Some compare governments' take from lotteries to a vice tax, such as the taxes on cigarettes or alcohol, but in the case of lotteries, government is doing everything it can to sell the "vice" product to as many people as possible. Yet, many lotteries in the twenty-first century have leveled off, even as states have desperately sought to increase gambling through "creative" or "innovative" games such as video horse racing or keno. States spend millions to ramp up and renew excitement among the public through advertising. When sales slow down, state lotteries redouble their efforts.

Massachusetts has the most successful formula. But having squeezed their players to the limit through scratch tickets. Massachusetts has decided to try cartoon horse racing in bars. It's a bid for the 30 percent of people who never play, an attempt to get nongamblers to gamble. And for each dollar spent, about twenty-one cents will go back to the public.

The Massachusetts instant-game formula, as Cavanagh says, is something more states are following—a cheap, instant-win game with high return to the customer. In 2006, lotto drawings and similar games resulted in about $22.3 billion in sales. Instant scratch-ticket sales were $29.7 billion. While lotto-drawing sales are flattening out, instant-ticket sales have grown every year since 2001. The Virginia Company of London learned the same lesson four hundred years ago: a chance for instant prizes is great for sales. In Massachusetts, it's no accident that the state lottery has both a heavy dependence on scratch tickets and massive player spending.

What lotteries know is that while most Americans play once in a while, about 80 percent of lottery sales are made from the top 20 percent of customers. Studies of the core group of gamblers has shown that the top 10 percent of players make up 70 percent of sales in some states. Lottery officials know that the heavy gamblers, the regulars, are responsible for state lottery profits. It is easier and more cost efficient, from a business perspective, to get current players to spend more than it is to get nonplayers to spend dollar one. The pressure to make the sale rolls downhill from the legislature, which generally knows little about lottery operations but sees the games as a way to help cover dangerous budget gaps; to the lottery offices, which are mandated to squeeze as many dollars from players as they can in order to return money to the public treasury; to retailers, such as Tony Amico, who have to encourage sales and encourage the compulsion for instant gratification if they want to profit from the business at 5 percent commission; and finally to the players. All the pressure comes down to a convenience-store transaction. If the adults of Massachusetts spend *on average* $700 per capita, it means that the hard-core players—people such as Robert and Ed Rader—are spending much more than that to account for the 30 percent of people in the state who never play.

From the 1990s and into the twenty-first century, more and more casinos have cropped up. In an odd recognition of their role in compulsive gambling, some have created self-banning programs. People who know they can't control their gambling have themselves barred from entering. Tens of thousands of people have signed up. The measures are a partnership of public and private interests—casinos working with the state. If people who have signed up for a self-ban are caught gambling, their winnings can be forfeited and, in some places, they can be arrested. The Iowa lottery instituted a self-ban program in 2005.

Since 1987 the Massachusetts Lottery has taken some responsibility for gambling addiction by funding the Massachusetts Council on Compulsive Gambling, a private, nonprofit organization that refers problem gamblers to counseling and promotes education about gambling addiction. At one time the lottery gave $2 million annually, but in 2002, acting governor Jane Swift cut the lottery's share of funds to $655,000. At the time the lottery was setting sales records. Governor Romney later suggested cutting all funds to the council. In 2004 and 2005, the lottery donated $100,000 to gambling-addiction services. Under pressure from advocacy groups and media attention, in 2006 the lottery gave more than $1 million from its advertising budget to a gambling-awareness campaign for the council. The $1 million is a tenth of 1 percent of the state's lottery profits.

"We don't think one million dollars is enough," says Kathy Scanlon, executive director of the council. The state should pay for gambling-addiction services as part of the cost of owning the lottery business, she says. The million dollars in lottery funds is almost the only funding that the council receives. It pays for ad campaigns using the lottery's marketing firm, pamphlets, and educational outreach, and the signs that are posted wherever lottery tickets are sold. The signs list a hotline number for problem gamblers—the same number Robert called.

Gambling addicts are divided roughly into two groups. Some have trouble controlling their spending. Others are pathological gamblers and have a more severe problem. The distinction is made based on how people answer a series of questions about their gambling and how much it has altered their decision-making and behavior. Someone who gambles to feel better may be a "problem" gambler, but someone who uses food or rent money to gamble would likely be considered a "pathological" gambler.

In Massachusetts, it has been estimated that 4 percent of the state's residents—some 250,000 people—have experienced a gambling problem, and an additional 2 percent have experienced a severe gambling problem. That's in the general population. But it's not the whole picture, because gambling problems can vary widely among specific populations. In Massachusetts, among adolescents, 14.6 percent say they've had a gambling problem, and 4.8 percent report a severe problem. People who've been treated for gambling addiction in the past or have been in prison share similar rates of problem gambling, with 17 percent reporting having problems controlling their spending and 15 percent saying they have had a severe problem. Problem gambling is also correlated with depression or other mental illnesses.

Not surprisingly, the greater the availability of legal gambling, the more problem gamblers there are. But those who study gambling addiction or work in counseling avoid blaming the casinos or lotteries. Clinicians don't moralize gambling. The problem lies in people's relationship to gambling and their seeming inability to control their compulsion for it. Despite that reluctance to blame the game, evidence suggests that some games are more "addictive" than others. What often separates these games out is the speed of play. Faster games, instant games, that allow quicker bets tend to be more addictive or to feed compulsion more than slower games, Scanlon says.

In Massachusetts in 2007, more than one third of the calls to the gambling hotline came from people unable to control their lottery gambling. Scratch tickets and keno lead the games among problem lottery gamblers. "The quick results," Scanlon says. "They don't want to wait. People came into our office joking about the twenty-dollar scratch-ticket sweepstakes."

Video Lottery Terminals, or VLTs, are lottery products sold in many states, but they are in a different category. The games are video terminals for fast-paced poker, bingo, blackjack, and keno. They often pay players back a high rate of about 65 cents on each dollar wagered. They mimic the slot machine experience and appeal to serious gamblers. If lotteries say they market to average consumers by pitching lotto and scratch tickets with dreams of life-changing money, VLTs are about the rush of gambling. More than keno, the games have been criticized for being addictive. VLTs have been called the "crack cocaine" of lottery products. Not many states have them; Delaware, Rhode Island, and West Virigina banded together to offer Ca$hola, a video game in which they share profits. New York like several other states relegates its VLTs to race tracks. South Dakota, Montana, and Oregon also have VLTs.

The South Dakota Lottery was the first state to offer them in 1989. Despite approval, the state's heavy dependence on their profits has kept the controversy alive. In 1992 and 2000, they were reapproved in public referendums. In 2006, the South Dakota Supreme Court ordered the state to hold another ballot referendum on VLTs, which turned about $220 million a year in profits split between the state's education budget and the businesses that have the games. More than 60 percent of voters chose VLTs.

In 1994, in between ballot referendums, the state tried an experiment. It turned the machines off for three months. The number of gamblers seeking help for addiction fell by more than 90 percent. Nearly all of South Dakota's compulsive gamblers that had been in treatment reported problems controlling their VLT spending. At the time South Dakota had more GA meetings per capita than any other state besides Montana, which was the only state that had more VLTs than South Dakota.

VLTs, like keno, turn instant profits for the states that have them. Despite lobbying efforts most states seriously consider them only in times of fiscal crisis.

"Prohibition is not the answer," Scanlon says. Most people gamble and have fun. The problem is not the lottery ticket or the horse track or casino. The problem lies not in the game or gambling device but the gambler's compulsive behavior. But most gambling-addiction specialists acknowledge that it doesn't help addicts that the lotteries and casinos put out advertisements promoting attractive prizes and the excitement of gambling.

For Cavanagh, addiction is an unfortunate side effect of any gambling operation, but the minority 6 percent who might have trouble with their gambling is outweighed by the needs of the state and the nearly $1 billion annually it profits from gambling. "With more advertising and more aggressive campaigning, I can reach more people that I can entice to play our games to the benefit of the greater good than would be affected negatively by what I do," Cavanagh says.

The lottery has a great sales pitch. Who, besides a wealthy person, doesn't occasionally dream about being wealthy? It's a popular dream and the lottery sells it cheap. "It's a dollar," Cavanagh says. "It's the change in the floor of your car. When you open up the idea, am I creating someone with a gambling problem? I certainly hope not. I hope they don't go on to robbing banks to try to win it, but if I can get them to buy a piece of that dream for a buck, it helps the state. And they get a kick out of it. And somebody's got to win, too. I think there are a lot of people out there that I can get to like that."

It was the lottery's ability to "get to people" that bugged Tom Birmingham. Around the same time that Robert was buying his first scratch tickets in the early 1990s, Birmingham, the state Senate president, attacked the lottery for targeting the poor in their advertisements.

More than altruism motivated Birmingham's fight with the lottery—
there was money. He represented Chelsea, a low income suburb just
north of downtown Boston, where residents spend an average of
$900 per capita on lottery tickets every year. The people of Chelsea
spend more than the state average and triple what wealthy towns
such as Milton spend on lottery tickets. Birmingham saw a lot of
money leaving his hometown, but didn't see much coming back.
The state disperses its lottery profits to 351 towns and cities, but not
based on how much money they spend on the lottery. Strictly by the
math, residents of Chelsea were paying for public services in towns
such as Milton because they gave so much more to the lottery than
they got back.

   "We could demonstrate the Robin Hood in reverse nature of the
lottery," Birmingham says. "We are asking poor people to finance
government. There's no question about the regressivity of participation in the lottery." To add insult to injury, Birmingham felt that the
lottery took advantage of this imbalance by targeting the poorer districts in advertisements. He recalls one ad that asked, "How do you
become a millionaire?" It offered the suggestion to work hard in high
school, get great grades, work hard in college, get more great grades,
get a job with a big company and work real hard, and after forty years
you'll be a millionaire. Or, the ad suggested, play the lottery. The
message was hardly geared to people on the professional track. He
moved to kill their ad budget. Lottery officials complained that slash-
ing their marketing budget was going to hurt the state budget. But
lottery spending kept rising even without the ads. "Every corner store
was a bookie joint when I was a kid, and nobody advertised," says
Birmingham.

   Not only do states advertise their lottery games, they are exempt, as government bodies, from the Federal Trade Commission standards that govern truth in advertising. In some cases, under pressure from lottery critics, states such as Missouri, North Carolina, and others have adopted their own broad, yet vague restrictions, banning ads that induce people to gamble or depict the lottery as a way of solving personal financial problems. Often these restrictions are scaled back when they conflict with strong sales. In accordance with its determination to protect states' rights, the Federal Communications Commission does bar broadcasters in nonlottery states from advertising lotteries in neighboring states. The Supreme Court upheld this rule in a 1993 case against a North Carolina broadcaster, 90 percent of whose viewers were in Virginia, that ran ads for the Virginia Lottery.

Birmingham has a law degree from Harvard but is the son of a longshoreman and a secretary from Chelsea. In 1992, the town was approaching bankruptcy, and according to one report, citizens of the town spent more on lottery tickets than they did on property taxes. The same year, the Massachusetts Lottery spent more then $11 million on advertising.

In his battle to win equitable lottery revenue for his district, Birmingham could have copied the playbook of Chicago's Mayor Richard J. Daley, who announced in 1976 that he was starting a city-only lottery to compete with the lucrative Illinois Lottery. The Illinois game, little more than a year old, had sold $144 million in tickets, most of them in the Chicago metropolitan area. Daley wanted the city to get its fair share of profits.

Birmingham chose to play hardball by gutting the state lottery's advertising budget. In 1993, he led the state legislature to cut the lottery's ad budget by half, over objections from Governor William Weld, who wanted to protect the money. The ad budget would have been slashed further but Birmingham let the lottery keep some marketing money in exchange for restrictions on direct-mail ads in poor districts. He also tried to force a bill through that would have required the state to print the odds of each prize, but the governor struck the idea down. The fight was heated and personal. The Republican governor and treasurer accused Birmingham of playing politics with the state budget, warning citizens that Birmingham was risking shortfalls in public funding. But lottery sales kept rising, year after year. And year after year Birmingham kept pushing for more cuts, until by 1996 the lottery was limited to $400,000 worth of advertising, plus in-store signs.

"This level of funding and restriction places the lottery in 'unknown territory,'" the lottery commission's executive director wrote to the governor's budget director. "The distinct possibility exists that no revenue growth will occur." Lottery sales rose again that year.

On its Web site, the Massachusetts Lottery offers an official chronology of significant events in its history. This time line does not mention the protracted fight over its advertising to the poor. The chronology does point out that in 2003 the lottery secured $5 million in advertising funds. The $5 million was secured a few months after Birmingham left office following a failed run for governor.

For a brief period, on the heels of Birmingham's attack on lottery advertising, a number of states were inspired to try to restrict their lotteries' marketing. In Nebraska, a proposal to prohibit ads that were "enticing" people to play died on the vine. Iowa's legislature took one look at their House majority leader's bill to prohibit the lottery from using broadcast ads and killed it before it even reached a committee.

After leaving the state Senate, Birmingham joined a white-shoe law firm. A few years removed from the Massachusetts political slugfest, he enjoys an office twenty floors above Copley Plaza. The glass-enclosed conference room has views of the Charles River and Boston Harbor. From his perch in the statehouse Birmingham helped to give Massachusetts a minimum wage of $6.75 and to reform education funding, but as soon as he went out the door, the tide swept the lottery advertising budget back in.

"The Massachusetts Lottery, for better or for worse—and I really mean you can characterize it either way—is well run and efficient as a business," Birmingham says. "Whether that's a badge of honor or an emblem of shame depends on what you think about the relationship between government and the people and gambling."

By 2005, the lottery had doubled its ad budget to $10 million. It stretched its wings with a new ad campaign: "Did you know that when you play the lottery, you can't lose?" The slogan received some criticism. The lottery argued that everybody who plays the lottery wins because the money goes back to towns and cities. It still doesn't go back proportionate to local spending on tickets.

WHEN HE GOT to work, Robert closed his office door behind him, sat down, and called the help line posted on a sign in the store. A woman answered, listened to him, and suggested he attend a Gamblers Anonymous meeting. "Can't I take care of this by myself or at least gamble less?" he asked. That doesn't usually work, she replied.

No one had ever told him that he was gambling too much. In the gas stations and convenience stores where he lost thousands of dollars, the cashiers and owners never suggested that he spent too much on lottery tickets. They were only too happy to take his money. He understood. He was a businessman, too. A few days after the phone call, he went to a GA meeting. More than four years later, he hasn't gambled since, he says. Hundreds of people come through the meetings; only a handful stay clean a year or more, he says. Many come in once and are never seen again.

If Robert had landed the big one, a quarter of a million or half a million, he says, "I would be still gambling. All of the drudgery and losses would have been wiped out by the great win. But I only had all the losses and the drudgery and the misery and the anxiety and the heartache, and I never had any big wins. It was so bad, I don't want to dip my foot in that mess again." Robert chased his dream of winning riches for nearly a decade. The closest he came was the $10,000. "That's part of my disaster," he says. "I expected to have won many huge amounts of money the way I was gambling."

Everybody in his GA meetings expected that day. On the day he won that $10,000, he had been playing scratch tickets for seven years and had spent about $200,000. The losses didn't matter to him because he knew that he was going to win $500,000 or $1 million any day. The big win would justify all of his losses, prove himself a winner to all the people who looked down their noses at lottery players. "I was on my way to getting a huge amount of money," he says, and slaps his desk. "I was on my way."

As much as he respects GA's teachings, he doesn't accept the GA mantra that gambling addicts are "powerless" over their habit, that it is an illness. "When I was gambling I was powerless over gambling, but am I still powerless now that I'm clean?" he asks. Robert does not believe that he is powerless or sick. He believes that he quit gambling through personal resolve. "Are you a man or are you a bum? That's what it amounts to," he says. He keeps this opinion to himself because he knows it would insult some members and conflicts with Gamblers Anonymous teachings. He still depends on the meetings because the stories he hears from other compulsive gamblers remind him of what's at risk if he slips up, and he enjoys helping the others with his own advice.

It was the convenience of lottery gambling that drew in Robert. "I would love at any time to take a $20 bill and get two $10 tickets because it might be a winner. When I walk into a convenience store and I look up and there's a $10 ticket—I want to gamble." He trembles with anger toward the lottery and toward the governor for proposing casinos in Massachusetts. If only the lottery officials or the governor would come to one of his meetings, he says, and see how gambling can destroy people. Some lottery players at his meetings describe wrestling with their addiction every time they enter a grocery store. "There are numerous cases where people only have two or five dollars and they enter convenience stores to buy food and they end up buying lottery tickets," he says. Some describe spending their last dollar on tickets.

One friend with a gambling problem got a $300 coupon for an online casino. The friend had been clean for three months. "I can't believe you're even thinking of using it," he told his friend. "You should sue the casino for interfering with your efforts to stay clean."

"I want to gamble," Robert says. "Every day I want to gamble, but I can't start on that road."

Robert stopped gambling cold after his first GA meeting because the stories he heard stunned him. He feels that he got out before he was too badly hurt. He stopped before it destroyed his life. Other compulsive gamblers lost wives and families, are buried in debt, suffer depression, and, in some cases, commit suicide. His family is now proud of him, more so than for anything else he's done in his life.

During Robert's lottery years, the bills got paid, but not without resentment. When his wife would mention bills or something she needed to buy he cut her off. She tried to stop him from gambling for two or three years before he finally quit. There were times when she took tickets from his hands and threw them away.

Once, he left a $1,000 prize–winning scratch ticket in the car door compartment. His wife found it and showed it to their son. When Robert asked if she had seen the lost ticket she told him that they had looked at it and decided it wasn't a winner. They tore it up and threw it away. Robert found the ticket in shreds in a trash can at the office and carefully taped it back together. At the lottery headquarters they told him he would have to wait for the ticket to be verified. When he raised a fuss and called over a state trooper standing nearby, the lottery paid him the money.

Now that he's clean, his wife reminds him of how mean he would be to her over money. If he ever gambles again, she tells him, she'll leave him. Now, when she wants to buy something for herself or to take a trip, he quickly agrees. "It's only gambling money," he tells her.

"I say to her, 'You should have bought two pairs of shoes. I'm way ahead. I'm not gambling.'"

Not long after he gave up scratch tickets, Robert stopped at a convenience store on his gambling route. It was the same store where he had cashed checks. The owner lit up, happy to see a regular and valued customer. "I'm not going to do this anymore," Robert told him. The man looked at him and marveled out loud over how much Robert had spent in the store—maybe $50,000. Robert didn't respond. People were standing behind him in line; other players were within earshot, scratching away.

"This is bad," Robert finally said loudly, pointing to the scratch cards behind the counter.

The owner gestured him to the side and said in a low voice, "I know, but I'm making a hundred thousand a year."

As the first year went past, workers in Robert's favorite stores, without asking, would pull $10 tickets down from the dispenser as soon as he walked up to the counter. He takes an enormous amount of pride in ignoring their actions. Outwardly, he puts on an expression of total indifference to the lottery tickets they offer. It feels good, he says.

CHAPTER 8

THE BUSINESS

IN APRIL 2007, two months after Governor Arnold Schwarzenegger officially appointed her to run the California State Lottery, Joan Borucki boarded a plane for Washington, D.C. For the next two days she would attend a lottery-industry conference and, briefly, leave behind the headache she had just accepted. The conference provided an opportunity to mingle with lottery executives from other states, hear some new ideas in an industry she was still learning, and present a bit of good news in what had been a miserable year for the California State Lottery. Sales were down after two years of record profits. One of her first tasks on the job had been to inform the legislature that the lottery could not deliver the money it had promised for schools that year.

The lottery had tried to get out in front of the bad news before making a public announcement about the drop-off in sales. Its officials told legislators, education officials, newspapers, anyone in a position to know. They hoped it would soften the blow about what was happening. They didn't want scare stories in the newspapers about budget shortfalls or grandstanding condemnations from elected officials. No surprises.

Like many lottery states, California earmarks its lottery profits for education. In California at least thirty-four cents of every dollar players spent on the lottery must go to K–12 public schools. As Borucki held her first staff meetings in 2007, it was clear that educational revenue from the lottery was about $160 million short. In the grand scheme of things, this was not a lot of money; California's education budget was about $66 billion for the year. The lottery contributes just over $1 billion—less than 2 percent. The $160 million deficit wasn't good, but it was almost a rounding error when everything was counted.

Nevertheless, the perception persists that public education is propped up by lottery dollars. Much of the blame for the confusion lies with government. Nearly every state has, at one time or another, sought public approval for its lottery by exaggerating the benefits of lottery dollars to government. The California Lottery openly blames the state for overselling it as a source of education funding to win approval in a public ballot initiative in 1984.

During the eighties and nineties, lotteries provided a fountain of cash for many states. But since the mid-1990s, lottery dollars have become less and less relevant as a percentage of government revenue, usually accounting for no more than 2 percent of the budget. Yet, in an effort to boost their brand, states continue to brag about the lottery's benefits to education, parks, sports programs, and other public trusts. The misperception lives on. And it had Borucki in hot water. If the lottery was short on cash, it was shortchanging kids—that's what people were saying. By getting out and explaining the situation and how lottery funding works, Borucki hoped to win over some key sympathetic ears.

"It's relatively small, yet the perception is that schools are flush with funding as a result of all this lottery money," the California schools superintendent, Jack O'Connell, told the *Los Angeles Times* when Borucki's bad news was released. But his words were largely lost in the bigger story: the California State Lottery was failing kids and teachers.

And the story was true in a more significant way. California's lottery was failing, but a kid without books was not Borucki's biggest problem. The real challenge was that the California State Lottery was, by many measures, the worst in the country. At heart, lotteries are a retail business, and California's had been underperforming for years. California has thirty-six million people and a $1.6 trillion gross domestic product. It is practically a nation unto itself. Yet, its lottery sales rank last among the ten most populous states. The most successful state, Massachusetts, has a population of 6.4 million people; it sold $4.5 billion in lottery products in 2006. California had $3.5 billion in sales. While residents of Massachusetts spend $700 a year on their lottery, Californians wager just $98 a head. It follows that it also ranks last among the ten largest states in per capita lottery dollars sent to government.

Schwarzenegger gave Borucki control of a multibillion-dollar business in drastic need of help. She had worked for the lottery for less than a year, but she had one significant qualification to run the agency. She was unafraid. During the twenty-five years she had worked for the state, mostly on transportation, she had established a reputation for rattling bureaucracy with aggressive, if unpopular, initiatives.

In the late 1990s, Borucki sued the state Department of Transportation with a group of four other women, for gender discrimination. The women alleged that they were unfairly targeted for demotion under a new director. The suit was settled out of court. Schwarzenegger appointed her director of the California Transportation Commission, and later to the California Performance Review, which was created to come up with ways to cut the fat from state bureaucracy.

Borucki recommended gutting the Transportation Commission. Her reputation as a bureaucrat with steely nerves grew.

"It probably was not the smartest political thing to recommend that your own job be eliminated or merged into someone else's," she says. "But in my mind it made sense for government. It was the right thing to do."

In 2004, Schwarzenegger named her interim director of the state Department of Motor Vehicles. Running the DMV is no pencil pusher's job in the state that put road rage on the map. Borucki immediately ran into trouble with an idea she had to tax drivers based on the mileage they drove (rather than on their gas consumption). It smacked of favoring gas-guzzlers such as the governor, who famously drove a Hummer. The other roadblock was logistical: all drivers would have to outfit their cars with a global positioning device so the state could track them. Borucki's idea was ridiculed in the legislature and the press. She was accused of trying to turn California into a Huxleyan Brave New World. Her popularity in the legislature fell even lower when she sided with Governor Schwarzenegger against giving driver's licenses to undocumented immigrants. When the governor nominated her to run the DMV full-time, the legislature blocked her. "Given the magnitude of the job and the magnitude of the challenges facing us, the candidate was not prepared for those challenges," one state Senate opponent told the *Sacramento Bee*.

After that fiasco, she was more than prepared to weather the migraine of declining lottery-ticket sales. Already, as her plane touched down in Washington, D.C., the lottery had prepared a three-year plan to turn the business around. But the California Lottery was a slow ship to turn and it was on the governor's radar. As a native of Massachusetts, the state's first lady, Maria Shriver, had noticed the miserable performance of the lottery compared to her home state.

"Her issue was always 'Why aren't we like them?'" Borucki says. "'Why aren't we selling like them? What's going on?'"

One of the problems was that the California Lottery operates under legal restrictions no other large-state lottery has, such as the insistence that, after overhead, 34 percent of everything go back to the state, regardless of the game. Nearly every other state has rewritten its lottery laws to make its lottery products more attractive, particularly scratch tickets, by giving more back to players. Massachusetts, which returns 76 percent of its scratch-ticket sales in prizes, leads the pack. New York gives back 68 percent to players. It's a profitable formula that lowers odds on scratch tickets and keeps players coming back for more. In an instant-win game, players get frustrated fast when they never see an instant win.

Hampered by legislation, California gives only 56 percent of scratch-ticket sales back to players, meaning there are fewer prizes. And while other states pile on profits from $10 and $20 scratch tickets, California's most expensive is $5. More than a quarter of national instant-ticket sales come from high-end scratch tickets—a percentage that is growing—but California doesn't even sell them. It cannot afford $100,000 or $1 million prize payouts because the legislature demands the lion's share for state education across the board.

"That would be one of the legislative changes we would like to see happen," Borucki says. "But it's also one of the more controversial changes, in particular with our beneficiary, their fear being that somehow if they're not guaranteed the thirty-four percent on every dollar, that they're going to get something less than they get today."

Still, in the gambling industry it's nearly irrefutable that more money for prizes means more sales because the games have better odds and better prizes. In general, casinos return about 90 percent of the money gamblers spend on slot machines back to players as prizes.

If no one ever won anything, few people would gamble. Over the years, most state lotteries have crept closer to this sales formula—occasionally satisfied customers will play more often, even if they lose more than they win. California had always balked at the idea—the games were for government, not gambling.

State laws bar the lottery from updating its technology and from using popular scratch-ticket themes such as Lucky 7s, dice, and slot machines because they reference gambling. The state and the lottery can't agree on how to run the operation. "Show me another private company that's making thirty-four percent profit with only three percent overhead," Borucki says. "You're not going to find anything out there like that. They have to think of us, and compare us to, something like Williams-Sonoma that has about the same kind of annual sales numbers as the California Lottery. That's a phenomenal thing to be able to do. So when they start criticizing me about the per capita and comparisons with other lotteries, and all that, it's 'Okay, remember, you've got me in this box, and we have been in that box since day one.'"

Borucki needed the legislature to loosen the chains. That was the real challenge, made nearly impossible because she and the lottery were unpopular in the state capital. She needed to make inroads with elected officials, but it was hard to build clout as a virtual lame duck: Borucki was the nineteenth lottery director in twenty-two years. There was no track record for the job. Luckily, Arnold had her back. She had proven her loyalty.

The legislature was three thousand miles away when her plane touched down on a cloudless day at the height of the Washington's cherry-blossom festival. She had good reason to be optimistic. Borucki had saved a bit of sunshine to present to her colleagues at La Fleur's 12th Annual Lottery Symposium. She was scheduled to share the good news on the morning of the first day of the conference: despite the legal chains that bound it, the lottery had managed to expand into a new market. Lottery tickets were for sale in Costco and other big-box chains. It was a breakthrough into mainstream retail that state lotteries have dreamed of for years.

"I was really touting at the time a change in the basic business model that the lottery uses with its retailers, which I think is just so critical if we're going to move forward in any vein with new retail-trade styles," Borucki says. "I was anxious to get some feedback." Her upbeat presentation was part of a two-day conference of PowerPoint presentations from lottery workers from around the country and their attendant industries. The attendees controlled the full life span of lottery products from conception to cash register. There were state lottery directors, their marketing and production executives, representatives of GTECH and Scientific Games, the printing companies that make scratch tickets, manufacturers of the plastic shelving units that hold the cards, and nearly everyone with a hand in bringing lottery games to market.

Most of the people worked for the government. The men and women who run state lotteries inhabit a small, unique corner of the world. They don't talk like civil servants. Instead, they speak in terms from the retail industry: point of purchase, product cannibalism, customer base, and emerging markets. Many lottery directors earn salaries that are close, if not equivalent, to those for a private company with several billion in sales. Most notable among them, in part for her salary, is the veteran Tennessee Lottery director, Rebecca Paul Hargrove, whose salary, including bonuses, has reached $750,000. States defend the high lottery salaries because these state employees compete in the retail sales industry, not government.

"You're basically a private corporation that's all about sales, and what it takes to get those sales, but at the same time trying to stay cognitive of the social responsibility that you have as an arm of state government," Borucki says. "Sometimes those things work together, sometimes they don't."

Whether in government or sales, at the end of the day it's all about the bottom line. But straddling the line between public and private can be awkward. On one hand, lottery bosses—state governors and legislatures—want lottery workers to bring home as much money as possible. If they fail to increase sales of their gambling product, they catch heat. On the other hand, the workers' job is to encourage the public to gamble, not something most politicians want to be associated with. Back home, most of the conference attendees are isolated from government. Lotteries are low on most political priority lists. Few elected officials understand or take an interest in how they operate beyond the amount of revenue they return. Politically, lotteries are dangerous. As a result, most state governments do not want to hear from the lottery unless it's to announce that sales are rising and more money is going into education or senior-citizen programs or the state general fund. "We went around and actually met with every one of the legislators or their staff. Almost every one of them said, 'We haven't heard from the lottery in years,'" Borucki says.

Most lotteries, particularly in larger states under greater media scrutiny, are wary of press coverage unless it's a feel-good story about a big winner, or a lost ticket found, or an upcoming mega-jackpot. Stories outside those areas are often negative. There are a few boilerplate stories about winners who ended in ruin—"the curse of the lottery," as one television documentary called it. Analytical articles often point out sales demographics to show that lotteries exploit the poor. If a lottery tries to boost sales through marketing and it misfires, it can find itself accused of predatory advertising. The lottery gets called on the carpet for duping the gullible and stealing dollars from the poor by advertising impossible dreams of wealth. At the time of the La Fleur's conference, several states were smarting from the bad press they were getting over low sales. Nationwide, sales were slow. Reports were coming out, not just in California, that disappointing sales meant that the state government wasn't getting what it is supposed to from the lottery. Everyone was searching for new ways to make more money and stave off criticism back home. Borucki wasn't the only lottery director under the gun to improve her product.

It is not surprising, then, that lottery officials, caught between their sensitive government overseers and unpredictable press attention, tend to be reticent. I was told that I could attend the La Fleur's symposium without paying the $1,400 registration fee, but only if I agreed not to print the name of the conference or its location. The host, La Fleur's Lottery World, is a small, family-run business that collects and sells worldwide lottery data, publishes a trade magazine, and hosts industry forums. It was under no obligation to let reporters in for free. While their finances are public, lotteries are not accustomed to discussing their business and marketing practices and strategies so openly with the public and are not particularly trustful when journalists examine the business. I paid the fee.

Annual conferences such as the La Fleur's symposium or the North American Association of State and Provincial Lotteries gathering are some of the few chances lottery officials have to discuss the business in their own language. They share information on what products show potential for sales growth and which are lost causes. They discuss how the lottery ticket comes to market. A lot of research and thought goes into each product before it reaches the convenience store. Scratch-ticket colors have to be chosen for optimal sales; the print run of a raffle game has to be calculated against estimated sales to make sure it sells out quickly. What game can draw in new users to the product? How can we interest younger players? The questions are all aimed at the bottom line. The lottery is a retail business more than a government bureaucracy.

In April 2007, the sense across the industry was that the mature lotteries, now more than twenty years old, had saturated their markets. The boom years of the lotteries in the 1980s and 1990s, which saw double-digit growth, were gone forever. Lotteries have slowed down to annual increases of 2 percent, or even zero in many states. Inflation was rising faster than lottery revenue. Keeping the numbers up meant a constant battle for customers and keeping governors and legislatures happy.

Over the two-day conference several states presented their recent attempts to boost sales with new or revamped lottery games. Because they are not in competition with one another, there are no real trade secrets. State lotteries routinely "borrow" one another's ideas. Take the recent spate of raffle games.

"Isn't it a great industry?" a Virginia executive said to the audience. "You look at what everybody did right and say, 'Let's go do that.'" Virginia was one of more than a dozen states that have rolled out million-dollar raffles over the last two years. All of them were modeled after the first one in Pennsylvania. Pennsylvania's "groundbreaking" raffle started in late 2005. The game, though it seemed fresh and creative, was actually a retread of the live lottery drawings that had been popular since the seventeenth century. People bought prenumbered tickets in anticipation of a heavily promoted drawing. The "new" game's appeal was the simplicity of its marketing—the "best chance to win $1 million." In every state that ran a raffle, the odds were about the same—1 in 125,000. The phrase was repeated in marketing around the country. Tickets were $20 or more. The print runs were limited—in Pennsylvania to half a million tickets—giving the game built-in drama and exclusivity. One of the raffle's goals was to make a $1 million prize exciting again. If it worked, it would bring in new players and interest jaded lotto players.

Florida's Millionaire Raffle was the most ambitious entry in the trend and the subject of a talk to the La Fleur's crowd given by Florida's online-product manager, Vicki Munroe. Florida wanted to disprove the industry belief that raffles have a short life span: the novelty starts to wear thin after the first drawing and drops every time the game is repeated. Florida's campaign set out to "brand" its raffle game and make it a staple of their gambling line. The state trumpeted the message—borrowed from Pennsylvania—that it was a player's "Best Shot at a Million!" "We created a sense of urgency," Munroe said. "We used words like 'hurry,' 'limited,' 'sellout.' We just used it all the way through any of our materials and anything that we said."

They kept their print run low, 1.25 million, to ensure the $25 tickets would sell out fast and become a hard-to-get, and seemingly exclusive item. Inspired by the odds and the ads, players bought 250,000 tickets the first day. The tickets were gone in eleven days. Through the computer network that connected the convenience-store terminals that printed the tickets, the lottery officials watched the sales in real time from their Tallahassee headquarters. As the tickets dwindled, the state broadcast text messages to the store computers— "Don't let the excitement pass you by." They watched sales jump within minutes.

"We had a fully integrated communication plan for every stage of this game's life," Munroe said. As soon as the last ticket was sold, the Florida Lottery kicked in phase two. They flashed the message SOLD OUT across convenience stores' ticket machines and on their Web site. They gave the raffle the rock-concert treatment. The SOLD

OUT notice was immediately followed with the reminder that "scratch-off games make good gifts."

"People said the reason they didn't play was because it was sold out," Munroe told her colleagues. "The truth of the matter is they may not even have been planning to play, but the fact that they saw that it sold out, it makes it more valuable for next time." The raffle mania made local news. "We haven't gotten that kind of press for a lotto in a long time," Munroe said. People tried to sell tickets on eBay, which was illegal. Eventually, someone was clever enough to sell a paper bag that happened to contain some raffle tickets.

For all of the energy expended, the $31.25 million in raffle ticket sales was almost invisible in Florida's $4 billion gross sales. It did add to the bottom line, however. Perhaps more important, the lottery believed the raffle brought in new players. There was reason to listen to what Florida was doing because unlike in many states, lottery sales there had grown by almost 10 percent.

Munroe stepped away from the podium to join conference organizer Terri La Fleur in a semicircle of chairs in the middle of the stage. "You repackage an old idea and suddenly it seems brand-new to the public out there," La Fleur said excitedly.

Borucki and others in the room took mental notes; Florida was doing something right. California had plans of its own to boost sales, including a big New Year's Raffle for 2008 and a revamped televised lottery drawing.

In the search for increased sales Georgia had succeeded in repackaging an old idea as well. The lottery needed a boost in revenue after meager 2.5 percent profit growth the previous year. The state's sales and marketing executives recounted for the conference how they had resurrected their dying keno game by marketing as a social game to play in bars. It was no small feat, considering that keno gets criticized for turning its devotees into zombies. Keno players stare as if hypnotized at numbers flashing on television screens. Because of its quick pace—the game resets every few minutes—keno is widely believed to be more addictive than lottery tickets. Keno also carries a darker taint of gambling than do lottery tickets because it's a staple in casinos.

Georgia voters had approved the lottery by the meager majority of 52 percent in 1993, so the state tucked controversial keno games into convenience stores, mostly in rural areas. The young lottery didn't want to push keno down people's throats and be accused of encouraging gambling. The game, suffering from lack of support and bad placement, had slowly been dying for a more than a decade. Sales were down from a peak of $1.5 million a week to about $650,000. It needed a makeover. "We wanted to brand ourselves as entertainment, not gaming," said Jack Dimling, the Georgia Lottery's vice president for sales.

After ten years the moral objections to keno had subsided, so the state undertook an aggressive relaunch, focused on bars in urban areas. One of their first steps was to go to the Web site of the Alcohol and Tobacco Division of the Georgia Department of Revenue and print out a list of all the liquor-license holders. "We wanted locations that had regulars in there," said James Hutchinson, the lottery's vice president of marketing. "People who came in and hung out. The *Cheers* kind of places . . . Of course we wanted locations that worked to keep patrons in there, that offered happy hours and karaoke and other entertainment pieces."

The state pulled its keno games from half of the convenience stores. Near comatose people staring at a television in the back of a convenience store did not jibe with the game's new slogan: "Great friends. Great fun. Keno." They printed scorecards in McDonald's colors—yellow letters on a red background. The lottery's ad agency created a mascot, Keno Master, a white-bearded, Zen-like teacher copied from kung fu movies. Keno Master delivered catch phrases to players: "If no keno seed planted, how can wallet grow?" "Keno slip in hand is better than two in holder." They fiddled with the computer-programmed game so that it paid out more money on Saturday afternoons and Monday nights when the bars were filled with sports fans. "We kind of owned Mondays in a lot of bar businesses," Dimling said. They ran on-site promotions, letting people try the game for free, teaching people in bars how to fill in the scorecards and place bets.

In 2007, a little more than a year after the relaunch, Georgia's keno had sales of $1.4 million a week and was projected to reach $2 million a week by the end of 2008. Like Florida's raffle revenue, the $75 million or so from keno was not a massive influx of cash to the Georgia Lottery or state education. It was an incremental profit increase with expectations for a long life. More significant, it was a profit increase made under pressure to increase sales.

Few speakers directly addressed the pressure and responsibility of funding government during the conference. But it was the motivation behind such aggressive product placements as Florida's Millionaire Raffle and Georgia's keno. The Florida Lottery made $1.26 billion for public schools, school construction, state universities, and college scholarships in the fiscal year that spanned 2006 and 2007. Like the California State Lottery, Florida's lottery provides just a fraction, 4 percent, of the $32 billion spent on education. In Georgia, the $822 million in lottery dollars has a greater impact and accounts for 4.5 percent of all state revenues. The money is earmarked for college scholarships and pre-K programs, to avoid the chance that it could be used to replace the core K–12 public education budget of about $9.5 billion.

A unique solution to the pressure to increase sales came from outside the United States, when Jussi Isotalo, executive vice president of Finland's lottery, Veikkaus Oy, stepped to the microphone. There are lotteries on every continent and the few companies that service them are increasingly international, so it was not unusual to have a representative of the Finnish lottery at the conference. What was unique was his call for restraint.

"How many of you have been there to witness your lottery revenue rise over twenty percent a year?" Isotalo asked the audience. About two dozen people raised their hands. "Those who raised your hands, did you get a pay raise or a promotion?" They laughed. "Did the governor tell you that's all very nice, but next year we won't need any more? How about public reactions? Were you being praised by the media for good work?" Some listeners tittered.

Isotalo recalled that one year he returned more than a 20 percent sales increase. He happily reported back to the Ministry of Cultural Education, where he was told, "You guys are creating problems. Your marketing is too aggressive. Next year we expect you to get the same growth rate, but no more aggressive marketing."

"I learned quickly," Isotalo told his colleagues in his heavily accented, joking manner. "I haven't done it since." Finland's lottery maintains a goal of slow, incremental increases of about 2 percent a year, he said. Money spent on lottery games has increased slightly more than the average purchasing power of the Finnish public.

"If a game attracts people, it is also addictive," Isotalo said. "Thus if we want our lottery to be socially responsible, a good corporate citizen, we must only offer games so dull that nobody gets hooked." That line got the biggest laughs. "You've got the answer. Of course not. Doing so, we would only be pushing our customers into the arms of unscrupulous gaming operators."

Maximizing profits is a Pyrrhic victory, he said. Lotteries needed to step on the brakes sometimes. The boom-year profits come at the cost of increased gambling addiction among the public or unrealistic expectations from politicians. "Greed is not good for this brand," Isotalo told the lottery crowd. "You might not take my advice, but I give it anyway."

Isotalo was in startling contrast to the other speakers, who waxed enthusiastically about their aggressive efforts and success in getting people to buy more lottery tickets. "Aggressive supply and problem gambling may ruin our brand," Isotalo said. "We do want people to love us." He entertained the crowd with his humor, but no one rallied around his message. It was, after all, a sales conference, and held in a time of widespread stagnation. There was too much risk of coming up short.

"That's a worry I have about the industry overall. How far can we really take this industry? Where is the new product development in this industry? You can only sell the same old product so often," Borucki says.

Most players in California are more than forty years old. For an industry with plateauing sales it's not a good demographic to build a future on. There is little growth with an older customer base. People who are older have set expenses and responsibilities to caution them against lottery tickets. Everyone in the lottery industry talks about capturing the youth market. A youthful customer can become a customer for life and ensure the future life of the product. Every retailer wants to capture the youth market. The difference with lotteries is that it is the government and it's talking about selling gambling to youth. The oddity of this, on an ethical or moral level, does not register during conversations about sales at industry conventions, however. Sales are sales. The executives need to maximize sales or they have failed in their job.

Borucki, facing decreases in sales, says she'd prefer moderate annual growth, a few percentage points, rather than the old days of double-digits increases. It's easy to say that since those days aren't coming back, but flattening profits have created a psychological change in the lottery industry—stable growth is better because it means no shocks to government. Slow and steady growth is better than dramatic ups and downs, in other words.

"They've got to put together their budget each year based on what they think they're going to get from the lottery," Borucki says. "I'd rather give them some kind of an even number each year that's growing enough to keep them satisfied."

The primary culprit behind the national slowdown in lottery sales was the decline of the lotto-style, jackpot game. Small states that can't generate enough sales to put up their own large, attractive jackpots belong to multistate cooperatives such as Mega Millions or Powerball. Large states hold their own in-state drawings and offer multistate games. Once the financial heartbeat of lotteries, lotto games have topped out and are widely seen as unpredictable. A group of regular, mostly older players adhere to the games consistently, but to get large turnouts the jackpots have to be stratospheric, at least $100 or $200 million for the multistate games. The industry calls it jackpot fatigue. The free press attention and hype will only follow the largest drawings. A jackpot has to break records or top some understood standard of impressiveness to be "newsworthy." As multistate games started reaching $200 and $300 million, the press and the players became jaded over jackpots of $10, $20, or even $90 million. Lotteries became dependent on the flood of sales that followed big jackpots, but they're rare and impossible to predict—a long string of winnerless drawings is needed to get the purse sufficiently large. To counter this problem, lotteries have to increase the number of picks in the game, or the field of numbers to choose from, to make jackpots harder to win. Decreasing the odds in this way should, in the long run, increase play by building large jackpots. But all of this interplay between the lotteries and fickle players has made lotto revenue increasingly unpredictable.

For years now, most states have focused on their scratch tickets. Scratch tickets have overtaken lotto drawings as the bread and butter of the lottery business, selling $28.4 billion in 2006. Scratch-ticket sales tripled over the last ten years as lotto-draw games flatlined. As much as lotteries experiment with new games such as raffles or remake old ones in search of profits, scratch tickets remain the workhorse of all state lotteries. The games offer instant gratification, and better odds (1 in 3 or 1 in 4) of winning something—even if it's only a dollar. Each game usually has a life span of a year or so before it is cycled out of rotation and replaced with a new scratch game. As a product, the games are the most basic form of the lottery. There is little player involvement—no favorite or lucky numbers to pick and no drawing to wait for. The rush of anticipation lasts a few seconds. Many players scratch their tickets inside the store and, if they win a small amount, put the money right back into more tickets, making the glut of small prizes that allow for high odds of winning cost-effective. And because of the lack of fuss, lottery officials understand that these games depend heavily on regular players who don't need or want all of the promotional bells and whistles that come with raffles, keno, or lotto jackpot games.

That isn't to say that scratch-ticket players aren't fickle. States offer players dozens to choose from, each designed in the belief that within the confines of a few square inches of paper stock there is some irresistible draw for players. The latest successful experiment has been to increase profit margins by convincing players that a scratch ticket is worth $10, $20, and even $50 if it promises millions in prizes. In 2006, the $10 scratch tickets made up 19 percent of sales nationwide, while the $1 tickets—once the only tickets available—accounted for 13 percent of sales. Beyond tweaking the price and the odds, marketing innovation in scratch tickets is limited to the face of the ticket itself. That is Gary Smith's area of expertise at the Maryland Lottery, where he is the instant-ticket product manager. Smith oversees the production of fifty-two new games every year for the Maryland Lottery. He shared his arcane knowledge in a presentation entitled "Breaking Through the Clutter at Retail."

"It's no accident that fire engines are the color they are: bright red, bright yellow, bright white, a lot of shiny chrome," he said. "It's certainly no accident that when Ray Kroc designed the golden arches, he picked these colors. Black, believe it or not, is very hot. Not only is it hip, for some strange reason every time we print a primary black ticket in Maryland, it's a winner."

For hard-core ticket scratchers, the color matters less than the basic facts of the game—price, prize payouts, and the odds. But to grab the attention of someone who doesn't play often, a ticket that pops out from the display case can lead to an impulse gambling purchase, just like a candy bar or magazine. One of the companies that makes eye-catching tickets for lotteries is Canada-based Pollard Banknote. About 60 percent of its business comes from U.S. lotteries. The hundred-year-old printing company makes a wide variety of scratch tickets: scented, fluorescent, ones that change colors, or have holograms. "I'm not sure what that says about our society, but for whatever reason the scratch-ticket market is just very healthy," the company's co-CEO, John Pollard, told investors in early 2007.

The company's director of U.S. marketing, Nancy Bettcher, followed Smith onto the stage with her talk: "Capturing Attention at Retail: Quest for Eyeballs and Greenbacks." She related the results of a study of players' habits commissioned by her company. Canadian lotteries are known for their intensive market research. From 2002 to 2006, Pollard Banknote looked at sales patterns of more than four thousand different games from twenty-two different lotteries. She confirmed Smith's assessment that yellow and red tickets sell above average. So do games with the words *seven*, *cash*, and *holiday*. Also, people are more likely to buy a $1 scratch ticket when the top prize is under $1,500. One possible conclusion is that scratch-ticket players see a correlation between the cost of a ticket and the value of its prize—one shouldn't expect to win riches from a cheap ticket. "Overall, odds of winning had no significant relationship with the tickets' success," Bettcher said. "I think that goes quite counter to what a lot of people intuitively think."

If players do not pay attention to the odds, what do they look for? In some cases, it's mass appeal. For both seasoned and impulse players, choosing which scratch ticket to buy is a subjective decision. So a ticket offering a "dream vacation" or pictures of puppies and kittens will sell better than one that doesn't. The Maryland Lottery put out Kitty Cash and Doggy Dough scratch tickets through its contract with Pollard. Both sold well. Scratch tickets linked to licensed images accounted for just $150 million in sales in 2001. In 2006, they sold $2.5 billion. More and more lotteries have paid for the rights to use images from popular movies, TV shows, and professional sports teams on their scratch tickets. Several states put out King Kong scratch tickets when the blockbuster remake came out in 2005. American Idol scratch tickets were sold in California, Washington, Virginia, and other states in attempt to reach the younger market that watches the show. Virginia offered a second-chance drawing on its American Idol tickets, in which players could submit their losing tickets for a consolation-prize drawing. To encourage younger players the state accepted text messages of the losing tickets' code numbers as entries.

Borucki knew the California Lottery needed to join the rest of the country and sell more scratch tickets. It was too dependent on the tired lotto-jackpot draws. But with no sign of help from the state legislature, the lottery chose another avenue by rethinking the entire way it did business. When Borucki took her turn at the podium, she told the assembled executives that the California State Lottery had broken out of the liquor stores, gas stations, convenience stores, and supermarkets that have largely set the boundaries for the industry for thirty years. "That's not where they go anymore," she said of her customers. "They're changing the way they shop."

In deals with Costco, Sears, and the pharmacy chain CVS, the California lottery became one of the first in the nation to sell tickets to big-box retail shoppers. It was too inside-baseball for much newspaper coverage, but in the lottery world it was a big news. California had found a toehold in American family retail. Megastores have taken increasingly large chunks of the nation's retail profits for a decade. In all that time, lotteries had been unable to get their product into the stores. Although it was still an experiment, California had proved that tickets didn't have to be torn off one by one; they could be sold in bulk, at a discount, in plastic clamshells hung from a rack near the Costco cash registers.

The lottery packaged its "Holiday Gift Pack" just in time for the shopping season. For $50 customers got $60 worth of—mostly

$1—scratch tickets and coupons. With no advertising, sales were $500 million in six weeks. Sales at the some of the Sears stores matched convenience-store sales. "The nice part about this is Sears believes they are getting new customers," Borucki said. "Customers are coming in to buy lottery products. We've definitely gained new players. This is going to be a very powerful product for us."

The California Lottery had no choice but to reinvent the way it did business to get the contracts. Big-box chains don't like lottery tickets. They're a pain in the neck to sell. As a retail product, lotteries have three problems, which Borucki referred to as "the Three L's"— lines, labor, and losses. It sums up the complaints state lotteries hear from their convenience-store vendors. People who buy lottery tickets tie up employees, clog stores with lines that annoy people who just want a cup of coffee or some cigarettes, and only bring in a 5 percent or 6 percent profit. The situation was bad enough that in 1996 convenience-store owners hired Ernst & Young to study the effect lotteries have on their business. The consultants came back with good news and bad news. The good news was that 65 percent of the adult customers in convenience stores were playing the lottery. Frequent players—those who play at least once a week—made 4.5 trips to a convenience store each week and spent $7 per visit or $1,600 over a year. The bad news was that customers who buy lottery tickets cost the store more money than the other customers. To sell a lottery ticket the store has to deal with the customer, balance ticket sales against the cash register, cash winning tickets, check its ticket inventory and display cases, and deal with complaints about lost or stolen tickets. It was a lot of labor for a low-profit-margin product. Selling a candy bar turns a better profit margin without the headaches. The Ernst & Young study concluded that convenience stores make a 6 percent profit on lottery players' purchases and a 19 percent profit on

customers who don't gamble. The North American Association of State and Provincial Lotteries (NASPL)—the umbrella organization for American, Canadian, and Caribbean lotteries—responded to the study by issuing a set of suggested "initiatives" designed to speed up the sales process. Lotteries put bar codes on tickets and other time-saving devices to speed things up at the cash register.

It still wasn't fast enough for large-scale retail. Megastores have succeeded on a formula of high-volume, discounted sales, labor effi-ciency, and quick lines. The California lottery met those demands by selling a prepackaged, discounted collection of lottery tickets off the rack. It was not a product for regular players or those who wondered what tickets were lucky or due for a win or had the best odds. Those kinds of questions are for serious scratch-ticket players. People bought the gift pack on a whim as a stocking stuffer. "Why aren't we just sell-ing the product there like everybody else sells a product?" Borucki asked her colleagues.

Some supermarket chains elsewhere sold lottery tickets, and so did some Kmart stores, but California was first into big-box retail. Canada had beaten America into big-box retail. Before California's deals with Sears and Costco, the Ontario Lottery and Gaming Corpo-ration sold tickets at Home Depot and Wal-Mart, the two giants of the mega-retail industry. Roy Bortolussi, the Ontario Lottery's director of marketing, called them "power centers" in his presentation to the sym-posium. "It's considered a stage for the masses and we have a product that appeals to the masses, so the consumer fit is absolutely perfect," Bortolussi said. "Needless to say we were able to crack the nut."

For Ontario, getting inside had been the end of a long chase, during which the lottery's account director had kept a photo of Wal-Mart's Omaha headquarters on the wall across from his desk like

a great white whale. With three hundred stores and a dozen more opening each year, Wal-Mart was the fastest-growing thing in Canada. Once inside the doors, the Ontario Lottery sold aggressively. It set up brightly colored kiosks near the store's entrances, decorated with as many signs as possible, and handed out coupons for tickets. Sales at Home Depot and Wal-Mart soon rose faster than convenience-store sales.

But kiosks were too expensive for California. Besides, the lottery was trying to blend into the retail model of the big chains, not pitch a tent inside their stores. In Sears and Costco, it marketed scratch tickets as an impulse purchase. In the spirit of cutting out the labor, lines, and losses, California focused on automation and self-service. When the pharmacy giant CVS bought out a competing chain, Save-On, California offered to install scratch-ticket vending machines and do everything except count the money. The store manager's only job was to call if the machine broke. The state even offered CVS a discount that convenience-store owners didn't get. The contract was on a trial basis, but if it succeeded, CVS might put scratch-ticket vending machines in all 350 of its California stores. The vending machines had the added advantage of attracting younger customers, Borucki said. "The younger demographics prefer the self-service and are more comfortable than with face-to-face interaction," she said, repeating an industry truism. "Our older demographic prefers that face-to-face interaction."

There was one drawback. It turned out that CVS was responsible for making sure no one under eighteen years old bought tickets. "We're looking at adding some features to our game points to check driver's licenses for age," Borucki told the La Fleur's audience. "My staff cringes every time I say that, because they're just convinced we're going to lose at least half our sales." They worry that customers will get frustrated and give up if they have to submit to automated ID checks. Gamblers like their privacy. But as Borucki put it, "I'd rather face that than face the legislature taking my budget away from me because I'm contributing to underage gambling."

California's inroad into unexplored retail territory was Borucki's good news. After twenty years of selling tickets through cashiers at liquor and convenience stores, the California Lottery was looking for a sea change in its retail business, a new way to reach gamblers that was efficient and sold in bulk. It had enormous potential. Lottery tickets already saturated 80 percent of California's 15,000 gas-station and convenience stores. That market was covered—if underperforming. Only 350 of the state's thousands of big-box stores sold lottery tickets. The state could break through to them if it could change the way people bought lottery tickets by making them a faster transaction. If they could break through, growth would come overnight. Thousands of individual contracts are needed to get each convenience-store and gas-station owner to sell tickets. Big-box retail only requires one agreement from corporate headquarters. If the big-box retail chains are satisfied, they can put lottery tickets into thousands of stores right away.

When Borucki finished her presentation, Terri La Fleur recounted the years of frustration among lottery officials trying to break through into mass-market retail. When she finished, the audience broke into a loud round of applause. Borucki didn't notice, but it was the most enthusiastic applause of any presentation during the two days. California, an industry byword for weak lottery sales, was poised to blaze a trail for other states to follow. If it was successful, it could easily spread to other states. The chains were national after all. If California succeeded, that could add billions to the lottery sales and revenue for the rest of the states.

Warmed by the applause, Borucki returned to California with a plan to turn around the lottery. For the first time the lottery had come up with a forward-looking business plan, like a real retail operation. Borucki wanted to get away from the government-agency model of creating a new plan every year to bring before the legislature for approval. Selling tickets in big-box stores was one of more than a dozen ideas the lottery intended to pursue over its three-year plan.

But Governor Schwarzenegger had different plans formulating in the "horseshoe," as his inner offices were known. Two months after Borucki returned from the conference, the governor held a press conference to announce that he wanted to sell the lottery. The state could reap billions by selling its gambling business to private industry. "California has one of the lowest-performing lotteries in the country," the governor's communications director said. "Taxpayers could see two to three times more money go into state coffers." Privatization had already been suggested in a number of states. Illinois had given privatization serious thought when its governor proclaimed that the state could get $10 billion for its lottery.

"It was a surprise," Borucki recalls. "I put a phone call in to the horseshoe and said, 'It's kind of hard to rally the troops around a new business plan when you just set the governor up in front of cameras to say how mismanaged the lottery is, especially since I'm his appointee."

"Oh, we weren't talking about you" came the response. "We weren't talking about the current business plan."

The attacks stopped, but the damage had been done to morale. "I think we eventually got over that, but that was a surprise," Borucki says.

Later in the year the legislature shot down Schwarzenegger's plan to sell the lottery. But there was enough interest in the wide-ranging talk of $8–34 billlion to be had that a legislative committee held a hearing in October. A former treasurer of California, now a Goldman Sachs executive, Kathleen Brown, testified.

"My own personal view is the lottery is fundamentally retail sales, a marketing business," Brown told the senators. "It is driven by technology and it is driven by innovation, and a state's proper role in this gaming area is regulation. So regulate; do not operate."

On paper at least, California was a strong target for investors. It was much larger than Illinois, and Schwarzenegger was right—it underperformed miserably. In the eyes of investors, the California State Lottery was a diamond in the rough. It had potential to become like New York, which had annual sales of $6.8 billion in 2006, or Massachusetts. Many lotteries around the country felt they were bumping against the limits of their markets. California on the other hand was a vast untapped resource.

"A private company is not going to come in here until they take away some of those restrictions," Borucki says. "They're not going to put their money on the table until some of those are gone. It can only go up here. Most of the others are fairly well established lotteries that don't have the kind of restrictions to be removed that we do."

Loosen some government restrictions that were about ten years behind the times and watch it grow. Perhaps that's what the governor meant when he said, "I think the question really is, should we not really start thinking creatively here?" Borucki's plans for a surge in sales didn't pan out. In the 2007–8 fiscal year, California's sales continued to slide. Borucki entered the year with a modest goal: keeping sales level at $3.5 billion. The state was hurt by the national recession, the mortgage crisis, which hit California particularly hard, and national factors such as rising fuel costs and food inflation that affected the all-important gas-station and convenience-store lottery purchases. For the second year in a row, Borucki was forced to report that the lottery was short of its projections for education funding, by about $100 million. "The reasons behind the decline are complex, multifaceted and not always discernable," she wrote in May 2008. "We are aware of our poor brand image, and low prize payouts, have and will continue to contribute to declining playership levels."

Sales dropped despite the addition of a thousand retailers selling lottery tickets. Around the country many of the forty-two state lotteries had either flat or declining sales. That means that less than half of lotteries were hurt by a national recession. It is remarkable, considering the extensive reports of household belt-tightening, that twenty-nine states, including Illinois, New York, and Massachusetts, saw an increase in lottery sales. In 2008, many states continued to see sales rise as the national economy worsened.

Yet in California and elsewhere the political arguments for selling off the lotteries were strengthened as state budgets tightened. Twenty years ago lotteries were the golden goose. The states felt as if they had won the lottery themselves: the public was voluntarily handing over an annual check. Today, most lotteries account for less than 2 percent of their state's revenues, and even that amount has become unreliable. The problem, states have lately learned, is that lotteries are not unlimited. When the fickle sales of lottery tickets dip, there is going to be a budget shortfall. As they begin to take notice of their lotteries, some state governors see the industry they have created as a product, not an efficient government revenue stream. The sluggish growth in some areas, their operating inefficiency, and the pitched battles lotteries can spark over questions of ethics and public spending have led numerous states to consider selling their lotteries. So far, ten states have voiced interest in privatizing their lotteries by leasing or selling them for billions of dollars. Some states have merely dipped a toe in the water, while others, such as Illinois and California, have met with investment banks to seriously explore selling their branded gambling product to the private sector.

Such a sale would lead to the first privately run lottery in modern American history. It has been more than a century since the states banned private lotteries and the federal government drove the Louisiana Lottery into hiding in Honduras. It would be a return of the lotteries that government has alternately encouraged and prohibited since the 1700s.

CHAPTER 9

HISTORY REPEATS ITSELF

IN MAY 2006, Illinois governor Rod Blagojevich was gearing up for a reelection campaign when he stopped at an elementary school on the South Side to announce that the state would be taking meetings with investors to talk about selling or leasing the state lottery. Illinois, he explained, could get $10 billion cash—money that would go to educating children—if it privatized the lottery. "We want more money in our schools. The question is, how do you get it? We found a creative way to do it. This education plan is historic, it's ambitious, and it will fundamentally change the way we fund schools," he told the reporters who gathered.

It smelled of political opportunism. It was an election year; the governor was under attack for the state of the education system; he was politically unable and publicly unwilling to raise taxes. More important, the proposal to spend lavishly on schools had the immediate benefit of removing a potential rival from the polls on Election Day. State senator James Meeks, an independent at the time and a Baptist minister, had threatened to run against Blagojevich. Meeks accused the governor of neglecting education. Yet there he was with Blagojevich at the press conference to endorse the governor's lottery privatization plan. Meeks stepped out of the race and later that year joined the Democratic Party.

There was not much detail. The governor said that $4 billion of the supposed $10 billion in lottery money would be spent on schools as a massive infusion in the first four years after the deal was closed. The state would parcel out the remaining $6 billion in annual payments of $650 million—about the amount that the Illinois Lottery gives back as profit to the state each year. Those payments would last through 2024. After that the state would collect nothing, but presumably the lottery would still be held in private hands for years to come. The governor's estimates came from Goldman Sachs, which was advising his office on privatization.

Supporters of the proposal made the usual case for privatization of any government service. Namely, that government lacks the skills of private industry. In the case of the lotteries, a retail-sales industry, the states would be better off getting someone who was an expert to run the show. The natural choices were the two leading lottery operators in the United States, GTECH (Lottomatica) and Scientific Games, backed with money from one of the interested investment banks such as Macquarie, Goldman Sachs, UBS, Lehman Brothers, and others. The structure was inspired by the 2004 deal that teamed Macquarie bank with Cintra, the highway specialist, to lease the Chicago Skyway.

The Chicago Skyway was a white elephant for decades until its toll booths started to turn a profit in the 1990s. The city, which had tried in vain to unload the decrepit elevated road on the state, saw a potential source of government funding. Mayor Richard M. Daley announced that the city was going to lease the Skyway for ninety-nine years to private investors who would maintain it and keep the toll money. Daley announced the winning bidder in late 2004. With an upfront payment of $1.8 billion, the Macquarie Infrastructure Group, an arm of the Australia-based Macquarie investment bank, took over the highway. Macquarie financed the lease, referred to as a "concession agreement," and Cintra, a Spanish company that specializes in managing toll roads around the world, handled the day-to-day operations of the Skyway.

Two years later, the Macquarie-Cintra team signed a seventy-five-year concession agreement to run the Indiana Toll Road. The Indiana Toll Road runs right into the Chicago Skyway and controlling their operations in sync made business sense. The companies paid $3.85 billion for the Indiana lease. Again, the money, backed by a lot of debt, was paid up front. As with Chicago, the agreement included a set of predetermined toll increases that started soon after the signing. The Indiana agreement was announced just a few months after Blagojevich announced the his intention to privatize the Illinois Lottery.

The privatization of these toll roads, in particular the Chicago Skyway, was taken by investment banks—and some in government—as proof that public infrastructure could be given to private operators in a way that profited government and private investors. By collecting $1.8 billion up front, Chicago was able to cover a significant budget deficit. The sheer amount of the money overcame opposition.

Privatization is not new. Privately operated turnpikes were around before and after the Revolutionary War. In the 1790s, unable to fund the expansion and operation of their own infrastructure, several states had toll roads that were privately maintained. At the beginning of the twenty-first century, public-private partnerships are common in Europe, Australia, and South America. There are major shipping ports, airports, highways, and other pieces of complex and costly public infrastructure that are managed by private investment groups. In America, most suggestions for privatization have come up against public and political opposition.

The Skyway was a strong argument for privatization. It heralded a potential new era in infrastructure investments in the United States. Investment banks, eager to expand the profitable business, began to pitch state governments on the money their assets could bring.

Lotteries, like toll roads, seemed ripe for plucking. They were an awkward and cumbersome operation for governments. They also returned a steady cash flow that could be easily increased, especially if government restrictions were relaxed. There were numerous political hurdles to the selling off of lotteries, but the Skyway deal opened the door.

Of course, lotteries had a long history of being run by private companies; they had been used to fund numerous public causes. It turned out to be a terribly inefficient way to get money, however. It also wasn't a particularly popular history. The story of private lotteries had ended badly in the nineteenth century with the Louisiana Lottery. This time, however, the interested operators were investment banks and companies like GTECH and Scientific Games, not the shady gamblers who created the Octopus in Louisiana.

In December 2006, Indiana governor Mitch Daniels, a former budget director under President George W. Bush, followed Blagojevich with a proposal to privatize the Hoosier Lottery. Daniels was advised on his plan by Morgan Stanley. He estimated the Hoosier Lottery was worth $1 billion up front and $200 million annually over the life of the lease. The money would fund higher education, he said. The $1 billion would create an endowment for college scholarships and grants to state universities and colleges for attracting top-shelf professors. Daniels dubbed his idea the World Class Scholars Fund.

That's where lottery privatization stood in the spring of 2007 when Goldman Sachs sent two executives to the La Fleur's symposium in Washington, D.C. Goldman, which made some $9 million in fees through its work on the Chicago Skyway deal, was advising Blagojevich on lottery privatization. Working pro bono, their numbers crunchers had come up with his $10 billion figure. Of course, the bank hoped to profit as investors in a privatization deal. In fact, several investment banks were calling on statehouses and governors around the country. Because the market was just beginning to open and was politically sensitive, a soft approach was required. The Goldman executives came to the symposium to explain the fundamentals of privatization and allay the concerns of the state employees.

Adam Rosenberg, cohead of Goldman's Gaming Practice division, laid out the privatization scenario to the industry officials at the La Fleur's symposium by starting with a theoretical state that only wants to sell its lottery if the private operators agree to maintain the current regulations, restrictions, and games. "Our job is to try and move as far from that baseline as we can," Rosenberg told the crowd, "recognizing that there is a lot of complexity here, there is a lot of nuance, and there are a lot of difficult regulatory constraints on how we can really grow the business. But that's the tension. That's what we're going to see: how far we can move from that baseline in the next few lotteries that come out."

Over the next several months, many states announced their interest in privatizing their lottery. But no one knew just what a privately run lottery would look like. Would it be another Louisiana Lottery, another grasping Octopus with a reach that used the Internet or cell phones instead of the mail system?

Certainly, investors would like to group several state lotteries

together. Much like Macquarie and Cintra linked the Skyway with
the Indiana Toll Road, it would be more efficient to bundle neighboring state lottery operations together and share expenses. Why not
have a single owner of the Indiana and Illinois lotteries or, say, the
Midwest state lotteries, or the Pacific Coast lotteries? Already,
GTECH had experience running multiple state lotteries, including
the nation's largest operations.

Most industry officials agree that a privately run lottery would
have to be a more aggressive lottery—not a politically popular idea.
Some of the present restrictions, which vary widely from state to state,
would likely be loosened to increase sales under private operation.
Lotteries attracted investors because, like highways, they have steady
income and could be run more profitably. But a slim profit growth of
2 or 3 percent annually may not be enough to satisfy private investors.
State lotteries are charged with maximizing sales, but not by the standards of private industry. They have limitations, both ethical and political. Gradually, most states have relaxed their lottery rules because
doing so means more money. In the name of increasing state revenues,
states have increased their prize payouts to encourage players, allowed
more advertising, added games such as keno, and introduced lottery
coupons. They have also sought to interest younger players through
trademark licensing from *American Idol* and through other marketing
gimmicks and technological innovations such as text messaging. For
a chance to collect lottery profits, private industry will pay an amount
that is weighted by its ability to expand the lottery. The more it can
grow sales, the more states are willing to loosen the reins, and the
more investment banks will offer states. The limitations would have
to be spelled out in the lease agreements.

If legislators and governors are convinced that a massive up-front payment is in the best interest of the state, they will seek to loosen the chains and let private business take over. A private lottery might add or expand keno games or video lottery terminals or seek to market more aggressively or in different locations. Perhaps, they would get permission to partner with colleges by licensing, say, Notre Dame– or NCAA Final Four–themed scratch tickets and returning a portion to the schools? What if the tickets were sold on campus or marketed to students the way credit cards are? A private lottery would likely target its marketing more than state government dares. Such measures can really squeeze profits from a lottery by focusing on poor, middle-class, and minority neighborhoods. For a state-run lottery this would be political thin ice.

These are some areas of untapped profit growth. The largest of all is the youth market. Lotteries, in general, have an aging customer base. Younger players are drawn to scratch tickets and would be thrilled if they could play over the Internet, their cell phones, PDAs, or other direct handheld devices. Though still illegal in the United States, such wagering may only be a matter of time as it expands in Europe.

A private lottery would spend more on advertising; would likely be more aggressive in its advertising both in targeting players by desire and demographic group; would probably give back more in prizes to players; and would seek to engage in some kind of direct relationship with players through customer rewards.

Any state that makes a concession agreement would have to lay down the groundwork for what is and what isn't allowed. The language of the lease agreement would have to cover everything up front: regulations on marketing, types of games allowed, sale price. The state would essentially have to think up anything that could go

wrong and guard against it in advance by spelling out detailed guidelines for the lottery's operation. Because the length of the agreement
could run anywhere from ten to ninety-nine years the trick would be
to get it right the first time and consider all of the future possibilities.
It's a seemingly impossible task, particularly when one considers how
quickly technology is changing gambling around the world.

IN MAY 2007, Governor Schwarzenegger offered up the state's lottery.
Over the next year Michigan, Texas, New Jersey, New York, Okla-
homa, Florida, and Vermont all looked at how they could get some
up-front value from their lotteries. Powerful guns were pulled out. In
Texas, former senator Phil Gramm was pushing privatization for
UBS, the Swiss investment bank where he is vice president; in Cal-
fornia, former state treasurer Kathleen Brown represented Goldman
Sachs.

Even states that had little real interest or incentive to sell or lease
their lottery took meetings with investment banks to hear them out.
What state wouldn't listen to people who say that they can get a billion or several billion dollars for the budget?

GTECH was poised to run a privatized lottery. The company
said it was interested in Blagojevich's proposal to privatize the Illinois
Lottery—an understatement, no doubt—but would need to hear spe-
cifics. The company's chief Illinois lobbyist had served Blagojevich as
chief of staff during the governor's time in Congress.

Bank executives even pitched Rhode Island, only about a year
after GTECH had secured its unheard-of twenty-year contract to run
the state lottery.

Even in Massachusetts, where the lottery was the most efficient
and profitable in the nation, four Republican legislators said the

games, which bring in $1 billion a year, were showing their age through their shrinking profit margins and ought to be sold off. Former Massachusetts governor William Weld, who was known as a proponent of privatizing government operations and had fought to protect the lottery's advertising budget, made the rounds at the state capital trying to rally interest in the idea, accompanied by a former deputy governor from Illinois and representatives from Lehman Brothers investment bank. It wasn't long before Weld was told to register as a lobbyist.

"I've met with bankers and they put the idea in front of us and said we don't want to be operating behind your back," says Mark Cavanagh, director of the Massachusetts Lottery. "Some have come in because they were involved in Illinois, or they were involved in Indiana, or Texas or California, and Florida. Those are the five main states where it's gained some type of traction. In some cases it's just been political traction, really." Massachusetts, Cavanagh knows, could make more money if the rules of the lottery game were changed. When the bankers come in, they pitch the big selling price. Massachusetts, with $1 billion in annual revenues, could get a lot more than Illinois's estimated $10 billion. But Massachusetts is too successful to make a good investment. "One of the key ingredients that they're telling me that they need is a low-performing lottery or a poorly performing lottery," he says.

That means California. It is the worst-performing lottery in the country, in large part because of legislated restrictions on sales and types of games. If the ties that bind it were cut, California has enormous potential for expansion. But, as in Illinois, it's impossible to separate the lottery from politics. If Governor Schwarzenegger really wanted a stronger lottery, a more profitable lottery, he could have tried to win over legislators. Instead, he announced that the lottery was an underperforming asset that would be better run by private industry. He disavowed the lottery and distanced himself from it, which is exactly what the legislature had done by limiting its operations. Neither ever disavowed the profits from it, however. In a sleight of hand proposal, Schwarzenegger, in 2008, wanted to issue $15 billion in funds secured by future lottery profits. Five billion dollars in future revenue would go toward California's immediate deficit. Schwarzenegger wanted to spend gambling money he did not yet have.

Although a national conversation on lottery privatization has started, most states have not yet seriously considered selling off the asset. But many have played with the idea for political ends. It is provocative. It offers politicians a chance to rail against the inefficiencies of an agency that is supposed to bring in revenue. Lotteries are a convenient target to blame for budget shortfalls. One can attack a lottery and know that few, if any, other elected officials are going to stand up in its defense. It's not easy to find a governor or a legislator who publicly encourages citizens to go out and play the lottery.

In Illinois, at least, Blagojevich has not let go of the idea and into 2008 continued to revise his privatization plan in an effort to make it easier to swallow. Under his 2008 plan, the state could hold on to a 20 percent share of the lottery, along with 20 percent of its profits, and still collect $10 billion.

Considering the growing expenses of government—the skyrocketing costs of fuel oil, gasoline, construction, health care, and pension plans—states are casting about for ways to cover budget deficits just as investment banks are lining up to offer them billions. The forty-two lottery states, along with Washington, D.C., will calculate whether selling their games to private operators is an efficient way to maximize their lottery profits.

LOTTERY PLAYERS MAKE no such calculations. They buy tickets based on optimism or some variant emotional math such as hope, compulsion, or desperation. But the lottery, while designed to encourage optimism, is also engineered to exploit it: The vast majority of players lose. The more players gamble based on their hopes and dreams, the less they win. In the fall of 1986, a study found that the most popular combinations in Maryland's lotto game were 3-3-3, 7-7-7, and 5-5-5. Such "lucky" combinations have been popular since the nineteenth-century policy games allowed players to pick their own numbers and dream books assigned meanings. Of course, when lucky numbers hit, that's proof of their luck. But the trouble with such commonly picked numbers is that, when they win, it's guaranteed that the pot will have to be shared with other people who picked the same numbers. The lucky numbers, when they come up, bring less profit to the player.

On April 13, 2004, the Virginia Lottery drew 7-7-7-7 and had to pay more than $5.5 million in prizes on some fifteen hundred tickets. The payout was twenty-six times more than the game took in that day. The tickets won $5,000 for every $1 bet. The state's had its previous highest daily game payout when 7-7-7 had hit in 2001 and before that when 9-9-9-9 was drawn.

Player optimism or belief in luck is irrational, and the lottery encourages it, yet rationally calculates for players' behavior to protect its profits. Knowing player habits, some lotteries defend against such occasional lucky number hits. Pennsylvania, for one, calculated a saturation point for popular combinations, and when it was reached, the state stopped allowing players to pick those numbers. Another common irrational aspect of lottery play is the belief in lucky stores. A store that sells a winning ticket is deemed lucky, and state employees are not above encouraging the idea. In Missouri, between 1995 and 2005, a single St. Louis convenience store sold three jackpot winners. The Missouri Lottery issued a press release, in which their spokesman said, "This is one lucky location."

For a time, the luckiest lottery player in the country was believed to be Evelyn Adams, of New Jersey. Adams worked in a 7-Eleven that her boyfriend owned. She bought tickets every day. Over the first fifteen years of the New Jersey Lottery she spent about $25 a week, or $20,000, on tickets. Then on October 24, 1985, Evelyn Adams became a local celebrity when a GTECH Quick Pick computer picked six numbers from a field of thirty-nine for her. She took nearly $4 million from the $7.9 million jackpot. To the local papers and lottery officials she was proof that dreams do come true.

Evelyn saw no reason to let the sudden money go to her head. She kept her job at the convenience store. She began to spend more on the lottery: $100 a week on tickets, instead of her usual $25. Less than four months after becoming a newly minted millionaire, on February 14, 1986, her life took an even more unlikely turn: She hit the Pick 6 again. This time she won $1.5 million after the same machine guessed six numbers from a field of forty-two. No one in the nation, as far as lottery officials could tell, had ever won million-dollar jackpots twice. She was proof that miracles do happen.

The state lottery cited a Rutgers University statistics professor who proclaimed that the odds of Evelyn winning two million-dollar jackpots were 1 in 17 trillion. You're more likely to be hit by a meteorite. The *New York Times* reported the numbers as fact. Unfortunately, they were incorrect. Her first win beat odds of 3.2 million to 1. Her second jackpot was more unlikely, at 5.2 million to 1. But lottery odds do not compound. When Evelyn stood in line at the convenience store, she had the same chance to win as anyone. The state lottery acknowledged that the odds against winning the jackpot twice were really closer to 5.2 million to 1.

Evelyn wasn't the miracle that the lottery promoted her to be, and like many other lottery winners, she found that sudden life-changing money didn't necessarily change her life for the better. She set up a trust for her daughter, paid off debts, and gave some money to family. She also made frequents trips to Atlantic City and lost a chunk of the money, but plenty was still left. Family, friends, and acquaintances called asking for help. For some reason that help always required Evelyn to part with cash.

"Everybody wanted my money," she told a reporter. "Everybody had their hand out." In 2004, twenty years after she first won the lottery and the last year she received payouts, she said, "I wish I could go back and do everything differently." The millions had evaporated. Today Evelyn lives in a crowded mobile-home park on a busy intersection a few miles from her hometown. A few miles farther down a local highway is the small Cape Cod house with the leafy yard that she had bought with the winnings. The bank foreclosed on the house and took it in 2001.

"I was a big-time gambler," Evelyn told a reporter. "I didn't drop a million dollars, but it was a lot of money. I made mistakes, some I regret, some I don't. I'm human. I can't go back now, so I just go forward, one step at a time. I wish I had the chance to do it all over again. I'd be much smarter about it now."

But heavy players such as Evelyn are what make the lotteries tick. The game is less about their luck than it is about the desire, and sometimes compulsion, to gamble. Ed Rader was lucky enough to find a $10,000 scratch ticket in the garbage and regrets it. Robert, in Massachusetts, never had the luck to win the big jackpot after chasing the dream for years and spending a couple hundred thousand dollars. If he had gotten lucky, it would only have gotten worse, he says.

Evelyn Adams wasn't the only public miracle. At Shuttle Meadow Country Club in Berlin, Connecticut, a group of about two dozen staff each made a $10 contribution to lottery tickets when jackpots got large—at least a couple million. One week in 1985 they spent $230 on tickets and hit a $4.2 million jackpot. They did it again in 1987. The winning numbers they played that January 16 were 11-17-23-30-37-40. The twenty-six members of the group each won $1,600 a year over twenty years. The *New York Times* story on their win quoted Frank Reardon, who worked in the locker room. Reardon bought the tickets at the same store that had sold a $1 million winner a few months earlier. "I would say it's a pretty lucky place," he told the *Times*. Having learned from its earlier mistake, the *Times* story quoted a statistician at the University of Connecticut, who pointed out that the country-club workers in their second win faced the same odds as everyone else, about 1 in 3.8 million. "Whatever you think subconsciously," the lottery director, J. Blaine Lewis Jr., told the *Times*, "it doesn't change the mathematical odds."

And that's where we have trouble. When we perceive the lottery players as hopeful or optimists, we miss the point. In a 2005 study of sales in Texas, it was discovered that a "lucky" store that sells a winning ticket sells more lottery tickets for up to forty weeks. The study, "Lucky Stores, Gambling, and Addiction," also found that players chase the specific game that delivered the winner and will drive up sales by 12–38 percent in the week after a jackpot—despite the fact that prize money is at its lowest point after a big win.

Clearly, it's not just optimism that drives people to play the lottery. The purpose of the study was to see if such irrational behavior— there is no such thing as a "lucky" store, after all—was a sign of gambling addiction. The study decided it couldn't prove that players' pursuit of luck was a sign of addiction—the sales bump was too brief—but it couldn't rule it out.

What the study did find was that sales are higher in areas where people are less educated and poorer. More players sought out a "lucky" store in zip codes where more residents had less than a high school education—and if they made up 90 percent of adults, the study found, ticket sales doubled. Given the correlation between education and income, it's not surprising that the same zip codes also had lower incomes and greater numbers of welfare recipients.

Stories of wild luck whet the appetite, but they are hardly necessary to convince the core players to buy tickets. As early as the 1840s, Thomas Doyle, a former lottery-office employee turned opponent, had hit on one of the stranger phenomena of lottery gambling— "disappointment only sharpens the appetite."

If winning is a matter of sheer luck for the gambler, for the industry that luck has already been quantified in the odds and prize structure of each game. But every once in a while, the people who run the games are caught off guard, overwhelmed as it were by the "luck" of the players. In March of 2005, for example, more than one hundred people came forward with Powerball tickets that matched five of the six numbers pulled in the drawing. It was so unlikely that at first fraud was strongly suspected. It turned out they all got their numbers from the same fortune-cookie slip from Wonton Food's factory in Queens, New York. The Multi-State Lottery Association, which runs the Powerball game, paid out an unanticipated $19 million to the second-place finishers. They were one number off from winning the jackpot. But one player did have all six numbers, picked by a GTECH computer at a Tennessee convenience store. Human optimism and luck didn't beat the lottery, the industry's own computer calculated the winning numbers.

ACKNOWLEDGMENTS

I FIRST OWE thanks to those people who gave me their time and told me their stories. Curtis Sharp shared his past experience with lottery celebrity and his present devotion to Scripture. Sterling Plumpp provided a link between the present-day lottery and the policy games that were its bluesy past. Ed Rader and "Robert" in Massachusetts were courageous in allowing me to write about their personal struggles with lottery gambling. Tom Birmingham explained his winning strategy against lottery advertising. Tony Amico introduced me to the retailer's perspective on the lottery industry.

In North Carolina, many people shared their perspective on the battle over the creation of the state lottery. Among them are Charles Clotfelter and Philip Cook, authors of the seminal account of lottery business, *Selling Hope*; the Reverend Chester Debnam for taking me on a tour of Raleigh's backstreets; John Garwood, Chuck Neely, Rep. Bill Owens, John Rustin, Dr. Charles Sanders, and Rep. Paul Stam. Lottery directors Tom Shaheen of North Carolina and Mark Cavanagh in Massachusetts were generous with their knowledge of lottery operations and candid in their assessments of their sometimes awkward relationship with government overseers. Constance Laverty O'Connor, a veteran of the lottery world, generously gave me her time and her thoughts on the future of the industry.

I owe thanks to John Fox and Ronny West, who drove me through the fascinating history of beautiful Jackson County, Tennessee. They have helped keep alive Historic Avery Trace, a little known settlers' trail used by Andrew Jackson and many others that was cut through the wilderness with lottery dollars—a story that, unfortunately, did not make it into the final draft of this book. I would like to thank many others in Tennessee, such as Rep. Steve Cohen and Tennessee Lottery director Rebecca Paul Hargrove.

Professor Joan Zielinski, a former lottery director, shared her experiences of the early years of the state lotteries, as did Walter Szrek, a software engineer. Joan Borucki, California Lottery director, was open in her description of the challenges facing the games in that state. Thank you to Terri and Bruce La Fleur for compiling the most comprehensive database of the lottery industry's financial ups and downs, and for their symposium that provided a wealth of knowledge, and sympathy, for the unseen work done by state lottery employees.

In writing many sections of this book, I relied on the research and reporting of others. John Samuel Ezell's *Fortune's Merry Wheel* was an indispensable source and a definitive history of the early American lotteries. Ezell's bibliography is an excellent guide to documents from the early lottery wars. Columbia University's Butler Library, Rare Book and Manuscript Library, and Watson Library of Business and Economics provided access to endless articles, academic journals, and original nineteenth-century writings on the lottery, not to mention a quiet place to think and write.

In researching this book, I read too many newspaper and magazine articles to count. They provided much of the information used to write brief accounts of lottery winners, such as Jack Whittaker, Don Temple, and Evelyn Adams, as well as the accounts of Kevin Geddings's travails in North Carolina, lobbyist David Smith's career and court cases, GTECH's rise and occasional scandals, and many of the events in the lottery from the 1970s and 80s. My thanks to the reporters who did the work.

Others provided inspiration and helpful guidance. Jonathan Englert was there from the outset. His suggestions and comments were a second pair of eyes throughout the creation of this book. Samuel Freedman, whose class at Columbia University's School of Journalism is a breeding ground for book writers, made the whole thing possible. Claudia Cross, an enthusiastic supporter of this book, shepherded it—and me—to publication. My thanks also to Annik LaFarge, who chose the book for Bloomsbury, and Benjamin Adams, whose skillful editing shaped and focused it.

Finally, Sarah Garland, my wife, gets a lifetime of gratitude for always keeping a hand at my back for support and forward momentum.

BIBLIOGRAPHY

INTRODUCTION: GARBAGE STORIES

Austin, Liz. "Texan Finds Lost $25,000 Lottery Ticket." Associated Press, December 8, 2005.

Cain, Charlie. "$26M left unclaimed last year in lottery, $512M in jackpots lost over 35 years." *Detroit News*, November 26, 2007.

Consumer Federation of America. "How Americans View Personal Wealth vs. How Financial Planners View This Wealth." January 9, 2006. www.consumerfed.org/pdfs/Financial_Planners_Study 011006.pdf.

Davis, Chase. "Man Says He Found $1M Scratch Ticket in Trash." *Boston Globe*, October 16, 2005.

Devlin, Keith. "Lottery Mania." June 2000. Column at Mathematical Association of America. www.maa.org/devlin/devlin_ 6_00.html.

"Fortune Hunter's Hopes Rest on Grubby Lottery Tickets." Associated Press, February 7, 1983.

"Gambling: As the Take Rises, So Does Public Concern." Pew Research Center, May 23, 2006.

Guerrero, Lucio. "Lottery winners claim $10.5 million." *Chicago Sun-Times,* November 27, 2003.

Kropko, M. R. "Woman drops claim that she had winning lottery ticket." Associated Press, January 8 and 9, 2004.

Laverty O'Connor, Constance. Interview, May 7, 2008.

"Lottery Loser's Shady Past." *Smoking Gun*, January 6, 2003. www.thesmokinggun.com/archive/lottoreport1.html.

"Man Ends Search for $10,000 Lottery Ticket." Associated Press, February 5, 1983.

"Man Searches Trash for $10,000 Lottery Ticket." Associated Press, February 4, 1983.

"Man who plucked winning lottery ticket from trash settles suit." Associated Press, August 25, 2006.

Mooney, Tom. "Clash over $1-million lottery ticket outlives buyer." *Providence Journal*, June 19, 2006.

Nichols, Russell. "Lottery Ticket Finder to Keep Most Winnings." *Boston Globe*, August 26, 2006.

North American Association of State and Provincial Lotteries. www.naspl.com.

"Once-Lost Lottery Ticket Finally Pays Off." Associated Press, December 19, 2005.

Rader, Ed. Interview, November 16, 2007.

Schulte, Sarah. "Lottery winners saved by garbage strike." ABC News, November 26, 2003.

"Trashed Lottery Ticket Nets California Pair $8 Million." *Greensboro (NC) News & Record*, November 1, 1995.

CHAPTER 1: THE FIRST LOTTERY

Brown, Alexander. *The First Republic in America*. Boston: Houghton, Mifflin & Co., 1898.

————. *The Genesis of the United States.* Boston: Houghton, Mifflin & Co., 1891.

Chambers, Robert. *Chambers Book of Days.* Edinburgh: W & R Chambers, 1864.

Ellis, Joseph J. *His Excellency: George Washington.* New York: Alfred A. Knopf, 2004.

Ezell, John Samuel. *Fortune's Merry Wheel: The Lottery in America.* Cambridge, MA: Harvard University Press, 1960.

————. "The Lottery in Colonial America." *William and Mary Quarterly,* 3rd ser., 5, no. 2 (April 1948): 185–200.

————. "When Massachusetts Played the Lottery." *New England Quarterly* 22, no. 3 (September 1949): 316–35.

France, Clemens J. "The Gambling Impulse." *American Journal of Psychology* 13, no. 3 (July 1902): 364–407.

Hamilton, Alexander. "Ideas Concerning a Lottery." Reprinted in Joseph Stancliffe Davis, *Essays in the Earlier History of American Corporations.* Clark, NJ: The Lawbook Exchange, Ltd., 1965. Originally, Cambridge, MA: Harvard University Press, 1917.

Kingsbury, Susan M., ed. *Records of the Virginia Company of London.* 4 vols. Washington, D.C.: Government Printing Office, 1906–35.

McMaster, John Bach. *History of the People of the United States.* New York: D. Appleton & Co., 1883, 1: 587–88. Quote: "In a short time there was a wheel in every town . . ."

Pearson, Edward A., ed. *Designs Against Charleston: The Trial Record of the Denmark Vesey Slave Conspiracy of 1822.* Chapel Hill: University of North Carolina Press, 1999.

Report and Proceedings of the Senate Committee Appointed to Investigate the Police Department of the City of New York. Vol. 3. June 29 to October 18, 1894. James B. Lyon, state printer.

Robertson, David. *Denmark Vesey: The Buried History of America's Largest Slave Rebellion and the Man Who Led It.* New York: Alfred A. Knopf, 1999.

Smith, Adam. *An Inquiry into the Nature and Causes of the Wealth of Nations.* 1776. Reprint, London: Penguin Books, 1999. Quote: "Instead of piddling . . . ," 206, bk. 4. Quote: "The soberest people . . . ," 210, bks. 1–3.

Spofford, A. R. "Lotteries in American History." American Historical Association. Annual report for the year 1892. Washington, D.C.: Government Printing Office, 1893.

Three Proclamations Concerning the Lottery for Virginia, 1613–1621. Providence: John Carter Brown Library, 1907.

Wiencek, Henry. *An Imperfect God: George Washington, His Slaves, and the Creation of America.* New York: Farrar, Straus and Giroux, 2003.

CHAPTER 2: THE PROFESSIONALS

Aitken, Hugh G. J. "Yates and McIntyre: Lottery Managers." *Journal of Economic History* 13, no. 1 (Winter 1953).

Barnum, P. T. *The Life of P. T. Barnum, Written by Himself.* New York: Redfield, 1855.

Channing, Edward. *A History of the United States.* Vol. 4, *Federalists and Republicans, 1789–1815.* 1917. Reprint, New York: Macmillan Company, 1949.

Clotfelter, Charles T., and Philip J. Cook. *Selling Hope: State Lotteries in America.* Cambridge, MA: Harvard University Press, 1991.

Dasgupta, Anisha S. "Public Finance and the Fortunes of the Early America Lottery." Yale Law School Student Scholarship Series, Paper 9, 2005.

Kropko, M. R. "Woman drops claim that she had winning lottery ticket." Associated Press, January 8 and 9, 2004.

Laverty O'Connor, Constance. Interview, May 7, 2008.

"Lottery Loser's Shady Past." *Smoking Gun*, January 6, 2003. www.thesmokinggun.com/archive/lottoreport1.html.

"Man Ends Search for $10,000 Lottery Ticket." Associated Press, February 5, 1983.

"Man Searches Trash for $10,000 Lottery Ticket." Associated Press, February 4, 1983.

"Man who plucked winning lottery ticket from trash settles suit." Associated Press, August 25, 2006.

Mooney, Tom. "Clash over $1-million lottery ticket outlives buyer." *Providence Journal*, June 19, 2006.

Nichols, Russell. "Lottery Ticket Finder to Keep Most Winnings." *Boston Globe*, August 26, 2006.

North American Association of State and Provincial Lotteries. www .naspl.com.

"Once-Lost Lottery Ticket Finally Pays Off." Associated Press, December 19, 2005.

Rader, Ed. Interview, November 16, 2007.

Schulte, Sarah. "Lottery winners saved by garbage strike." ABC News, November 26, 2003.

"Trashed Lottery Ticket Nets California Pair $8 Million." *Greensboro (NC) News & Record*, November 1, 1995.

CHAPTER 1: THE FIRST LOTTERY

Brown, Alexander. *The First Republic in America*. Boston: Houghton, Mifflin & Co., 1898.

Doyle, Thomas F. *Five Years in a Lottery Office; Or, An Exposition of the Lottery System in the United States*. Boston: S. N. Dickinson, 1841.

Executive Documents of the House of Representatives for the 2nd Session of the 46th Congress, 1879–1880. Report of the Postmaster, General, Nov. 8, 1879. Washington, D.C.: Government Printing Office, 1880.

Ezell, John Samuel. *Fortune's Merry Wheel: The Lottery in America*. Cambridge, MA: Harvard University Press, 1960.

Fabian, Ann Vincent. *Card Sharps, Dream Books, and Bucket Shops: Gambling in 19th Century America*. Ithaca: Cornell University Press, 1990.

Farrar, Edgar Howard. *The Louisiana Lottery: Its History*. *Charities Review* 1, no. 4 (February 1892).

Geisst, Charles R. *Wall Street: A History: From Its Beginnings to the Fall of Enron*. New York: Oxford University Press, 1997.

Gordon, John Steele. "Born in Iniquity." *American Heritage* 45, no. 1 (February/March 1994).

Kendall, John. *History of New Orleans*. Chicago: Lewis Publishing Company, 1922, 483–501.

Klebaner, Benjamin J. "State-Chartered American Commercial Banks, 1781–1801." *Business History Review* 53, no. 4 (Winter 1979): 529–38.

Larson, Henrietta M. "S. & M. Allen—Lottery, Exchange, and Stock Brokerage." *Journal of Economic and Business History* 3, no. 3 (May 1931).

MacLeod, William Christie. "The Truth About Lotteries in American History." *South Atlantic Quarterly* 35, no. 2 (April 1936).

McGinty, G. W. "The Louisiana Lottery Company." *Southwestern Social Science Quarterly* 20, no. 3 (March 1940).

Dillon, John. "Could state lottery success spawn supersize US numbers game?" *Christian Science Monitor*, July 16, 1985.

"Dixie, Doxie & Dewey." *Time*, February 14, 1938.

"56 Seized in Raids Involving Gaming." *New York Times* (UPI), February 6, 1971.

"$5.73 Million in Tickets Sold in New Hampshire Lottery." *New York
Times*, September 9, 1964.

"Fortune Shifts View of a Refund-Seeker in the State Lottery." *New
York Times*, July 28, 1976.

Gentry, Curt. *J. Edgar Hoover: The Man and His Secrets*. New York:
Norton, 1991.

Gould, John. "The Lottery, the Puritan and the Devil." *New York
Times*, May 19, 1963.

Kaplan, Lawrence J., and James M. Maher. "The Economics of the
Numbers Game." *American Journal of Economics and Sociology*
29, no. 4. (October 1970): 391–408.

Khalfani, Lynnette. "Managing a Windfall." *Black Enterprise*, November 2006.

Lawrence, Curtis. "Bronzeville's policy kings were early venture capi-
talists." *Chicago Sun-Times*, July 7, 2003.

Light, Ivan. "Numbers Gambling Among Blacks: A Financial Institu-
tion." *American Sociological Review* 42, no. 6 (December 1977):
892–904.

Lombardo, Robert M. "The Black Mafia: African-American Organized Crime in Chicago, 1890–1960." *Crime, Law & Social
Change* 38 (2002): 33–65.

"The Lottery Staff: All Losers." *New York Times*, November 30,
1975.

"Lottery Winner Cooly Cashes In." *New York Times*, November 22,
1967.

"New York Lottery Will Be Directed by Michigan Man." *New York Times*, April 13, 1976.

"Old-Lottery Drawing Held." *New York Times*, July 17, 1976.

Plumpp, Sterling. Interview, April 6, 2006.

———. *The Mojo Hands Call, I Must Go*. Thunder's Mouth Press, 1982. "Clinton," lines 239–41.

———. *Steps to Break the Circle*. Third World Press, 1974. "Steps to Break the Circle," lines 168–78.

"Poet Sterling Plumpp Hits Lottery Jackpot." University of Illinois at Chicago Office of Public Affairs, press release, August 21, 2001.

Powell, Adam Clayton. *Adam by Adam: The Autobiography of Adam Clayton Powell, Jr.* New York: Kensington Publishing, 2002.

Powledge, Fred. "Pick a Number From 000 to 999." *New York Times*, December 6, 1964.

Prial, Frank J. "Carey to Overhaul Lottery and Dismiss Entire Staff." *New York Times*, November 29, 1975.

———. "Sabotage Added to Inquiry on State Lotteries Errors." *New York Times*, October 24, 1975.

———. "State Lotteries Thrive Despite Problems." *New York Times*, February 7, 1976.

———. "Why the Lottery Lags." *New York Times*, August 20, 1967.

The Region, *New York Times*, November 9, 1975.

Riis, Jacob A. *How the Other Half Lives*. New York: Charles Scribner's Sons, 1890.

Schanberg, Sydney H. "Lottery." *New York Times*, June 4, 1967.

Schatzbery, Rufus, and Robert J. Kelly. *African American Organized Crime: A Social History*. New Brunswick, NJ: Rutgers University Press, 1997.

Sitomer, Curtis J. "State lotteries: At any odds, a bad bet." *Christian Science Monitor*, August 30, 1984.

Smith, Stanley S. "Lotteries." *Journal of Criminal Law and Criminology*, 38, no. 6: (March–April) 1948: 659–669.

Sullivan, Ronald. "Lottery in Jersey Will Begin Today." *New York Times* (AP), December 16, 1970.

———. "Lottery Referendum Approved in Jersey." *New York Times*, May 2, 1969.

———. "New Jersey's Proposed Lottery." *New York Times*, October 17, 1969.

Swanson, Al. "College professor wins $1 million." UPI, August 21, 2001.

Thomas, Robert McG., Jr. "Carey Suspends Lottery over Duplicate Numbers." *New York Times*, October 23, 1975.

Thompson, Nathan. *Kings: The True Story of Chicago's Policy Kings and Numbers Racketeers.* Chicago: Bronzeville Press, 2003.

Tomasson, Robert E. "'Instant Lottery' Begins in New York Next Week." *New York Times*, September 1, 1976.

United States v. New Jersey Lottery Commission. U.S. Supreme Court 420 U.S. 371 (1975).

U.S. Senate Special Committee to Investigate Organized Crime in Interstate Commerce. Final Report, August 31, 1951. Washington, D.C.: Government Printing Office, 1951. "Kefauver Committee."

Yronwode, Catherine. "Hoodoo in Theory and Practice." Luckymojo .com.

CHAPTER 4: THE BOOM YEARS

Anderson, Susan Heller. "2 Lotteries Provide $13.6 Million Worth of Dreams." *New York Times*, December 1, 1982.

"Experts Tell How to Stay Rich After Winning the Lottery." *Jet*, March 25, 2002.

Goodman, Robert. *The Luck Business: The Devastating Consequences and Broken Promises of America's Gambling Explosion*. New York: Free Press, 1995.

Heard, Alex. "In with the Out Crowd on Fight Night." *Washington Post Magazine*, July 24, 1988.

"Living Well Is the Best Revenge." *Newsweek*, September 2, 1985.

Martinez, Jose. "Lottery's Winner's Cash Cow Dries Up." *Daily News*, December 10, 2002.

Peterson, Lisa. "Lottery Winner's Odyssey: Rags to Riches to Religion." *New Orleans Times-Picayune*, November 9, 1997.

Sharp, Curtis. Interviews, February 4, 5, 6, and 7, 2006.

Trescott, Jacqueline. "Parties & Politics All Around the Caucus." *Washington Post*, September 26, 1983.

CHAPTER 5: ONE VOTE

Beinart, Peter. "The Carville Trick." *Time*, November 16, 1998.

Bell, Adam, and Jim Morrill. "Lottery lures low incomes: Lesser-paid spend triple what the more affluent do." *Charlotte Observer*, March 18, 2006.

Binker, Mark. "State lottery beat the odds." *Greensboro (NC) News & Record*, March 26, 2006.

Christensen, Rob. "Final odds: 26–24 against the lottery; Curious left-right coalition prevails; Democratic leaders say they'll try again." *Raleigh (NC) News & Observer*, August 14, 2005.

Clotfelter, Dr. Charles. Interview, February 28, 2007.

Clotfelter, Charles T., and Philip J. Cook. "What if the lottery were run for lottery players?" *Raleigh (NC) News & Observer*, March 1, 2007.

Curliss, J. Andrew, and Dan Kane. "E-mail disclosure has witness in tears." *Raleigh (NC) News & Observer*, September 27, 2006.

———. "Lottery lowers bar on school funds goal." *Raleigh (NC) News & Observer*, June 14, 2006.

———. "Lottery tickets sold to minors." *Raleigh (NC) News & Observer*, November 16, 2006.

———. "More lottery money may go for prizes." *Raleigh (NC) News & Observer*, February 23, 2007.

Curliss, J. Andrew, Lisa Hoppenjans, and Rob Christensen. "Under the Dome." *Raleigh (NC) News & Observer*, December 20, 2006.

Debnam, the Reverend Chester. Interview, February 27, 2007.

———. "Not getting better" (op-ed). *Raleigh (NC) News & Observer*, November 10, 2006.

Dodd, Scott, and Amy Baldwin. "Games boring to start but easy." *Charlotte Observer*, March 29, 2006.

"Five people connected to former Speaker Jim Black have pleaded guilty to, or been found guilty of, breaking the law." *Raleigh (NC) News & Observer*, February 14, 2007.

Garwood, John. Interview, February 28, 2007.

Hansen, Alicia. "Gambling with Tax Policy: States' Growing Reliance on Lottery Tax Revenue." *Tax Foundation*, July 2007.

Ingram, David. "He made millions through concepts such as 'Bubba': But he now faces up to 100 years in prison." *Charlotte Observer*, October 14, 2006.

Ingram, David, and Mark Johnson. "Geddings looked at mayoral run." *Charlotte Observer*, September 27, 2006.

Johnson, Mark. "Another Lottery Official Resigns." *Charlotte Observer*, November 15, 2005.

———. "Judge convicts lottery lobbyist." *Charlotte Observer*, October 26, 2006.

———. "Lottery figures scratched: Sliding sales force N.C. officials to revise revenue forecasts." *Charlotte Observer*, December 25, 2006.

———. "Supporters win a war of attrition." *Charlotte Observer*, August 31, 2005.

"Judge rules North Carolina lottery law was passed legally." Associated Press, March 22, 2006.

Kane, Dan. "Gaming raises lobbyists' rankings." *Raleigh (NC) News & Observer*, November 15, 2006.

Kane, Dan, and J. Andrew Curliss. "Black-Norris alliance raised eyebrows; Feds investigate depth of influence." *Raleigh (NC) News & Observer*, November 26, 2006.

———. "Geddings guilty on five counts." *Raleigh (NC) News & Observer*, October 13, 2006.

———. "Trial looks back to S.C." *Raleigh (NC) News & Observer*, September 27, 2006.

"Lottery's skeptic-in-chief" (editorial). *Raleigh (NC) News & Observer*, September 15, 2006.

"A Lotto Sleaze Already" (editorial). *Wilmington (NC) Star News*, November 3, 2005.

Neely, Chuck. Interview, February 28, 2007.

Owens, Representative William. Interview, February 28, 2007.

"Raising the ante." *Raleigh (NC) News & Observer*, February 25, 2007.

Ranii, David. "Oompah oomph: Lotto ads set." *Raleigh (NC) News & Observer*, March 24, 2006.

Rawlins, Wade. "Odds Improve for N.C. Lottery." *Raleigh (NC) News & Observer*, December 6, 1998.

Rice, David. "GOP: Take Your Chances." *Winston-Salem (NC) Journal*, August 31, 2005.

———. "Legislature Adjourns After Historic Session: Lottery, Cigarette Tax Are Landmark Laws." *Winston-Salem (NC) Journal*, September 3, 2005.

———. "Lottery May Get Vote in Senate Today, with 2 Opponents Absent." *Winston-Salem (NC) Journal*, August 30, 2005.

———. "State Lottery Becomes Official as Governor Signs Bill into Law." *Winston-Salem (NC) Journal*, September 1, 2005.

Rustin, John. Interview, February 28, 2007.

Sanders, Dr. Charles A. Interview, February 27, 2007.

Sexton, Scott. "Wilkes Acts While Senator Takes a Walk Leg Infection or Not." *Winston-Salem (NC) Journal*, September 1, 2005.

Shaheen, Tom. Interview, February 27, 2007.

Skolnick, Jerome H. "The Social Transformation of Vice." *Law and Contemporary Problems* 51, no. 1 (Winter 1988): 9–29.

Stam, Representative Paul. Interview, February 27, 2007.

"Summary Judgement." *Greensboro (NC) News & Record*, April 15, 2006.

Szakmary, Andrew C., and Carol Matheny. "State Lotteries as a Source of Revenue: A Re-Examination." *Southern Economic Journal* 61, no. 4 (April 1995): 1167–81.

"Wednesday at the General Assembly." Associated Press, August 24, 2005.

CHAPTER 6: GTECH: LOTTERY GIANT

Bartlett, Ron. "Battle over hefty contract getting ugly." *Tampa Tribune*, February 19, 1995.

Bousquet, Steve. "Rival wins bid to run Florida Lottery." *St. Petersburg Times*, September 6, 2003.

Bredemeier, Kenneth. "D.C. Awards Contract for Daily Game." *Washington Post*, March 16, 1983.

———. "D.C. Blacks Join Lottery Bidders." *Washington Post*, February 24, 1983.

Burka, Paul. "You Lose Again!" *Texas Monthly*, March, 1998.

"Business People." *New York Times*, August 11, 1989.

Dyckman, Martin. "The lottery wars." *St. Petersburg Times*, November 9, 1995.

Eichenwald, Kurt. "Market Place; In a long shot, an indictment actually benefits a gaming stock." *New York Times*, March 4, 1993.

Elkind, Peter. "The Numbers Crunchers." *Fortune*, November 11, 1996.

Gold, Jeffrey. "Founder testifies lottery firm hired consultant for political ties." *Newark (NJ) Star-Ledger* (AP), September 26, 1996.

———. "Jury Told of Alleged Kickbacks." *Bergen County (NJ) Record* (AP), September 18, 1996.

"GTECH Holdings Corporation." Hoover's Company Records, March 25, 2008.

GTECH PR Newswire, March 3, 1981; May 18, 1981; October 7, 1981; April 12, 1982; June 21, 1982.

Herman, Ken. "Investigators subpoena files of GTECH's top Texas worker." *Austin (TX) American-Statesman*, January 22, 1997.

Hiday, Jeffrey L. "The Big Deal; The game is on the line and GTECH, the world's biggest lottery company, goes wherever it takes to win." *Providence Journal-Bulletin (Rhode Islander Magazine)*, June 19, 1994.

Kleinknecht, William G. "Ex-lottery-firm exec guilty in bribe case." *Newark (NJ) Star-Ledger*, October 5, 1996.

Laverty O'Connor, Constance. Interview, May 7, 2008.

Ledbetter, James. "Press Clips." *Village Voice*, June 17, 1997.

Lim, Kadir, and Anil Daswani. "China Lottery Market." Citigroup Research, Asia Pacific, August 11, 2006.

McNichol, Dunstan. "D.C. fines Jersey lottery operator $1.4 million in ticket scam." *Newark (NJ) Star-Ledger*, September 25, 2008.

Meier, Barry. "Rules of the Game: A Special Report; Behind the Glow of Jackpots, Scrutiny for a Lottery Giant." *New York Times*, December 19, 1994.

Moss, Bill. "Fight gets nasty for lottery contract." *St. Petersburg Times*, January 31, 1995.

Nash, James. "Rival: Lotto group doesn't stack up." *Columbus (OH) Dispatch*, May 17, 2008.

———. "Vendor has been pushing Ohio to play Keno for years." *Columbus (OH) Dispatch*, February 11, 2008.

Nash, James, and Alan Johnson. "Want to Play Keno?" *Columbus Dispatch*, February 2, 2008.

Precious, Tom. "The high-stakes lobbying for keno." *Albany (NY) Times Union*, May 8, 1995.

Ratcliffe, R. G. "Former Gtech official reportedly boasted about bribing Texas legislators." *Houston Chronicle*, February 7, 1997.

Sandberg, Lisa. "Overseas bribery among claims against state lottery service firm." *Houston Chronicle*, August 16, 2006.

Stape, Andrea L. "A Winner Again." *Providence (RI) Journal*, January 12, 2006.

Stodghill, Ron, and Ron Nixon. "Divide and Conquer: Meet the Lottery Titans." *New York Times*, October 21, 2007

Sullivan, Joseph F. "Lottery Company Executive Is Indicted in Kickbacks." *New York Times*, October 4, 1994.

Szrek, Walter. Interview, May 17, 2008.

Texas Department of Public Safety Criminal Intelligence Service. GTECH Overview for the Texas Lottery Commission Meeting on Wednesday, July 19, 2006.

"A thumbnail sketch of Guy Snowden." Associated Press, February 4, 1998.

Tooher, Nora Lockwood. "Guy Snowden: The Gentleman Farmer." *Providence (RI) Journal-Bulletin*, June 28, 1998.

Trigaux, Robert. "GTech has winning lottery ticket, checkered past." *St. Petersburg Times*, September 8, 2003.

"Where It All Began: A History of GTECH" (corporate history). www.thecaribbeanlottery.com.

CHAPTER 7: TICKET SCRATCH FEVER

Amico, Tony. Interview, November 13, 2007.

"Robert." Interview, November 12, 2007.

Belkin, Douglas. "Lottery Scratch Fever." *Boston Globe*, December 26, 2004.

Benner, Tom. "Lottery Gambles; $5M Ad Blitz Begins." *Quincy (MA) Patriot Ledger*, January 23, 2004.

Birmingham, Tom. Interview, November 12, 2007.

Bryson, Bill. "Americans spend over $550 billion a year on legalised gambling. Has it become the country's favourite pastime? You bet." *Mail on Sunday* (London), August 16, 1998.

Carr, R. D., et al. "'Video Lottery' and Treatment for Pathological Gambling: A Natural Experiment in South Dakota." *South Dakota Journal of Medicine* (January 1996).

Cavanagh, Mark. Interview, November 13, 2007.

Collins, Monica. "State Can Spread Lottery Fever Without Ad Budget" (editorial). *Boston Herald*, July 9, 1995.

Cullen, Kevin. "Worse Than Wiseguys." *Boston Globe*, August 20, 2007.

English, Bella. "Old Game, New Players." *Boston Globe Magazine*, February 21, 1999.

Gambling Impact and Behavior Study. The National Opinion Research Center at the University of Chicago Report to the National Gambling Impact Study Commission, April 1, 1999.

Gianatasio, David. "Lottery Chief Seeks Sales Boost: Increased Ad Spending to Be Put on the Table." *Adweek* (New England edition), December 14, 1998.

Halbfinger, David. "Lottery's profit slump blamed on ad budget cut." *Boston Globe*, July 2, 1996.

Halbfinger, David M., and Daniel Golden. "Lottery Halts Free Coupons After Abuse." *Boston Globe*, February 14, 1997.

———. "The lottery's poor choice of locations; Boom in instant games, Keno widens sales gap between white and blue collar." *Boston Globe*, February 12, 1997.

Howe, Peter J. "Aides Say Weld Seeks to Restore Lottery Ad Funds." *Boston Globe*, June 21, 1995.

Information Packet, 1971–2006. Massachusetts State Lottery Commission.

Kearney, Melissa Schettini. "The Economic Winners and Losers of Legalized Gambling." *National Tax Journal* 58 no. 2 (June 2005).

Lange, Mark. "The Gambling Scam on America's Poor." *Christian Science Monitor*, May 2, 2007.

Lehigh, Scot. "Three Who Stood Up to Their Challenges" (op-ed). *Boston Globe*, January 1, 2003.

Lewis, Raphael. "As Lottery Marks Holiday with Ads, Some Critics Object." *Boston Globe*, December 17, 2003.

———. "Firms Tied to Treasury Boost Cahill Coffers." *Boston Globe*, December 31, 2004.

Lopatin, Marc. "Has Camelot lost the plot? The lottery's prospects have taken a dive." *Independent* (London), December 6, 1998.

Mohl, Bruce. "An abrupt end for collectors who turned lottery ticket trash into cash." *Boston Globe*, May 26, 2007.

———. "Under pressure from municipalities to generate ever more money, the state lottery says it may have maxed out revenue from conventional games." *Boston Globe*, May 6, 2007.

Mooney, Brian C. "With No Regrets, Birmingham Set to Leave as Term Ends, He Sums Up." *Boston Globe*, December 26, 2002.

Paige, Connie. "Pol Says Malone Pushing His Luck in Lottery Promo." *Boston Herald*, April 19, 1996.

"The Poor Play More." *Hartford Courant*, October 7, 2002.

Rader, Ed. Interview, November 16, 2007.

———. "Byproducts of Lottery Addiction" (letter to the editor). *Boston Globe*, May 30, 2007.

Scanlan, Kathleen M. Interview, November 20, 2007.

———. Op-ed. *Boston Globe*, July 7, 2007.

"State Lottery Commits One Million Dollars to Increase Awareness About Problem Gambling" (press release). Massachusetts Council on Compulsive Gambling, May 11, 2006.

Taylor, Mia. "O'Brien Predicts Limit to Lottery Windfalls." *Quincy (MA) Patriot Ledger*, August 6, 1999.

Van Voorhis, Scott. "Lottery Hits Marketing Jackpot." *Boston Herald*, March 6, 2007.

———. "Lottery's big play; $20 game goes for historic numbers." *Boston Herald*, April 25, 2007.

Viser, Matt. "Lottery Usage, Payoffs Vary; Some Towns Doubt Their Share Is Fair." *Boston Globe,* February 22, 2004.

Zuckman, Jill. "Malone, Cellucci Sharpen Swords." *Boston Globe,* July 30, 1998.

CHAPTER 8: THE BUSINESS

Benson, Clea, Jim Sanders, and Gary Delsohn. "Driver's license bill faces new veto; The governor again will kill illegal-immigrants measure." *Sacramento Bee*, September 9, 2005.

Borucki, Joan. Interview, December 21, 2007.

"California Lottery, 2007–2010 Business Plan."

Furillo, Andy. "New Bid Made for a State Post." *Sacramento Bee*, November 2, 2005.

Gledhill, Lynda. "Medina Eased Out as Caltrans Director." *San Francisco Chronicle*, April 15, 2000.

"Governor Schwarzenegger Announces Appointments." States News Service, March 15, 2006.

"Governor Schwarzenegger Appoints Joan Borucki Director of California State Lottery." States News Service, February 15, 2007.

Halper, Evan. "Gov. may gamble on privatized lottery." *Los Angeles Times*, May 10, 2007. Quote: "lowest-performing . . ."

La Fleur's 12th Annual Symposium. Presentations at the Mayflower Hotel, Washington, D.C., April 2 and 3, 2007.

Lin, Judy. "Lottery privatization plan keys on middle-class sales, more outlets." *Sacramento Bee*, June 24, 2007.

Lucas, Greg, and Tom Chorneau. "Educators cool to lottery going private." *San Francisco Chronicle*, May 11, 2007.

Matier, Phillip, and Andrew Ross, "Road warrior: Gov. Arnold Schwarzenegger's pick of a longtime bureaucrat to head the

Department of Motor Vehicles wasn't meant to grab headlines—but it sure did." *San Francisco Chronicle*, November 22, 2004.

Nissenbau, Dion. "Caltrans Director Named in Complaint; Discrimination Charges Spark Federal Probe." *San Jose Mercury News*, February 18, 2000.

Sifuentes, Edward. "Lottery Sales Slipping." *Escondido (CA) North County Times*, March 8, 2007.

The True Value of the California Lottery. Senate Governmental Organization Committee. Dean Florez, Chair. Testimony, October 17, 2007.

Vogel, Nancy. "After Three Flush Years, Lottery Sees a Downturn." *Los Angeles Times*, March 1, 2007.

———. "State lottery to up the ante with its first raffle." *Los Angeles Times*, January 27, 2007.

Wiegand, Steve. "More than luck to fix lottery ills." *Sacramento Bee*, October 18, 2007.

Zezima, Katie. "Sweet Dreams in Hard Times Add to Lottery Sales." *New York Times*, September 12, 2008.

CHAPTER 9: HISTORY REPEATS ITSELF

Anderson, Jenny, and Charles Duhigg. "Illinois Seeks to Privatize Its State Lottery." *New York Times*, January 22, 2007.

Cameron, Doug. "Illinois Aims for Win with Lottery." *Financial Times*, May 24, 2006.

Cavanagh, Mark. Interview, November 13, 2007.

"Chicago Skyway Public Policy Issues: A Template for Asset Privatization?" (PowerPoint presentation). National Association of State Treasurers, Lake Tahoe, Nevada, September 20, 2005.

cFadden, Robert D. "Odds-Defying Jersey Woman Hits Lottery Jackpot 2d Time." *New York Times*, February 14, 1986.

cKinney, Dave. "Who Would Want to Buy Illinois Lottery?" *Chicago Sun-Times*, May 24, 2006.

IcLean, Bethany. "Would you buy a bridge from this man?" *Fortune*, October 2, 2007.

Iysak, Joe. "States Should Follow Illinois, Get out of Gambling." Bloomberg News, January 26, 2007.

Powerball takes big loss, but that's the way the cookie crumbles." *Grand Rapids Press*, May 12, 2005.

Ratcliffe, R. G. "Perry wants to 'sell' lottery." *Houston Chronicle*, February 3, 2007.

ichwartz, Nelson D., and Ron Nixon. "Some States Consider Leasing Their Lotteries." *New York Times*, October 14, 2007.

Segal, Geoffrey. "Several States Consider Privatizing Their Lotteries." Reason Foundation. www.reason.org, February 23, 2007.

Edelman, Susan, and Heather Gilmore. "Million to None. N
Post, November 28, 2004.

Friendly, Jonathan. "Double Millionaire Odds Put at On N
lion to 1." New York Times, February 27, 1986.

Ginsburg, Elisabeth. "Lottery Winners Years Later." New Y N
January 31, 1993.

Goodstein, Ellen. "Unlucky Lottery Winners, Who Lost Thei
www.bankrate.com, March 29, 2006.

Gregg, Katherine. "Looking to buy R.I.—Lured by budge
investors cast an eye on state assets." Providence Journal,
5, 2008.

Guryan, John, and Melissa S. Kearney. Lucky Stores, Gambl
Addiction: Empirical Evidence from State Lottery Sales. N
Bureau of Economic Research, Inc., Working Papers, Apr

Hakim, Danny. "Questions Surround Idea of Privatizing tl
tery." New York Times, January 26, 2008.

Halper, Evan. "Democrats split on lottery plan." Los Angeles
May 11, 2007

Hamilton, Robert A. "Country Club Workers Are Lucky T
New York Times, January 25, 1987. Quote: Connecticut Lo
director, "Whatever you think subconsciously . . ."

Ma, John, and Adam Rosenberg. "U.S. Lottery Privatization Tre
Presentation by Goldman Sachs executives at La Fleur's 12th
nual Symposium, Washington, D.C., Mayflower Hotel, Ap
2007.

McDermott, Kevin, and Philip Ewing. "Governor: Let's Sell Off L
tery." St. Louis Post-Dispatch, May 24, 2006.

———. "Sale of state lottery could start a trend." St. Louis Po
Dispatch, May 25, 2006.

INDEX

A NOTE ON THE AUTHOR

Matthew Sweeney is a journalist who has written for both the *New York Times* and the *New York Post*. He lives in Brooklyn.